Buffets & Casual Parties

ROBERT CARRIER'S KITCHEN

Buffets & Casual Parties

Marshall Cavendish   London Sydney & New York

Editor	Roz Fishel
Editorial Staff	Caroline Macy
	Penny Smith
	Kate Toner
	Anne Wiltsher
Designer	Alan White
Series Editor	Pepita Aris
Production Executive	Robert Paulley
Production Controller	Steve Roberts

Photography
Paul Bussell: 14, 16, 17, 31, 34, 44, 55, 94, 105
Chris Crofton: 13, 29, 38, 74
Laurie Evans: 13, 20, 23, 24, 41, 43, 54, 71, 86, 89, 95, 101, 107, 108, 110
Melvin Grey: 46
James Jackson: 8, 24, 27, 29, 30, 51, 58, 60, 61, 62, 68, 70, 82, 100, 104, 106
Chris Knaggs: 28, 57
David Levin: 17
Peter Myers: 10, 12, 18, 21, 25, 33, 35, 36, 39, 42, 48, 50, 52, 53, 56, 64, 66, 72, 75, 76, 80, 84, 90, 97
Roger Phillips: 77
Paul Williams: 76, 77, 78, 92, 102
Cover picture: **Paul Bussell**

Weights and measures
Both metric and imperial measurements are given. As these are not exact equivalents, please work from one set of figures or the other. Use graded measuring spoons levelled across.

Time symbols
The time needed to prepare the dish is given on each recipe. The symbols are as follows:

 simple to prepare and cook

 straightforward but requires more skill or attention

 time-consuming to prepare or requires extra skill

 must be started 1 day or more ahead

On the cover: Stuffed tomatoes, Italian pepper salad and Italian sausage platter, page 16

This edition published 1985
© Marshall Cavendish Limited 1985

Printed in Italy by
L.E.G.O. S.p.a. Vicenza

Typeset by Quadraset Limited, Midsomer Norton, Bath, Avon

Published by Marshall Cavendish House
58 Old Compton Street London W1V 5PA
ISBN 0 86307 264 X (series)
ISBN 0 86307 411 1 (this volume)

Contents

Entertaining a large number of people can make even the most experienced cooks apprehensive, but in my volume *Buffets & Casual Parties* you will find all the help and ideas that you need to ensure that the occasion runs smoothly. The first chapter includes an invaluable checklist for planning a buffet, as well as practical tips on menu choice, arranging the room and hiring crockery and cutlery.

Attractive presentation is important for buffets, and I've particularly borne this in mind when suggesting menus. My recipe for Smoked fish platter, for example, with its delicate pinks and greys, has plenty of visual appeal and is also easy to prepare. Casseroles are ideal main courses for casual parties where guests can help themselves to food. Mexican chicken casserole with sweetcorn, green peppers and black olives is one of my favourites — so are Chilli beans, cooked with lean minced beef. You will find the recipe in the Americana chapter.

Ingredients such as pork or fish fillets, prawns or liver, are excellent if you have to entertain friends at short notice. In my useful Cook-ahead party chapter I give details of 'nine emergency basics' and 'quick freezer garnishes', along with plenty of recipes to cut down preparation time.

Wine and cheese parties are a classic and ever-popular idea; my chapter tells you all you need to know. Fondues are fun, too. These are 'dip-in' meals invented by thrifty Swiss villagers who mixed melted cheese with wine and ate it with pieces of bread. Modern recipes include marinated steak or firm fish cubes dipped in a variety of sauces. My section on Food for crowds includes chapters on Cooking for large numbers (recipes for 18, 24 or 30 people) and plenty of tempting ideas for both hot and cold finger food.

Finally, I include information on what to drink at your party and how to serve it, with a dozen or so recipes for wine cups and punches. Cocktail recipes are included, too: Platinum blonde, Harvey Wallbanger and Deb's delight are on the circuit again and I show you how to mix them — as well as 'hair of the dog' drinks to help you revive the morning after!

Happy cooking and bon appétit!

Robert Carrier

Buffet Parties

PLANNING A BUFFET

A buffet party for 20 or 30 people sounds daunting, but with careful planning it can be perfectly manageable. Here I give you some practical tips on organization and on choosing the menu.

Buffet parties are often planned when the number you wish to entertain exceeds the number you can fit round your dining-room table, so your party could be as small as 12. On the other hand, once you have got down to cooking, it is almost as much work to give a party for 12 as it is for 20, and the larger number will help to create a good party atmosphere.

Send out the invitations at least a month ahead if you can — this will help you to get an idea of the final number of guests in advance. Once the invitations are sent, draw up a menu and work out what food and equipment you will need.

Planning the menu
You should serve simpler food at a buffet than at a dinner party, but give your guests more choice.

Consider the amount of refrigerator space you have. A grand cook-in a week before the party is practical if you have a large freezer, or an obliging neighbour with one, but don't land yourself with a lot of ready-prepared, perishable food 1–2 days before the party, with nowhere safe to store it.

Make a realistic estimate of the amount of time you can give to preparation. Remember also that if the guests are going to eat standing up, the food should be easy to eat with just a fork.

Choose one or two starters that can be made ahead of time and frozen. A soup and some type of pastry, such as vol-au-vents, might fit the bill. To go with the main course, choose a selection of salads and follow this with a choice of two or three desserts.

Remember that the salad ingredients should be chopped fairly small for easy eating. Huge, round tomato slices may look very pretty, but they are difficult to cut with a fork and impossible to eat in one mouthful. Don't choose more than one salad that involves last-minute preparation; for example, using apples or avocados that need acidulating to prevent discoloration. At least one salad should be largely prepared the day before — green salad, rice, pulses or potatoes are suitable. Dress them on the day.

Choose contrasting desserts, some rich and others light and refreshing, and avoid too much last-minute fiddling. For serving a large number of people, ice creams or sorbets can be a nuisance. They tend to be too hard for the first serving and melted by the time the last guests have reached them.

If you are serving cream, several small jugs of pouring cream, discreetly replenished, are better than a rich-looking mound of whipped

cream because the first guests may over-help themselves, leaving insufficient for later, however generously you have catered. Better still, serve a dessert where cream is already used: meringues sandwiched with cream, trifles and jellies with piped swirls on top.

Match the drink to the food, then finally sit down and make a vast list of what to buy, dividing it into three sections: those items which can be bought well ahead, those 2–3 days ahead, and last minute purchases. Next, make a detailed timetable. Work this out backwards from the party time, starting with the items that positively must be done within an hour of serving. Remember tasks like dressing salads and piping cream, which although quick for a small party, take much longer if you are serving 20 or more.

Make your timetable realistic. Allow adequate time for salad washing and chopping up large quantities of vegetables, which always takes longer than you think. Remember too, to allow for telephone calls — inevitable if you are giving a party — and the normal family meals of a household. Consider again whether you can cope with

---

Plan-ahead timetable

Four to six weeks before the party
Make a list and send out invitations. Plan the menu.

Three to four weeks before the party
Make lists for crockery, cutlery and glasses, plus tables, chairs, trays, etc, if needed. Organize hiring or borrowing as necessary. Order wines and hire glasses. Make food lists and shop for non-perishables, including napkins, candles, tablecloths, etc. Cook any dishes that can be frozen.

One week before the party
Check that all hire orders and wine orders are acknowledged. Order flowers and fresh foods such as vegetables, fruit and cream. Check that nothing has been forgotten. Make ice cubes.

Four days before the party
Make meringues, mayonnaise and pastry.

Two days before the party
Start cooking dishes such as glazed meats, fish, galantines.

One day before the party
Defrost the frozen dishes. Make jellied dishes, if using; cook meat, wash salads, etc.

Take delivery of crockery, glasses, wine, flowers, fresh fruit and vegetables. Clean and arrange the buffet rooms, lay the table if practical. Put glasses and coffee cups on trays. Arrange the flowers and the candles, if using.

Four hours before the party
Partially assemble the salads and make the dressings. Chill white wine and chambré red wine.

Two hours before the party
Whip the cream and assemble meringues, if using. Put the food to be heated into pans on the hob. Open the red wine.

Thirty minutes before the meal
Put all the food on the table, except possibly the cream and dishes to be served chilled. Unmould the jellies; pipe desserts and refrigerate.

Just before the meal
Pour on dressings and toss the salads.

During the buffet
Combine identical salads and remove empty dishes and used plates. Bring out chilled desserts.

After the dessert
Make pots of coffee.

your chosen menu — a party is supposed to be fun, not a marathon. What can be done the weekend, two days or one day before?

Equipment

Having sorted out the menu, and with a definite figure of how many you are catering for, make a list of all the crockery, cutlery and glasses you will need. Paper plates are not as pretty or practical as china ones, so hire or borrow any extra crockery. Some firms will even collect the plates dirty so you don't have the chore of washing up. Use large plates for the main course, as salads piled on a small plate may end up on the floor!

You will need extra plates for people who abandon their plates 'somewhere' but come back for second helpings. Bowls will be needed for serving dessert, and don't forget coffee cups and spoons. Check your serving dishes too. A serving dish should complement the food; white is a good colour, except perhaps for very pale-coloured food which needs a darker container, or at least a contrasting garnish. You may also need to order extra large jugs to make coffee for 20–30 people.

Shop around when hiring and see what is available. Place orders well in advance and ask for the delivery to be the day before the party. Check up a week before to make sure that all is in order. Ask a friend or member of the family to collect any plates, etc, that you intend to borrow the day before the party.

Glasses can often be obtained from wine merchants, if you buy your drink from them. There may then be no hire charge, but a returnable deposit and a charge for any breakages that occur.

Organization

The table will be the focal point of the buffet party, so plan it carefully. For a large party of 30 guests you will need two tables, one for starters and the main course, the other for desserts and coffee. If you don't have a table large enough, try using a trestle table or a decorators' paper-hanging table. Make sure it is secure and hide the legs with a large table-cloth or well-laundered sheet, pinning up the corners so that no-one trips on them. Wine is best served from a separate table, but do not put all the supplies on show from the start or

Centre, Pork stroganoff (page 67), with bowls of pasta and Three-pepper green salad (page 68)

you are likely to end up with dozens of half-empty bottles.

Whilst a stand-up buffet will be necessary for 20 or more guests, it may be possible to provide some seating for smaller numbers. In any case, you should ask your guests to move away from the table once they have served themselves, in order to make room for others. Small card or coffee tables with extra dining-room or kitchen chairs, placed in other rooms, will enable your guests to eat in a comfortable way.

Do make the food look attractive. You may like to plan a centrepiece for the tables, if there's room. To avoid long queues, divide the starters and salads and arrange them at each end of the buffet table. Provide two serving spoons for each dish; two piles of plates and the cutlery needed per person for each course, wrapped in a napkin. Provide extra napkins for the dessert — and don't forget to arrange for someone to remove the used plates.

9

A BUFFET FOR TWELVE

Smoked fish platter

Boeuf en daube
Green grape salad

Roquefort pâté with nuts

Brazilian chocolate cakes
Cream moulds with
blackcurrant sauce

Twelve is a good number to entertain when you want a lively party. However, many homes can't accommodate twelve people around one table, so here's a menu to serve as a buffet. The meal consists of four courses. To begin with I have chosen an easy-to-prepare fish platter. Follow this with Boeuf en daube, a rich casserole that can be cooked the day before the meal, allowing the flavours to blend and develop. Offer my Roquefort pâté with nuts instead of a cheese board. Serve it French-style before the sweets.

When you are cooking for this number of people, it is a good idea to have a choice of desserts. I have included Brazilian chocolate cakes and cool Cream moulds with blackcurrant sauce. You may like to serve small helpings — in case your guests want to try both dishes!

Plan-ahead timetable

On the day before the party
Brazilian chocolate cakes: make then cool the cakes. Store in an airtight container until needed.
Boeuf en daube: marinate the beef. Cook, cool and then reserve the casserole in the refrigerator.
Green grape salad: wash then chill the lettuce leaves.
Cream moulds with blackcurrant sauce: make the moulds. Chill.
Roquefort pâté with nuts: make then chill the pâté.

Early on the day of the party
Smoked fish platter: prepare, cover with cling film and chill.
Make the horseradish chantilly, cover and chill until needed.
Brazilian chocolate cakes: finish preparing and reserve.
Green grape salad: make and chill salad. Make vinaigrette.
Cream moulds with blackcurrant sauce: purée the blackcurrants. Beat in the icing sugar, cover and chill.

One hour before the party
Boeuf en daube: reheat the casserole, then add the olives and allow them to heat through.
Roquefort pâté with nuts: slice, arrange, cover and chill.

Just before serving
Green grape salad: toss the salad in the vinaigrette.
Cream moulds with blackcurrant sauce: turn the moulds onto serving plates and then spoon the blackcurrant sauce over them.

Smoked fish platter

30 minutes

Serves 12
12 thin slices smoked sturgeon
12 thin slices smoked salmon
12 thin slices smoked haddock or tuna
6 smoked trout fillets, halved lengthways
12 smoked sprats
freshly ground black pepper
For the garnish
watercress sprigs
lemon wedges

For the horseradish chantilly
60 ml /4 tbls grated horseradish
30 ml /2 tbls white wine vinegar
150 ml /5 fl oz thick cream

1 On a very large serving platter or tray, arrange the thicker slices of smoked fish across the dish and the smoked trout fillets and sprats around the edge. Fold the thinner slices and arrange them at either end of the dish. Alternatively, arrange the fish attractively on 2 small platters. Season lightly with freshly ground black pepper.
2 Garnish the dish with sprigs of watercress, and lemon wedges. Cover with cling film and chill until ready to use.

3 Meanwhile, make the horseradish chantilly. In a small bowl, combine the grated horseradish with the white wine vinegar and mix thoroughly.
4 In a separate bowl, whisk the cream until it is very thick, then fold in the horseradish and vinegar mixture. Transfer to a serving bowl, chill in the refrigerator until ready to use. Serve with the fish.

● Serve this Smoked fish platter with thin slices of buttered brown bread, cut into neat triangles, and arranged on either a large serving plate or several smaller plates.

Smoked fish platter with horseradish chantilly

Boeuf en daube

This traditional French beef casserole takes its name from *daubière*, a heavy cast-iron cooking pot.

5 hours marinating, then 4–5 hours

Serves 12

2.7 kg /6 lb braising beef
6 Spanish onions
6 carrots, sliced
bouquet garni
salt and freshly ground black pepper
850 ml /1½ pt red wine
275 ml /10 fl oz brandy
olive oil, for frying
700 g /1½ lb streaky bacon, diced
425 ml /15 fl oz beef stock, home-made or from a cube
12 garlic cloves
3 thin strips orange zest
350 g /12 oz black olives, stoned

1 Cut the beef into 25 mm /1 in cubes, discarding any fat or gristle. Put the meat into a large bowl. Slice 3 of the onions and add them to the meat with the sliced carrots, bouquet garni, freshly ground black pepper, the red wine and the brandy. Stir to coat the meat thoroughly, then cover it and marinate for at least 5 hours, stirring occasionally.
2 Heat the oven to 150C /300F /gas 2.
3 Quarter the remaining onions. In a large flameproof casserole, heat 60 ml /4 tbls olive oil and sauté the diced bacon and onion quarters for 12–15 minutes, or until golden brown, stirring occasionally. Remove with a slotted spoon. Drain and reserve. Keep the fat in the pan hot.
4 Using a slotted spoon and reserving the marinade, remove the meat and drain well on absorbent paper.
5 Add enough meat to the casserole to cover the base, then sauté it, turning it regularly, until evenly browned. Season with salt. Remove the browned meat to a plate using a slotted spoon. Repeat with the remaining meat, adding more oil if necessary and keeping the temperature constant.
6 Discard the excess fat from the casserole and pour in the marinade. Stir to remove the sediment from the base and sides of the pan and boil until the liquid is reduced to half its original quantity. Add the stock, then season to taste with salt and freshly ground black pepper. Bring to the boil.
7 Return the diced bacon and meat to the casserole and add the garlic cloves and orange zest. Bring to the boil, then cover and cook in the oven for 3–4 hours, or until tender.
8 Skim any fat from the surface with a spoon or absorbent paper. Add the olives, correct the seasoning. Return to the oven for 10–15 minutes to heat the olives, then serve from the casserole or transfer the contents to a serving dish.

Green grape salad

15 minutes

Serves 12

1 iceberg lettuce
225 g /8 oz fresh spinach
700 g /1½ lb green grapes, halved and seeded
100 g /4 oz walnuts, chopped
75 ml /3 fl oz Vinaigrette (½ × recipe page 21)

1 Separate the lettuce leaves. Wash them in cold water, then dry them thoroughly and wrap them in a clean tea-towel. Chill them until they are needed.
2 Wash the spinach, discarding any coarse stalks and damaged leaves. Dry the leaves.
3 Tear up the lettuce and spinach leaves by hand. In a large serving bowl, combine the lettuce and spinach with the prepared grapes and walnuts.
4 Before serving, add the vinaigrette and toss gently but thoroughly until coated.

Roquefort pâté with nuts

10 minutes, 1 hour chilling, then 5 minutes, plus chilling

Serves 12

100 g /4 oz Roquefort cheese, crumbled
250 g /9 oz cream cheese
15 ml /1 tbls thick cream
30 ml /2 tbls finely chopped fresh parsley
15 ml /1 tbls finely chopped fresh chives
50 g /2 oz hazelnuts, roughly chopped

1 In a bowl, combine the crumbled Roquefort, the cream cheese and the thick cream and beat them together, with a wooden spoon, until they are smooth. Fold in the chopped parsley and chives.
2 Shape the cheese into a cylinder, wrap it in foil and chill it for about 1 hour, or until it is firm.
3 Unwrap the pâté and roll it in the chopped hazelnuts to coat. Chill again until just before serving.
4 To serve, cut the pâté carefully with a serrated knife into slices about 10 mm /⅓ in thick and arrange them on a serving plate.

● Serve this pâté as a savoury at the end of a meal, or French-style before the sweets.

Brazilian chocolate cakes

1½ hours, plus cooling and assembling

Serves 12

125 g /4 oz butter, plus extra for greasing
225 g /8 oz flour, plus extra for dusting
6 eggs
4 egg yolks
225 g /8 oz caster sugar
10 ml /2 tsp vanilla essence
200 g /7 oz flaked almonds, toasted and finely chopped, to decorate

For the cream filling
6 egg yolks
425 g /15 oz caster sugar
650 g /1¼ lb unsalted butter, softened
105 ml /7 tbls strong black coffee
105 ml /7 tbls cocoa powder

For the rum syrup
225 g /8 oz caster sugar
225 ml /8 fl oz dark rum

1 Heat the oven to 180C /350F /gas 4.
2 Grease the base and sides of two 22 cm / 8½ in cake tins with butter. Line the bases of the tins with circles of greaseproof paper and grease the paper with more butter. Lightly dust with flour and shake off any surplus.
3 Sift the flour 3 times onto a sheet of greaseproof paper.
4 Choose a large mixing bowl and select a saucepan over which it will fit firmly. Pour about 5 cm /2 in water into the pan and bring it to the boil. Reduce the heat.
5 Place the butter in another smaller bowl. Lower it into the water so that the butter melts without sizzling or bubbling. Remove the bowl from the water.
6 Combine the eggs, the egg yolks, the caster sugar and the vanilla essence in the large bowl. Set it over the barely simmering water and whisk for 10 minutes with a hand-held electric whisk, until the mixture is very thick, light and lukewarm.
7 Remove the bowl from the heat. Stand it on a cool surface and continue to whisk for about 5 minutes, or until the mixture leaves a trail on the surface when the beaters are lifted and the mixture has cooled.
8 Gradually sift the flour over the surface of the egg mixture, at the same time gently folding it in with a large spoon.
9 Carefully pour off the clear liquid from the surface of the melted butter, leaving the sediment behind. Discard the sediment.
10 Pour the butter gradually into the batter, folding it lightly until it has been completely absorbed. Work as quickly and lightly as possible so as not to lose any of the air in the mixture.
11 Divide the batter between the prepared tins and bake in the oven for 40–45 minutes or until the cakes shrink slightly from the sides of the tins and spring back into shape when lightly pressed with a finger.
12 Remove the cakes from the oven and leave them for 2 minutes. Turn them out onto a wire rack, remove the greaseproof

Roquefort pâté with nuts

Brazilian chocolate cakes

paper and leave them until they are cold.

13 Meanwhile, prepare the cream filling. In a mixing bowl, combine the egg yolks and caster sugar. Beat until pale and frothy.

14 In another bowl, cream the butter. Add the butter to the egg yolk mixture and mix until well blended and smooth.

15 Divide the creamed mixture in half. Add the black coffee to one half and the cocoa powder to the other half; beat until well blended, then reserve.

16 Next, make the rum syrup. Combine the caster sugar and 225 ml /8 fl oz water in a saucepan. Heat gently, stirring, until the sugar is completely dissolved. Now bring to the boil and boil without stirring for 8 minutes. Remove from the heat, stir in the rum and leave to cool.

17 To assemble, carefully cut each sponge cake horizontally into 3 rounds. Reserve a quarter of the rum syrup and sprinkle the rest over the sponge rounds.

18 Take the 2 base layers and spread each with a thick layer of coffee cream filling. Spread the 2 middle layers with a thick layer of chocolate cream and place them on top of the bottom layers.

19 Use the remaining rum syrup to moisten the top layers of sponge again. Place on top of the chocolate cream layers.

20 Add the remaining chocolate cream to the remaining coffee cream and blend them together well. Spread the tops and sides of both cakes with the mixture, smoothing it with a palette knife.

21 Press the chopped almonds over the top and sides of both cakes. Keep cool until ready to serve, but do not refrigerate.

Cream moulds with blackcurrant sauce

🔪 1 hour, plus chilling,
then 15 minutes finishing

Serves 12
1.1 L /2 pt milk
225 g /8 oz semolina
15 g /½ oz powdered gelatine
4 medium-sized eggs, separated
175 g /6 oz caster sugar
1.5 ml /¼ tsp vanilla essence
juice of 1 lemon
125 ml /4 fl oz thick cream, whipped
900 g /2 lb blackcurrants, fresh or defrosted frozen fruit
225 g /8 oz icing sugar

1 In a saucepan, bring the milk to the boil. Stir in the semolina and simmer, stirring frequently, for 15–20 minutes, or until the mixture is thick and the semolina is well cooked. Remove it from the heat and allow it to cool slightly.

2 In a small bowl, sprinkle the gelatine over 60 ml /4 tbls water and leave it to soften. Place the bowl in a pan of boiling water until the gelatine is dissolved. Allow it to cool slightly.

3 In another bowl, combine the egg yolks and the caster sugar. Whisk until thick and light, then beat in the semolina mixture, together with the vanilla essence and the lemon juice. Beat in the dissolved gelatine.

4 Line two 1.4 L /2½ pt decorative moulds with cling film. Whisk the egg whites until they are stiff but not dry.

5 Using a large metal spoon, fold the whipped cream into the semolina mixture, then carefully fold in the whisked egg whites. Divide the mixture between the 2 prepared moulds and chill in the refrigerator until set.

6 Put the blackcurrants in a blender and blend them to a purée, then rub the purée through a sieve into a bowl. Sift the icing sugar into the blackcurrant purée, then beat it in thoroughly.

7 To serve, dip each mould briefly into hot water and then invert onto a serving plate. Remove the cling film. Spoon the blackcurrant sauce over each cream mould and serve immediately.

● For a delicious flavour and texture contrast, try serving the smooth cream moulds with ratafia biscuits.

A Cream mould with blackcurrant sauce

Italian pepper salad
Italian sausage platter
Stuffed tomatoes

Lasagne bolognese
Lettuce and cucumber salad

Caramelized oranges

Plan-ahead timetable

On the day before the meal
Italian pepper salad: prepare peppers and leave to marinate.
Stuffed tomatoes: prepare stuffing(s); store in airtight
container(s) in refrigerator. Organize the garnishes.
Lasagne bolognese: make both sauces; refrigerate.

On the morning of the meal
Caramelized oranges: make and chill.

Two hours before the meal
Lettuce and cucumber salad: prepare the salad and the
dressing and refrigerate.

One and a half hours before the meal
Stuffed tomatoes: prepare the tomato cases.
Italian pepper salad: arrange in serving dish(es) and garnish.

One hour before the meal
Lasagne bolognese: heat the oven, gently heat both the sauces
and put the lasagne in boiling water to soak for five minutes.
Assemble the dish and put it in the oven.

Thirty minutes before the meal
Italian sausage platter: assemble and garnish, then cover
loosely with foil.
Stuffed tomatoes: fill the tomato cases, arrange and garnish.

Just before the main course
Lettuce and cucumber salad: toss the salad.

AN ITALIAN THEME

For a relaxed, informal buffet party for a large group of friends, Italian food is hard to beat. Not only is it tasty, but it is also colourful and inexpensive. Serve it with Italian red or white wine, and if you want to warm to your Italian theme, buy some red, white and green paper napkins, the colours of the national flag.

The _antipasto_ featured here looks particularly inviting. It comprises a variety of salads: a platter of assorted Italian cold meats, a dish of succulent marinated sweet peppers and beautifully decorated stuffed tomatoes. Use either melon balls or cucumber to garnish the cold meat

platter. Melon is a good choice for this particular menu since cucumber appears later on in the menu, in the Lettuce and cucumber salad. Two different fillings are given for the Stuffed tomatoes; you can offer either one or both, as you wish.

Buy some *grissini* (Italian bread sticks) to go with the antipasto. Stand them in tall glasses or, for an added party touch, tie 2 or 3 together with a trio of red, white and green ribbons and lay one bundle on each napkin.

Black or green olives, either stuffed or stoned, also go well with antipasto and they look pretty served in pottery bowls as part of the buffet. You can also provide spiced mustard and Italian pickles.

Pasta is always popular, and what could be more convenient than Lasagne bolognese, cooked in the oven and produced, golden and bubbling, at the right moment? Serve it with Lettuce and cucumber salad with Italian dressing. To follow this warming main course there is a delicious orange dessert — chilled Caramelized oranges.

The array of dishes for this menu is impressively large and may at first look rather complicated to organize, but it is actually very easy as most of the work is done the day before the party. As the plan-ahead timetable shows, the lasagne is your main task on the day. The two sauces, however, can be made the day before and gently reheated just before the dish is assembled. The Italian sausage platter must be arranged close to serving time if it is to be enjoyed at its best, but this is very straightforward as no cooking is involved. I have suggested making the dessert in the morning, but if it is more convenient, you could prepare it the day before.

Italian pepper salad

⏱🍴🍴 35 minutes,
plus marinating

Serves 8

6 large peppers, a combination of yellow, red
  and green
90–120 ml /6–8 tbls olive oil
30 ml /2 tbls wine vinegar
salt and freshly ground black pepper
a pinch of thyme
1.5 ml /¼ tsp ground fennel seeds or celery salt
100 g /4 oz green olives, stoned
100 g /4 oz canned, rolled anchovy fillets,
  stuffed with capers
30 ml /2 tbls finely chopped fresh parsley

1 Heat the grill to maximum heat. Arrange
the peppers in the grill pan, and immediately
reduce the heat to moderate and grill the
peppers until their skins blacken and blister,
turning them regularly so that they cook
evenly. (Do not increase the heat again: slow
steady charring gives the peppers their
delicious flavour.)
2 When the peppers are throughly charred
all over, place them under cold running
water and rub off the skins with your fingers.
Pat the peppers dry, cut them in half and
discard the seeds and stems. Slice the
peppers into thick strips.
3 In a cup or small bowl, combine the olive
oil and the wine vinegar with salt and freshly
ground black pepper to taste. Add the thyme
and the ground fennel seeds or celery salt and
whisk vigorously with a fork until emulsified.
4 Arrange the pepper strips in a shallow
dish, keeping the colours separate. Pour the
dressing over them and toss lightly. Cover
the dish with foil, then place it in the
refrigerator and leave the peppers to marinate
for 8 hours or overnight.
5 Before serving, arrange the peppers
attractively on 1 large serving dish or 3
separate dishes. Garnish with the olives and
rolled anchovy fillets and sprinkle with
freshly chopped parsley.

Italian sausage platter

🍴 20–30 minutes

Serves 8

1 lettuce (optional)
8–10 thin slices mixed Italian sausages,
  including salami
8–10 thin slices mortadella
8–10 thin slices Parma ham
2 large cucumbers or 2 small melons
salt
cucumber slices and a parsley sprig, to garnish
spiced mustard and Italian pickles in vinegar,
  to serve

1 Wash the lettuce leaves individually, if
using, then pat dry and use the crisp leaves
to line a large serving platter. Arrange the
slices of salami and other Italian sausages,
overlapping, at one end of the platter.
Arrange the mortadella at the other end.
Loosely roll up each slice of Parma ham and
lay these side by side in the centre of the
platter.
2 Peel the cucumbers, if using; cut them
lengthways in quarters and remove the seeds.
Cut the cucumber flesh into large dice and
place in a colander. Sprinkle with salt,
shaking the colander to coat the cucumber
evenly, and then leave to drain for 15
minutes. Thoroughly rinse the cucumber
under cold water and pat dry. Alternatively,
if you are using melons, cut each one in half
and scoop out the seeds with a spoon. If you
own a melon baller, cut the melon flesh into
balls, or quarter and peel the melons, cubing
the flesh.
3 Just before serving, decorate the platter
with melon balls, a few slices of cucumber
and a parsley sprig. Serve with spiced
mustard and Italian pickles.

Italian pepper salad

Italian sausage platter

Stuffed tomatoes

🍴🍴 50 minutes

Serves 8–10
For the smoked mackerel-stuffed tomatoes

8–10 large tomatoes
salt
350 g /12 oz smoked mackerel
150 ml /5 fl oz soured cream
150 ml /5 fl oz yoghurt
5 ml /1 tsp lemon juice
2 celery sticks
15 ml /1 tbls dry sherry
100 g /4 oz Cheddar cheese, grated
freshly ground black pepper

For the minted cheese-stuffed tomatoes

8–10 large tomatoes
350 g /12 oz medium fat cream cheese
45 ml /3 tbls natural set yoghurt
15 ml /1 tbls finely chopped fresh mint
30 ml /2 tbls finely snipped fresh chives
50 g /2 oz pineapple, finely chopped
12 capers, finely chopped
2 egg whites

For the garnish

8–10 crisp lettuce leaves (optional)
15–30 ml /1–2 tbls soured cream or yoghurt
parsley sprigs
3 hard-boiled eggs, quartered
75 g /3 oz black olives, stoned
gherkin fans (see page 87)
finely chopped fresh parsley

1 First make the smoked mackerel-stuffed
tomatoes. Cut a thin slice from the top of
each tomato. Using a small metal spoon,
carefully scoop out the pips and the pulp.
Sprinkle the cavities with salt, turn upside
down and cover loosely with foil. Leave the
tomatoes to drain for at least 30 minutes.
2 Skin and flake the mackerel. Combine
with the soured cream, the yogurt, the lemon
juice, the celery and the sherry. Mix in the
cheese using a fork. Season to taste.
3 Rinse the tomato cavities and pat them
dry. Fill the tomatoes with the smoked
mackerel mixture. Just before serving, if
using the lettuce leaves, arrange them on a
wide plate and place a stuffed tomato on each
one. Spoon or pipe a dab of soured cream or
yogurt on the top of each tomato and garnish
with sprigs of parsley.
4 Garnish the edge of the dish with wedges
of hard boiled eggs, olives and gherkin 'fans'.
5 Now make the minted cheese-stuffed
tomatoes. Prepare the tomatoes as in step 1.
6 Blend the cheese, the yogurt and the
mint in an electric blender for 30 seconds.
Turn into a bowl and combine with the
chives, the pineapple, and the capers.
7 Whisk the egg whites until they are stiff
and fold them into the cheese mixture. Chill
for at least 30 minutes.
8 Just before serving, rinse the tomato
cavities and pat them dry, then fill the
tomatoes with the cheese mixture. Arrange
on a serving plate and sprinkle with the
finely chopped parsley.

Lasagne bolognese

⏱ 2¾ hours for the sauces,
then 1 hour

Serves 8
500 g /1 lb lasagne
50 g /2 oz butter
100 g /4 oz freshly grated Parmesan cheese,
plus extra for serving
For the bolognese meat sauce
700 g /1½ lb Spanish onions, chopped
2 carrots, finely chopped
2 celery sticks, finely chopped
60 ml /4 tbls olive oil
100 g /4 oz butter
100 g /4 oz bacon, finely chopped
225 g /8 oz lean pork, minced
225 g /8 oz lean beef, minced
100 g /4 oz sausage meat
300 ml /10 fl oz dry white wine
90 ml /6 tbls tomato purée
425 ml /15 fl oz beef stock
225 g /8 oz button mushrooms, sliced
1–2 garlic cloves, crushed
30 ml /2 tbls finely chopped fresh parsley
For the cream sauce
100 g /4 oz butter
120 ml /8 tbls flour
1.3 L /2¼ pt milk
salt and freshly ground black pepper
a pinch of freshly grated nutmeg
1 garlic clove, lightly crushed
8 dried mushrooms, soaked in water
30 ml /2 tbls finely chopped fresh parsley

1 Make the meat sauce: in a casserole, sauté the onions, carrots and celery with 30 ml / 2 tbls olive oil and 50 g /2 oz butter until they are soft. Brown the bacon, pork, beef and sausage meat in 30 ml /2 tbls olive oil and 25 g /1 oz butter in a frying-pan. Add to the casserole with the wine. Simmer for 15–20 minutes.
2 Stir in the tomato purée with a little beef stock. Simmer, covered, for 1½ hours, stirring frequently and gradually adding the remaining stock.
3 For the cream sauce, cook 75 g /3 oz butter and the flour gently for 1–2 minutes. Gradually add 1 L /1¾ pt milk, stirring constantly. Boil for 3–5 minutes, still stirring. Season with salt, pepper and nutmeg, and reserve, covered with greaseproof paper.
4 Sauté the garlic in 25 g / 1 oz butter for 2–3 minutes, then discard the garlic. Simmer the soaked mushrooms until they are soft. Reserve the liquid. Finely chop the mushrooms. Toss them in the butter for 2–3 minutes over a low heat. Add 50 ml /2 fl oz of the mushroom liquid, 30 ml /2 tbls parsley and the remaining milk; simmer for 15–20 minutes. Mix into the cream sauce and season.
5 Finish the meat sauce: sauté the mushrooms and garlic in 25 g /1 oz butter and the parsley for minutes. Fold into the sauce.
6 Heat the oven to 190C /375F /gas 5. Spread out the lasagne in a roasting tin; pour on boiling water; soak for 5 minutes.
7 To assemble: butter a deep 22×35 cm / 9×14 in heatproof oven dish. Cover the base with a layer of lasagne, top with one-third of the meat sauce and then one-third of the cream sauce; sprinkle with Parmesan. Repeat

using all the meat sauce. Top with lasagne and cream sauce. Sprinkle with Parmesan cheese and dot with 50 g /2 oz butter.
8 Bake for 30–40 minutes, and serve sprinkled with more grated Parmesan cheese.

Lettuce and cucumber salad

⏱ 20 minutes

Serves 8
2 crisp lettuces
1 cucumber
For the Italian dressing
60 ml /4 tbls wine vinegar
2.5–5 ml /½–1 tsp mustard powder
150 ml /5 fl oz olive oil
1–2 garlic cloves, finely chopped
30–45 ml /2–3 tbls finely chopped fresh parsley
5–7.5 ml /1–1½ tsp dried oregano
salt and freshly ground black pepper

1 Trim and separate the lettuces, discarding any damaged leaves. Wash and dry thoroughly, then tear the leaves into 4 cm / 1½ in strips. Wrap loosely and chill until required.
2 Wipe the cucumber clean, then trim off the ends. Score the sides of the cucumber by drawing a citrus zester or the prongs of a fork lengthways down the skin. Now cut the cucumber into thin slices and reserve.
3 Make the Italian dressing. In a small bowl, combine the wine vinegar, mustard to taste and the olive oil and whisk well with a fork. Add the chopped garlic, parsley and dried oregano and season to taste with salt and freshly ground black pepper.
4 To serve, arrange the lettuce strips in a large salad bowl and top with the cucumber slices. Pour the dressing over the salad and toss it well.

Caramelized oranges

Lasagne bolognese

Caramelized oranges

A dessert from Sicily in the Mediterranean, caramelized oranges are one of the most attractive of all orange fruit salads.

⏱ 55 minutes,
plus chilling

Serves 8
8 large oranges
350 g /12 oz sugar

1 Using a potato peeler, remove very thin strips of zest from 4 of the oranges and reserve. Cut 4 strips from a fifth orange. Put all the oranges into the freezer compartment of the refrigerator to firm up for 10 minutes. Reserve 4 strips of zest and cut all the rest into julienne strips using scissors. Simmer the strips in boiling water for 5 minutes. Drain and pour cold water over the strips.
2 Put the sugar, 250 ml /8 fl oz water and 4 orange strips into a small saucepan. Stir over medium heat to dissolve the sugar, then boil for 5 minutes to form a syrup. Remove from the heat.
3 Take the oranges from the freezer and peel them with a very sharp knife, removing the peel and every trace of pith. Slice the oranges into rings. Reassemble and hold in shape by sticking a wooden cocktail stick through the rings. Arrange in a shallow dish.
4 Remove the orange strips from the syrup and discard them. Spoon the syrup over the oranges, scooping it up from the bottom of the dish so that each orange is well coated 2–3 times.
5 Transfer the oranges to a serving plate and pour the syrup back into the saucepan. Add the julienne strips, bring to the boil and boil for 2 minutes or until the syrup begins to turn brown around the edges of the pan. Remove the pan from the heat, stir once, then spoon a little heap of strips like a thatch on top of each orange. Chill before serving.

A SIT-DOWN BUFFET

Haddock and scallop bourride

~

Cold meat platter

Salade provençale

~

Red berry sorbet

Plan-ahead timetable

On the day before the party
Haddock and scallop bourride: prepare and chill the rouille and aïole sauces.
Salade provencale: soak the chick-peas.
Cold meat platter: cook the meats, if preparing at home.
Make the radish roses.
Red berry sorbet: prepare and freeze.

Early on the day of the party
Salade provencale: cook the vegetables. Make the vinaigrette.
Cold meat platter: assemble the platter. Garnish with the radish roses and chill. Make the Mustard mayonnaise and Horseradish chantilly (see page 11), if serving.
Chill the wine and lay the table.

One hour before the party
Cold meat platter: arrange on the buffet table.
Haddock and scallop bourride: cook the fish; keep warm.
Sauté the French bread rounds; keep hot. Make the soup; keep hot. Warm the bowls.
Salade provencale: assemble and arrange on the buffet table.

Just before the meal
Haddock and scallop bourride: assemble the soup bowls on trays and serve the soup with the rouille and sautéed French bread rounds.
Red berry sorbert: place in the refrigerator to soften.

Ten minutes later
Haddock and scallop bourride: bring in the fish and aïoli.
Guests serve themselves; any remaining soup can be served as sauce.
Remove all the soup plates before proceeding to the next course.

Just before the dessert
Red berry sorbet: scoop out, cover with raspberries, sprinkle with kirsch and serve.

This menu for 12 is ideal for an occasion when you want to serve an impressive buffet supper. Arrange the food attractively on the table and provide enough chairs, floor cushions and occasional tables to allow your guests to manage their food in comfort — most important with this particular meal which includes soup.

In this elegant menu I have chosen a combination of hot and cold foods. As an outstanding and somewhat unusual starter, try my Haddock and scallop bourride. The fish is gently poached, drained, then kept warm; some aïoli (a rich garlic sauce) is added to the poaching liquid to make a superb Mediterranean-style soup. Guests help themselves to the soup, adding to their individual bowls a round of sautéed French bread topped with a spoonful of rouille (a thick spicy sauce). The warm fish is served separately, immediately after the soup, accompanied by more aïoli.

Continuing the Mediterranean theme, prepare Salade provencale to accompany the Cold meat platter. This salad is a colourful mixture of chick-peas, cooked vegetables and canned artichoke hearts tossed in a vinaigrette dressing, to which you can add fresh herbs, if wished. Serve the salad in a glass bowl so that the colours are shown to their very best effect.

You can buy your selection of cold meats from a delicatessen if you decide not to cook them yourself. It is a bit more expensive, but worth it if you are pressed for time. Garnish the meat platter with radish 'roses'. To make these, choose very fresh, even-sized, unblemished radishes and slice off their stalks. With this end downwards, make three vertical rows of slits round each radish (see picture, page 20), which will open out into petals. Start at the bottom: holding a small sharp knife almost horizontally, with the point turned downwards, cut a series of round petals. Raise the knife and make a new row of petals which bridge the gaps in the line below. Make a third row if the radish is large enough. Soak the cut radishes in iced water overnight until the petals open.

Serve the Cold meat platter with Mustard mayonnaise (see recipe) and, if wished, Horseradish chantilly (see recipe, page 11).

To finish this excellent meal, try my delectable Red berry sorbet — mouthwatering scoops of strawberry sorbet nestling beneath a mound of fresh raspberries sprinkled with kirsch. The sorbet is not difficult to make and will be a delicious end to the meal, but do remember to take it out of the freezer about an hour before you wish to eat it and put it in the refrigerator to soften.

Which wine will best complement this menu? I recommend a chilled Frascati. This popular Italian wine comes from Rome and its country environs. DOC (Denominazione di Origine Controllata) regulations have brought the end of an era when any white wine from Rome could call itself Frascati. Now anything labelled as such is likely to be a pleasant, golden white wine with a strong taste of the whole grape. The extra flavour is obtained by keeping the must (the grape pulp during the fermentation process) in contact with the skins, and it is distinctive among Italian whites.

Frascati is usually dry now, labelled either *asciutto* or *secco*, but it may also be found in softer, sweeter styles called *amabile* or *cannellino* (the latter is the sweetest). Frascati *superiore* has a higher level of alcohol. It is definitely a wine to drink young — six months is fine, and two years old is the maximum.

To round off the occasion, serve your guests a pot of piping hot fresh coffee. Some people may like to have a liqueur with their coffee and, as kirsch is used to flavour the raspberries in Red berry sorbet, your guests may wish to continue with this liqueur. Kirsch is different from other cherry brandies in that it is a spirit distilled from cherries and is without any additional sweetening.

Haddock and scallop bourride

 1¼ hours

Serves 12

1.8 kg /4 lb haddock fillets
1 large Spanish onion, finely chopped
bouquet garni
salt and freshly ground black pepper
60 ml /4 tbls olive oil
50 g /2 oz butter
4 garlic cloves, crushed
12 slices French bread
12 scallops, shelled
1 shallot, finely chopped
a sprig of fresh parsley
a sprig of fresh thyme
60 ml /4 tbls finely chopped fresh parsley,
  to garnish

For the rouille

50 g /2 oz fresh white breadcrumbs
100 ml /4 fl oz chicken stock, home-made or
  from a cube
4 ml /¾ tsp cayenne pepper
4 ml /¾ tsp powdered saffron
3 small dried chillies, crushed
4 garlic cloves, peeled
100 ml /4 fl oz olive oil, warmed
salt and freshly ground black pepper

For the aïoli

8–12 garlic cloves, finely chopped
4 egg yolks
salt and freshly ground black pepper
800 ml–1.1 L /1½–2 pt olive oil
60 ml /4 tbls lemon juice

1 Prepare the rouille. In a bowl, soak the breadcrumbs in the chicken stock. In a mortar (or separate bowl), combine the cayenne pepper, powdered saffron, crushed chillies and garlic. Using a pestle (or the back of a wooden spoon), mash the garlic into the spice mixture to form a smooth paste.

2 Add the breadcrumb and stock mixture to the paste. Slowly beat in the warmed olive oil, drop by drop at first, then in a thin trickle as for mayonnaise. Season to taste with salt and freshly ground black pepper. Set aside.

3 Make the aïoli. In a bowl, combine the finely chopped garlic with the egg yolks. Season to taste with salt and freshly ground black pepper. Gradually whisk in the olive oil, adding it drop by drop at first, then in a slow, thin stream as for mayonnaise. Stir in the lemon juice. Reserve.

4 Bring 1.7 L /3 pt water to the boil. Meanwhile, cut the haddock into 12 even-sized pieces. Select a saucepan large enough to take the haddock pieces in a single layer, if possible. Lay the pieces in the pan and add the finely chopped onion and bouquet garni, then season to taste with salt and freshly ground black pepper. Add the boiling water, place over a low heat and simmer for 10 minutes, or until the fish flakes easily.

5 Remove the fish with a slotted spoon, drain it well on absorbent paper and transfer to a heated serving dish. Keep warm. Strain the cooking liquid and reserve.

6 In a frying-pan, heat the olive oil, butter and garlic cloves. Add the slices of French bread and sauté them for 2–3 minutes each side, or until they are golden. Drain them and keep them warm. Discard the garlic.

7 Place the scallops in a saucepan and add the shallot, parsley and thyme. Pour enough reserved poaching liquid over the scallops to cover them. Season to taste with salt and freshly ground black pepper. Bring to simmering point and poach the scallops gently for 3–5 minutes, or until they are cooked but still firm. Remove them with a slotted spoon, drain them well on absorbent paper and arrange them with the haddock on the serving dish. Keep warm.

8 Strain the scallop cooking liquid and return it to the reserved fish liquid.

9 Transfer 300 ml /10 fl oz aïoli to a serving bowl. Put the rest in a large bowl and gradually add the fish bouillon, blending

Cold meat platter with mustard mayonnaise

with a whisk. Pour the mixture into a heavy-based saucepan and cook it over a low heat for 10 minutes, stirring, until the soup coats the back of a wooden spoon. Do not let the soup boil, or it will curdle.

10 To serve, arrange 12 individual heated soup bowls, the sautéed bread, soup and rouille on the buffet table. Guests place a slice of bread in a bowl and help themselves to soup and rouille.

11 A few minutes later, sprinkle the fish and scallops with freshly chopped parsley and carry it to the buffet table with the separate bowl of aïoli. Let the guests help themselves to haddock and a scallop, put them in their bowls and top them up with aïoli.

Haddock and scallop bourride

Cold meat platter

Cold meat is always popular; buy it from a delicatessen if you are in a hurry, or cook it yourself at home, if you prefer.

🕐 🍴 preparing the radishes,
plus 45 minutes

Serves 12
12 slices cold roast veal
12 slices cold cooked tongue
12 slices cold rare roast beef
12 slices cold roast chicken
For the garnish
radish roses (see introduction)
lettuce leaves, washed and dried
For the mustard mayonnaise
2 egg yolks
15 ml /1 tbls wine vinegar
2.5 ml /½ tsp mustard powder
2.5 ml /½ tsp salt
freshly ground black pepper
275 ml /10 fl oz olive oil
30 ml /2 tbls grainy mustard

1 Prepare the radish roses for the garnish.
2 Prepare the mustard mayonnaise. Use an electric blender, if you have one, which will make it easier to combine the egg yolks, wine vinegar, mustard powder, salt, freshly ground black pepper to taste and 25 ml /1 fl oz cold water. Blend the ingredients until they are well mixed.
3 Add the olive oil in a thin, steady trickle beating briskly with the blender at maximum speed.
4 Turn the mayonnaise into a bowl and stir in the grainy mustard. Reserve.
5 To serve, cover 2 or 3 large platters with lettuce leaves. Arrange rings of sliced cold meats attractively in a concentric circle on the lettuce. Garnish them with radish roses, cover and chill them.
6 Transfer the mustard mayonnaise and the

horseradish chantilly (see page 11), if serving, to small separate serving bowls to accompany the cold meats on the platter.

Salade provençale

🕐 🍴 soaking the chick-peas overnight,
then 1 hour, plus cooling

Serves 12
350 g /12 oz chick-peas, soaked overnight
450 g /1 lb new potatoes
salt
175 g /6 oz baby carrots
350 g /12 oz green beans
325 g /11 oz canned artichoke hearts, drained and sliced
chopped fresh parsley, to garnish
For the vinaigrette
60 ml /4 tbls red wine vinegar
salt and freshly ground black pepper
175 ml /6 fl oz olive oil

1 Drain the chick-peas. Transfer them to a saucepan, cover them with twice their volume of water and bring them to the boil. Reduce the heat and simmer for 45–60 minutes, or until the chick-peas are very soft. Drain them throughly.
2 While the chick-peas are cooking, prepare the other vegetables. Put the potatoes in a saucepan of cold salted water. Bring them to the boil, then add the baby carrots and cook them for 10 minutes, or until the carrots and potatoes are tender but not too soft. Drain them and reserve.
3 Trim the green beans. Cut them into 25mm /1 in lengths. Bring a saucepan of salted water to the boil, add the beans and cook them for 5–6 minutes, or until they are just tender, but still crisp. Drain, refresh them under cold running water and drain them again.
4 Make the vinaigrette. Pour the red wine vinegar into a bowl and season to taste with

the salt and freshly ground black pepper.
5 Add the olive oil and beat with a fork or wire whisk until the mixture thickens and emulsifies.
6 Combine the cooked chick-peas, new potatoes, baby carrots and green beans in a large bowl. Pour the vinaigrette all over the salad and toss together gently until the vegetables are well mixed and all the ingredients are glistening.
7 Place the sliced artichoke hearts in a large serving bowl and top them with the chick-pea mixture. Sprinkle with the fresh parsley and serve immediately.

● For a change, make your vinaigrette herb-flavoured. After the vinegar, salt, freshly ground black pepper and olive oil have been thoroughly mixed and the mixture has thickened, add 15 ml /1 tbls each finely chopped fresh tarragon, chervil and chives.

Red berry sorbet

🍴 50 minutes,
plus 4½ hours freezing

Serves 12
1 kg /2 lb strawberries, hulled
225 g /8 oz sugar
juice of 1 lemon
2.5 ml /½ tsp red food colouring
4 egg whites
1 kg /2 lb raspberries, hulled
90 ml /6 tbls kirsch

1 Rub the strawberries through a fine sieve into a bowl. Discard the pips and any fibres.
2 In a heavy-based saucepan, combine the sugar with 600 ml /1 pt water. Stir over a gentle heat until the sugar dissolves, then bring it to the boil. Boil for 10 minutes, removing any scum that rises to the surface. Remove the pan from the heat, stir in the lemon juice and leave it to cool. Next, strain the syrup carefully through a muslin-lined sieve.
3 Combine the strawberry purée and the syrup and add enough red food colouring to make a pink ice. Pour the mixture into a shallow freezer container, cover and freeze it for 2 hours, or until it is firm to a depth of about 25 mm /1 in all around the edges of the container.
4 Remove the strawberry mixture from the freezer and whisk it with a fork or wire whisk to break up the ice particles. Cover and freeze it again for 30 minutes.
5 Whisk the egg whites until they are stiff. Remove the strawberry mixture from the freezer, whisk it again until it is smooth and then whisk in the stiffly beaten egg whites. Return the sorbet to the freezer container and freeze it for another 2 hours or until it is firm.
6 About 1 hour before serving, transfer the sorbet to the main part of the refrigerator to soften it slightly.
7 To serve, scoop the sorbet into 12 balls and arrange them in a single layer on a large, flat, chilled serving dish.
8 Cover the sorbet with a mound of raspberries and sprinkle them with the kirsch. Serve immediately.

MEXICANA

Mexican chicken casserole
Mexican rice
Red kidney bean salad
Orange salad

Mexican pineapple custard
meringues

Plan-ahead timetable

On the day before the party
Red kidney bean salad: put the kidney beans in water to soak overnight.
Mexican pineapple custard meringues: make the meringues. Cool and then store them overnight in an airtight container.
Mexican chicken casserole: grill, then crumble the bacon. Prepare, then arrange, the other ingredients in a large casserole. Cool, cover and chill until needed.
Mexican rice and Orange salad: make a quantity of vinaigrette sufficient for both these dishes, then cover it and store it in the refrigerator.

On the morning of the party
Mexican pineapple custard meringues: make the custard and allow it to cool.
Mexican rice: prepare the rice but do not toss it in the vinaigrette. Cover and keep cool.
Red kidney bean salad: drain the beans. Assemble the salad and make the dressing. Toss the salad and allow it to become completely cold.
Place beer or lager (if serving) in the refrigerator.

One hour before the meal
Mexican pineapple custard meringues: fill the meringues with custard, then decorate.
Mexican chicken casserole: heat the casserole through slowly, without stirring, and then sprinkle it with the grilled, crumbled bacon just before serving.
Orange salad: assemble, toss in vinaigrette, arrange on lettuce leaves and garnish.
Mexican rice: toss in vinaigrette.

Next time you are having a group of friends round for a meal, try introducing a theme to make the occasion different. The country that inspired the recipes in this chapter is Mexico — the land of brilliant sunshine, spectacular scenery, and spicy food.

If you are lucky enough to have a warm summer evening, then try to create the feel of Mexico by serving the meal outside in the garden. Lay the food on coloured cloths and use brightly coloured table-napkins.

When your guests arrive, serve them each with a tangy Margarita cocktail (see page 104) — which has a salt frosting around the edge of the glass. If your guests are likely to be thirsty, serve cold beer or lager in jugs straight from the refrigerator.

The main course of this meal consists of a marvellous Mexican chicken casserole which can be prepared the day before and then simply heated through and sprinkled with crumbled, grilled bacon at the last minute. With it serve a choice of three salads — Mexican rice, Red kidney bean salad and Orange salad.

Finish the meal on a sweet note with my version of Mexican pineapple custard meringues: pretty nests of meringue filled with pineapple and decorated with glacé cherries and almonds.

Mexican chicken casserole

 2 hours

Serves 12
3 × 1.6 kg /3½ lb chickens, dressed weight
120 ml /8 tbls flour
15 ml /1 tbls paprika
7.5 ml /1½ tsp cayenne pepper
salt and freshly ground black pepper
120 ml /8 tbls lard or chicken fat
6 green peppers, cored, seeded and chopped
3–4 large garlic cloves, chopped
3 Spanish onions, chopped
1.7 L /3 pt chicken stock, home-made or from a cube
3 × 400 g /14 oz canned peeled tomatoes, drained and chopped
24 black olives, stoned
6 × 350 g /12 oz canned sweetcorn kernels
12 slices grilled bacon, crumbled

1 Divide each chicken into 12–14 pieces, cutting each drumstick and thigh into 2 pieces and each breast into 2 or 3 pieces.
2 In a bowl, combine the flour with the paprika and the cayenne pepper, season with salt and freshly ground black pepper. Dust the chicken pieces thoroughly with the flour mixture.
3 In a large flameproof casserole, heat the lard or chicken fat, then sauté the chicken pieces, a few at a time, for 8–10 minutes, or until they are well browned. Transfer the browned chicken pieces to a very large saucepan, or 2 smaller ones, using a slotted spoon.
4 In the fat remaining in the casserole, sauté the chopped green peppers, the garlic and the onions for 15–20 minutes, or until the vegetables are soft.
5 Meanwhile, add the chicken stock to the chicken pieces and bring it all to the boil. Skim the stock, then lower the heat and simmer for 30–35 minutes, or until the chicken is tender.
6 Add the chopped, canned tomatoes and the stoned black olives to the vegetables in the casserole. Season them to taste with salt and freshly ground black pepper. Drain the chicken stock into the vegetables.
7 Assemble the casserole. Thoroughly drain the sweetcorn kernels, then place a layer of sweetcorn kernels in the bottom of a very large, clean, flameproof casserole, or 2 smaller ones, and cover with a layer of chicken pieces. Using a slotted spoon, top with a layer of tomatoes and vegetables. Repeat the process until all the ingredients are used, ending with a layer of sweetcorn kernels.
8 Boil the remaining chicken stock until it is reduced by half and then pour it over the chicken and the vegetables. If preparing the casserole for the next day, then chill it overnight.
9 Heat the casserole until it is thoroughly warmed. Top it with crumbled, grilled bacon and serve.

In the background, Orange salad; left, Mexican rice; right, Mexican chicken casserole

Mexican rice

 30 minutes,
plus cooling

Serves 12
a large pinch of salt
500 g /1 lb long-grain rice
2 red peppers, cored, seeded and diced
2 green peppers, cored, seeded and diced
2 yellow peppers, cored, seeded and diced
4 small chillies, seeded and very finely chopped
1 small canned pimento, well drained and chopped
500 g /1 lb cooked chorizo sausage, skinned and sliced
200 ml /7 fl oz Vinaigrette (see page 21)

1   Bring a large saucepan of salted water to the boil. Pour the rice into the water in a thin stream, then bring the water back to the boil. Stir once to dislodge any grains that have stuck to the pan, then simmer very gently for 15–18 minutes or until the rice is cooked but not soft. Drain, refresh under cold water and drain again thoroughly.
2   In a large serving bowl or dish, combine the cold cooked rice, the diced red, green and yellow peppers, the finely chopped chillies, the chopped pimento and the sliced chorizo sausage. Add the vinaigrette and toss well, then serve.

Red kidney bean salad

⏱ 🍴 overnight soaking, then 2 hours, plus cooling

Serves 12
700 g /1½ lb red kidney beans, soaked overnight
200 ml /7 fl oz olive oil
3 Spanish onions, finely chopped
3 garlic cloves, finely chopped
2 bay leaves
3 green peppers, cored, seeded and diced
125 ml /4 fl oz red wine vinegar
salt and freshly ground black pepper
For the dressing
1½ Spanish onions, finely chopped
120 ml /8 tbls finely chopped fresh parsley
3 garlic cloves, finely chopped
30 ml /2 tbls German mustard
2 egg yolks
salt and freshly ground black pepper
150 ml /5 fl oz olive oil
30 ml /2 tbls lemon juice
To garnish
Chinese leaves, shredded
thin lemon slices

1   Drain the beans thoroughly.
2   In a flameproof casserole, heat 60 ml /

Red kidney bean salad

4 tbls of the olive oil. Add the onions and sauté them for 8–10 minutes, or until they are just beginning to colour. Add the beans, the garlic, the bay leaves and about 2.8 L / 5 pt water. Bring to the boil, boil hard for 15 minutes, then simmer for 1½–2 hours, or until the beans are tender. Drain.
3   Place the drained beans in a large bowl. Add the diced green peppers, the remaining olive oil and the red wine vinegar. Season generously with salt and freshly ground black pepper.
4   Make the dressing: in a bowl, combine the onions, parsley, garlic, German mustard and egg yolks. Season with salt and black pepper, to taste. Mix well, then add the oil, drop by drop at first, then in a thin trickle, beating all the time until the mixture is thick. Flavour with the lemon juice.
5   Spoon the salad into a serving bowl, pour the dressing over the top and toss until the ingredients are well coated and thoroughly mixed. Leave to get completely cold. To serve, garnish with shredded Chinese leaves and thin lemon slices.

Orange salad

🍴 30 minutes

Serves 12

10 large oranges, peeled and thinly sliced
350 g /12 oz green seedless grapes
75 ml /3 fl oz Vinaigrette (½ × recipe page 21)
1 lettuce
16–20 large black olives, stoned
a pinch of paprika
a pinch of cayenne pepper

1 Toss the orange slices and the grapes in the vinaigrette until they are well coated.
2 Line a serving bowl with lettuce leaves. Arrange the orange slices and the grapes on top. Garnish with the black olives and sprinkle with the paprika and the cayenne. Serve the salad immediately.

Mexican pineapple custard meringues

1 hour 35 minutes, plus cooling

Serves 12

3 medium-sized egg whites
175 g /6 oz caster sugar
1.5 ml /¼ tsp salt
2.5 ml /½ tsp cream of tartar
5 ml /1 tsp vanilla essence

For the pineapple custard
375 g /13 oz well-drained, canned crushed pineapple
45 ml /3 tbls cornflour
375 ml /13 fl oz milk
6 medium-sized egg yolks, well beaten
90 ml /6 tbls sugar
5 ml /1 tsp pineapple essence

For the garnish
halved glacé cherries
toasted flaked almonds

1 Heat the oven to 110C /225F /gas ¼. Cover 2 baking sheets with greaseproof or silicone baking paper.
2 Now make the meringues. Put the egg whites into a large clean bowl. Whisk them until they are stiff, then whisk in the sugar, the salt, the cream of tartar and the vanilla essence and continue whisking until the mixture is stiff and glossy.
3 Drop tablespoons of the mixture onto the paper-lined baking sheets to make 12 meringues. Use the back of the spoon to make an indentation in the centre of each. Alternatively, put the meringue mixture into a piping bag fitted with a large round nozzle and pipe 12 'nests' onto the paper.
4 Bake the meringues in the oven for 50–60 minutes or until they are set and dry but not coloured. Cool them on wire racks and, if

making in advance, store them in an airtight container until they are needed.
5 To make the custard, purée the crushed pineapple in a blender and reserve. Dissolve the cornflour in half the milk, then beat the rest of the milk with the egg yolks and the sugar. Next add the cornflour milk mixture to the egg yolk milk mixture and beat until well blended.
6 Pour the mixture into the top of a double boiler and stir constantly, with a wooden spoon, over simmering water until the mixture thickens enough to coat the back of the spoon — about 20 minutes.
7 Remove the pan from the heat and stir in the pineapple purée and the essence. Cool the custard to room temperature before using it to fill the meringues, then decorate with the halved glacé cherries and the toasted flaked almonds. (If this dessert is to be served to children, try leaving out the almonds.) Serve any extra custard handed separately.

● For a slight variation on this recipe, make Pineapple niñons (see photograph). Place the meringues on slices of fresh pineapple, and then decorate with strawberries instead of the glacé cherries and almonds.

Pineapple niñons are a variation of Mexican pineapple custard meringues

AMERICANA

Ranchburgers
Chilli beans
Bronco strips
Cabbage and pepper slaw

⌒

Strawberry ice-cream rolls
Shoo-fly pies

Plan-ahead timetable

The day before the party
Ranchburgers: slice the tomatoes, cucumber and spring onions for the garnishes. Cover tightly with cling film and keep in the refrigerator.
Bronco strips: make the topping and chill.
Chilli beans: soak the kidney beans.
Cabbage and pepper slaw: soak the raisins.
Strawberry ice-cream rolls: make the ice cream. Freeze in two chilled freezing trays.

The morning of the party
Ranchburgers: mix, form and chill until required.
Chilli beans: cook the beans; cool.
Cabbage and pepper slaw: prepare the cabbage 'bowl' and fry the bacon.
Shoo-fly pies: make the pastry and spicy filling, and then cook the pies.

Just before the party
Chilli beans: gently reheat; place serving dishes in the oven to warm.
Cabbage and pepper slaw: combine the ingredients in a large mixing bowl. Chill.
Strawberry ice-cream rolls: transfer from the freezer to the refrigerator.

While the party is in progress
Ranchburgers: cook the burgers and keep them warm. Toast the baps. Assemble, quickly grilling any burgers topped with cheese slices, serve with garnishes and accompaniments.
Bronco strips: toast the bread, spread on the topping, bake and serve.
Chilli beans: transfer to warmed serving dishes and serve.
Cabbage and pepper slaw: pile the filling into the cabbage 'bowl'; garnish and serve.
Strawberry ice-cream rolls: unmould and decorate with strawberries and cream; serve.
Shoo-fly pies: cut the pies into wedges and serve.

For a big party, when you are expecting 30 or more guests, try this Americana menu. It features a big pot of Chilli beans to dip into — serve it with rice if you like, or with chunks of crusty bread — or beefy Ranchburgers.

The Chilli beans can be made well in advance and gently reheated just before the party. They are spicy but not too rich, and everyone will love them. My Ranchburgers, which will have to be cooked while the party is in full swing, are served on toasted baps — with or without slices of cheese, added at the last moment — and a selection of garnishes: deep-fried onion rings, sliced tomato and cucumber. Offer a range of colourful relishes, pickles and ketchups, too.

Bronco strips — slices of toast with a pizza-like topping — will fill any corners your guests may have left; bake them just before you want to eat them so they are golden and bubbling. One good, big salad should be sufficient to go with the hot food and my Cabbage and pepper slaw with a mayonnaise dressing certainly fits the bill. The dressed salad is served in a hollowed-out 'bowl' made from a Savoy cabbage.

Ice cream is not just for youngsters, every one enjoys it. So make my gorgeous Straw-

berry ice-cream roll to please your guests. As a second choice serve Shoo-fly pie, a very rich and sweet dessert which is a speciality of the Pennyslvania Dutch community. This combination of desserts will win you compliments all down the line.

Ranchburgers

 1¼ hours

Serves 30
3.4 kg /7½ lb lean beef, minced
3 Spanish onions, finely chopped
105 ml /7 tbls Worcestershire sauce
7.5 ml /1½ tsp curry powder
7.5 ml /1½ tsp paprika
salt and freshly ground black pepper
melted butter
30 baps, halved
slices of cheese (optional)
To serve
tomatoes, sliced
cucumber, sliced
spring onions, finely chopped
pickled onions and cucumbers
stuffed olives

1 In a large bowl, combine the minced beef with the chopped onions, Worcestershire sauce, curry powder and paprika. Season with salt and freshly ground black pepper. Mix well.
2 With wet hands, shape into 30 burgers. Heat the grill to high and heat the oven to 150C /300F /gas 2.
3 Arrange the burgers in grill pans or shallow roasting tins lined with foil. Brush each one with melted butter and grill in batches. Grill them 7.5 cm /3 in from the heat for 3–4 minutes on each side or until they are brown and sizzling. Transfer each batch, as it is cooked, to the oven to keep warm.
4 Grill the halved baps on one side until brown. Place a burger on one half and top with another half.
5 If using cheese, place a slice on top of the burger and put it under the grill just before serving, so that the cheese melts. Replace the top of the bap.
6 Serve the ranchburgers with tomato and cucumber slices, spring onions, pickles and olives. These garnishes can be placed in the bap, on top of the burger, or eaten separately.

Ranchburgers

Chilli beans

overnight soaking,
then 2 hours

Serves 30
1.7 kg /3¾ lb red kidney beans, soaked
   overnight
7 Spanish onions, finely chopped
10 garlic cloves, finely chopped
110 ml /7½ tbls olive oil
1.7 kg /3¾ lb lean beef, minced
65 g /2½ oz butter
12.5 ml /2½ tsp dried oregano
37.5 ml /2½ tbls tomato purée
150 g /5 oz flour
2.2–2.3 L /3¾–4 pt beef stock, home-made or
   from cubes
12.5 ml /2½ tsp ground cumin
12.5 ml /2½ tsp hot chilli powder
salt and freshly ground black pepper
37.5 ml /2½ tbls mild chilli sauce

1 Drain the beans and put them in a pan with fresh cold water to cover. Add 2 Spanish onions and 3 garlic cloves to the water. Bring it to the boil, boil hard for 10 minutes, then simmer for 50 minutes, or until the beans are tender. Drain and reserve the beans and onion and garlic flavourings.
2 Meanwhile, in a flameproof casserole, heat the olive oil. Add the minced beef in batches and cook it over a high heat, stirring it until it is browned. Remove the meat from the pan with a slotted spoon and set it aside.
3 Add the butter to the pan and when the foaming subsides add the remaining onions and garlic cloves. Sauté for 5 minutes, stirring occasionally, until they are golden.
4 Return the meat to the pan, add the oregano and tomato purée and sprinkle in the flour. Cook for 2–3 minutes over a moderate heat, stirring.
5 In a separate pan, bring 2.2 L /3¾ pt beef stock to the boil. Add the ground cumin and the chilli powder to the meat and gradually pour the hot stock over the meat mixture, stirring. Season to taste with salt and freshly ground black pepper.
6 Add the reserved cooked beans and flavourings to the meat and stir in the mild chilli sauce. Simmer, stirring occasionally, for 45 minutes. Add extra stock if it thickens too much. Adjust the seasoning with more salt and black pepper if necessary. Serve it, piping hot, in warmed serving dishes.

Bronco strips

1 hour

Makes 60
45 g /1¾ oz canned anchovy fillets, chopped
225 g /8 oz green olives, chopped
400 g /14 oz canned tomatoes, drained and
   chopped
150 g /5 oz freshly grated Gruyère cheese
2.5 ml /½ tsp dried oregano
2 small garlic cloves, crushed
20 slices of white bread, crusts removed
softened butter

1 Heat the oven to 230C /450F /gas 8.

Chilli beans

Bronco strips

2 In a bowl, combine the chopped anchovies, chopped green olives, chopped tomatoes, grated Gruyère cheese, dried oregano and crushed garlic. Blend well.
3 Toast the bread and spread it with the softened butter.
4 Spread the topping mixture on the buttered slices of toast and place them on baking sheets. Bake, 2 sheets at a time, in the oven for 10–15 minutes, or until the cheese is melted and bubbling.
5 Cut each slice into 3 strips and serve.

Cabbage and pepper slaw

soaking the raisins, then 1 hour, plus chilling

Serves 30
1 large Savoy cabbage
salt
2.3 kg /5 lb crisp white cabbage
900 g /2 lb back bacon, chopped
about 300 ml /10 fl oz lemon juice
about 600 ml /1 pt Mayonnaise (see page 84)
freshly ground black pepper
3 large green peppers, seeded and chopped
275 g /10 oz raisins, soaked until plump and
*   drained*
10 celery sticks, chopped
150 g /5 oz onion, finely chopped
60 ml /4 tbls finely chopped fresh parsley

1 Carefully cut out the centre of the Savoy cabbage, leaving the large outer leaves attached to the centre stalk to make a 'bowl'. Reserve the centre. Trim any damaged leaves from the cabbage bowl and trim the base of the stalk flat. Put it, upside down, in a large bowl of salted water to soak for 20 minutes; drain it upside down.
2 Finely shred the white cabbage and the centre of the Savoy cabbage.
3 In a large frying-pan, sauté the chopped bacon in its own fat until it is golden and crisp. Remove it from the pan with a slotted spoon and drain on absorbent paper. Pour the bacon fat into a measuring jug and leave it to cool slightly.
4 Combine the bacon fat with an equal quantity of lemon juice in the jug. Pour into a bowl and add mayonnaise to equal the quantity of the combined bacon fat and lemon juice (approximately 300 ml /10 fl oz bacon fat, 300 ml /10 fl oz lemon juice and 600 ml /1 pt mayonnaise). Season to taste with salt and freshly ground black pepper.
5 In a large bowl, combine the sautéed bacon, the finely shredded cabbage, the chopped green peppers, the drained raisins, the chopped celery and the chopped onion. Add the mayonnaise mixture and toss the salad until all the ingredients are lightly coated. Chill until needed.
6 To serve, pile the salad mixture high in the cabbage bowl and sprinkle with the chopped parsley. Any left-over mixture can be served in a separate dish.

Cabbage and pepper slaw

Strawberry ice-cream rolls

 45 minutes,
plus 4 hours freezing

Serves 16
350 g /12 oz caster sugar
900 g /2 lb strawberries
300 ml /10 fl oz redcurrant juice
30 ml /2 tbls lemon juice
600 ml /1 pt thick cream, lightly whipped
fresh strawberries, to decorate
whipped cream, to decorate

1   If using the freezing compartment of the refrigerator, turn it down to the lowest temperature (the highest setting) 1 hour before starting. Put the sugar into a pan with 300 ml /11 fl oz water and stir over a low heat to dissolve the sugar. Bring to the boil and boil for 10 minutes until the syrup forms a thread when 2 cold spoons are dipped into the syrup and then pulled apart. Leave the syrup to cool.
2   Blend the strawberries to a purée, then mix together the purée, redcurrant and lemon juice. Stir in the cold syrup. Gradually pour the mixture onto the lightly whipped cream, stirring gently.
3   Divide the mixture between 2 chilled freezing trays, cover them and freeze for 45–60 minutes. Turn into a chilled bowl and whisk until the mixture is smooth.

4   Pour the ice-cream mixture into 2 cleaned 1 kg /2 lb cans. Cover the open ends with foil and stand them upright in the freezer. Freeze for about 3 hours.
5   Put the cans in the refrigerator for 30 minutes before serving. Next, run a knife between the can and the ice cream to help to unmould it. Decorate with fresh strawberries and piped whipped cream. Serve as quickly as possible.

● Try coating the rolls with 350 g /12 oz coarsely chopped walnuts or hazelnuts. Place half of the nuts in a shallow dish, then gently roll the ice cream over the nuts to cover the outside. Repeat with the second roll.

Shoo-fly pies

 2 hours

Serves 16
225 ml /8 fl oz molasses
225 g /8 oz soft light brown sugar
5 ml /1 tsp bicarbonate of soda
4 medium-sized eggs, beaten
350 g /12 oz flour
2.5 ml /½ tsp salt
2.5 ml /½ tsp ginger
2.5 ml /½ tsp nutmeg
5 ml /1 tsp cinnamon
50 g /2 oz cold butter, diced
225 g /8 oz raisins
ice cream or thick cream, to serve

A Strawberry ice-cream roll

For the crust
300 g /11 oz flour, sifted
5 ml /1 tsp salt
225 g /8 oz lard or white vegetable fat
90 ml /6 tbls (or slightly more) iced water

1   To make the crust, mix the flour and salt in a large bowl. Cut in the lard or white vegetable fat with 2 knives until the mixture resembles oatmeal.
2   Sprinkle the mixture with iced water while stirring with a fork until the mixture forms a ball. Cut it in half. Flatten one half, then roll it on a floured board to a circle about 3 mm /⅛ in thick. Fit into a 25 cm /10 in pie plate or flan tin. Repeat for the other half of the mixture.
3   Heat the oven to 230C /450F /gas 8. Stir 250 ml /8 fl oz hot water into the molasses and soft light brown sugar in a bowl. Add the bicarbonate of soda and eggs and then stir well.
4   Mix the flour, salt and spices in another bowl. Work in the butter until the mixture resembles fine breadcrumbs.
5   Sprinkle the raisins over the pastry cases, then add the molasses mixture alternately with the crumb mixture, dividing it equally between the 2 pies, finishing with a layer of crumbs.
6   Bake for 10 minutes, reduce the heat to 180C /350F /gas 4 and bake for 20 minutes, or until the top of each pie feels fairly firm. Serve with ice cream or thick cream.

Impromptu Parties

BIG BREAKFASTS

Why not start the day with a party — a breakfast party. Much of the work can be done the night before so that you need not have to get up at dawn to organize everything before the guests arrive!

A hurried cup of instant coffee and a slice of toast — eaten standing up — are all many of us manage for breakfast on most days. But in the past huge breakfasts, which must have taken hours both to prepare and eat, were commonplace. The sideboard in the dining room would be laden with a variety of dishes so that guests came and helped themselves as often as they wished.

Today there usually isn't time for this sort of feast unless you make a special occasion of it, so for a different kind of party try serving a luxurious breakfast either to friends or your weekend guests.

Starting the meal
Begin the day refreshingly with long glasses of chilled orange juice. Squeeze fresh oranges — it's worth the time and trouble and can be done the night before. Fresh grapefruit, especially the large, juicy pink ones, are a delicious alternative. Or combine several exotic fruits such as figs, pineapple, lichees and kiwi fruits, to create a Tropical fruit cup (see recipe).

For those who like a more substantial beginning, serve home-made Apricot yoghurt muesli (see recipe). Oats also give a good, and warming, start to the day — try your hand at making real Scots porridge, which can be served with brown sugar, golden syrup, or lots of thick cream. The usual breakfast cereals can also be offered to guests with a choice of cream, milk, sugar or stewed fruit such as rhubarb or apple.

Pancakes are sure to be a popular attraction. You can prepare the batter the night before and keep it, covered, in the refrigerator. Cook the pancakes the next morning when the guests are ready. A more filling recipe is Apple pancakes with black pudding (see recipe) — and crisply grilled chipolata sausages make a good substitute for the black puddings, if you prefer.

Main courses
The possibilities for main courses are endless, so choose three or four dishes with contrasting tastes and textures.

The classic English combination of eggs, bacon, sausages, tomatoes, mushrooms and fried bread — with or without baked beans — always goes down well. Meat and eggs are a traditional mixture: fried or grilled bacon or sausage-meat and scrambled, poached, coddled or fried eggs are the usual items served, but thick slices of ham are also lovely with fried eggs, and the classic Australian combination, if you can manage it, is steak and eggs.

Bacon coils (see recipe), little rolls of bacon wrapped around sausage-meat with a mushroom in the middle for added taste, are another idea to accompany eggs, be they poached, scrambled or fried.

I have included in this section two unusual recipes which are well worth trying — Norman pork patties and Piquant kidneys. The pork patties are adapted from an old French recipe, but I also include the original recipe so that you can take your choice of how to cook them — or why not make both?

Piquant kidneys are a spicy way to start the day and make a lovely contrast to scrambled eggs. These kidneys can be prepared the night before and then quickly heated up in the morning.

A traditional British dish is Breakfast lamb cutlets (see recipe). These thin lamb cutlets, coated with redcurrant jelly, Dijon mustard and breadcrumbs, are delicious when served with potato cakes. Potato cakes are simple to make from left-over mashed potatoes mixed with grated cheese. Form them into flat cakes and then fry them in butter until they are golden brown. Sprinkle them with freshly chopped herbs before serving.

Succulent jugged kippers or Finnan haddock and poached eggs are popular, while for an unusual dish see if you can locate Arbroath smokies, from Scotland. Failing that, Bloaters (see recipe) are very acceptable.

Soft herring roes, fried in butter and then sprinkled with herbs, are a different idea for a breakfast dish. Serve them on rounds of fried bread, or spread them onto thin slices of well-grilled streaky bacon, then roll up and secure each coil with a cocktail stick — either way providing a pleasing contrast of textures.

Kedgeree is traditionally made with smoked haddock, but salmon and ham make an interesting flavour, while Kipper kedgeree (see recipe) is very subtle.

For a complete contrast, a typical German breakfast dish is a wonderful spread of raw smoked bacon and sausages, with soft, creamy cheeses and thin slices of nutty black bread spread with unsalted butter. This takes little or no preparation apart from arranging it attractively on the serving plate.

Finishing the meal
End your breakfast with freshly baked wholemeal bread, slices of toast, either brown or white, lovely soft baps or even Scottish oatcakes. Serve them with butter and a selection of marmalades, jams or honey.

What to drink
Serve several different kinds of tea — an Assam or Darjeeling, a blend of Ceylons or a smoky China tea such as Earl Grey or Lapsang Souchong.

Many people prefer to drink coffee in the morning, so provide jugs of delicious-smelling, freshly ground coffee: Blue Mountain coffee from Jamaica is an ideal blend for breakfast, as is the mild but by no means weak Kenya Peaberry. For those who like really strong coffee, serve Continental blend, with jugs of piping hot milk or cream.

Tropical fruit cup

⏱ 30 minutes,
then overnight macerating

Serves 8
½ a medium-sized water-melon or 1 large Ogen melon
1 small pineapple, peeled, cored and diced
8 lichees, peeled, halved and stoned
8 ripe apricots, peeled, halved and stoned
1 papaya, peeled, seeded and diced
4 kiwi fruit or 4 fresh figs, peeled and thinly sliced
175 g /6 oz Cape gooseberries, dehusked, or 175 g /6 oz seedless white grapes
2 large, sweet oranges, peeled, pith removed and thinly sliced
150 ml /5 fl oz clear honey
juice of 1 lime

1 If you are using an Ogen melon, cut a slice off the top. Scoop out the flesh of the water-melon or Ogen, being careful not to pierce the shell, and remove all the seeds. Chop the flesh coarsely and put it into a large bowl with its juice. Reserve the melon shell, wrapped in cling film.
2 To the melon flesh add the pineapple, lichees, apricots, papaya, kiwi fruit or figs, gooseberries or grapes, and the oranges, together with their juices.
3 Heat the honey gently in a small saucepan until it is liquid, then pour it all over the fruit. Put the bowl in the refrigerator so the fruit can macerate overnight.
4 Just before serving, pile the fruit into the melon shell and pour the lime juice over it.

Apricot yoghurt muesli

⏱ 5 minutes, overnight soaking,
then 10 minutes

Serves 4–6
juice of 2 large lemons
juice of 2 large oranges
60 ml /4 tbls clear honey
125 g /4 oz dried apricots, chopped
1 large pear, peeled, cored and diced
1 large dessert apple
30 ml /2 tbls hazelnuts, finely chopped
125 g /4 oz blackberries (optional)
125 g /4 oz coarse oatmeal or rolled oats
60–90 ml /4–6 tbls yoghurt

1 Gently warm the lemon and orange juices and honey together in a saucepan.
2 Put the apricots and pear in a shallow bowl and cover them with the warm juice mixture. If necessary, top it up with a little tepid water so that the fruit is completely covered. Leave it to soak overnight in the refrigerator.
3 Just before serving, grate the unpeeled apple into the fruit, stirring it in to avoid discoloration, then fold in the hazelnuts and blackberries, if using.

Tropical fruit cup in a water-melon and an Ogen melon, and Breakfast lamb cutlets (page 35)

4 Stir in the oatmeal lightly. Pour the yoghurt over the mixture — depending on how liquid you like it — and serve it at once.

Bloaters

Bloaters are dry-salted and very lightly smoked without being gutted first. Eat them within a day of buying them.

 25 minutes

Serves 4–8
8 small bloaters or smoked, cured herrings
125 g /4 oz unsalted butter, melted
juice of 1 lemon
freshly ground black pepper
thinly sliced buttered brown bread, to serve

1 Heat the grill to high. Put the bloaters in the grill pan, pour half the melted butter over them, then reduce the heat to medium-low. Grill the bloaters for 10 minutes.
2 Turn over the bloaters, pour the remaining butter onto them and grill for a further 10 minutes.
3 Put the bloaters on a warmed serving dish, pour on any butter from the grill pan, the lemon juice and sprinkle with pepper. Serve at once with thin slices of buttered brown bread.

● Alternatively, the bloaters may be split open and the bones and guts removed. Grill, open, for just 5 minutes.

Apple pancakes with black pudding

 15 minutes to make the batter, then 45 minutes

Makes 12 pancakes
12 slices of black pudding (about 225 g /8 oz)
120 ml /8 tbls apple jelly, melted
For the pancakes
225 g /8 oz flour
2.5 ml /½ tsp ground allspice
22.5 ml /1½ tbls icing sugar
1 egg
25 g /1 oz butter, melted, plus extra for frying
215 ml /7½ fl oz buttermilk or milk
1.5 ml /¼ tsp salt
1 large dessert apple

1 Sift the flour, allspice and sugar together into a bowl. In another bowl, beat the egg thoroughly. Little by little, add the flour alternately with the melted butter, to form a thick paste. If it gets too thick to beat, add 15 ml /1 tbls buttermilk.
2 Add the salt, then add the buttermilk or milk very gradually, beating constantly so no lumps form.
3 Peel the apple, cut it into quarters and core it. Grate it into the batter and stir it well. If you wish, cover the batter and then refrigerate it overnight.
4 Heat the grill to high, then reduce the heat to medium. Grill the slices of black pudding for 5 minutes each side while you make the pancakes.
5 Give the batter a good whisk before cooking the pancakes. Melt a tiny knob of butter, just enough to coat an 18 cm /7 in heavy-based frying-pan, over a high heat. Pour in 20 ml /4 tsp batter, swirl it so that it covers the pan thinly and then cook until bubbles start to appear on the surface of the pancake.
6 Turn over the pancake with a spatula and cook for a further 50 seconds. Slide it out of the pan onto a warmed serving dish.
7 Spread 10 ml /2 tsp melted apple jelly down the centre of the pancake and roll it up quickly. Keep it warm while you make the

other pancakes with the remaining batter and jelly. Arrange the black pudding around the pancakes and then serve them.

Norman pork patties

 30 minutes

Makes 12 patties
225 g /8 oz cooked pork, minced
2.5 ml /½ tsp dried marjoram
1.5 ml /¼ tsp ground caraway seeds
freshly grated nutmeg
1.5 ml /¼ tsp ground ginger
1 blade of mace, crumbled
2.5 ml /½ tsp caster sugar
salt and freshly ground black pepper
2.5 ml /½ tsp ground white pepper
½ medium-sized onion, grated
1 egg, beaten
25 g /1 oz butter

1 Put the pork into a large bowl, add the herbs, spices, sugar, salt and black and white peppers. Stir in the onion and then mix in the egg to bind.
2 Using 2 dessertspoons, form the mixture into 12 oval patties.
3 Melt the butter in a large, heavy-based frying-pan. When it sizzles, add the patties in 1 layer. Fry for 3–4 minutes, turning once. Drain on absorbent paper, arrange on a warmed serving dish and serve at once.

● Norman pork patties are an adaptation of a very old French recipe, Golden apples, where the pork mixture was dipped in batter before it was fried. If you want to make Golden apples, use the Apple pancake batter minus the apple (see previous recipe) as a coating batter. Deep fry the patties for 3–4 minutes or until they are golden.

Kipper kedgeree

55 minutes

Serves 8

salt
1.5 ml /¼ tsp turmeric
175 g /6 oz long-grain rice
75 g /3 oz butter
1 Spanish onion, finely chopped
4 large kippers
3 medium-sized eggs, hard-boiled and finely
   chopped
a large pinch of cayenne pepper
freshly ground black pepper
45 ml /3 tbls finely chopped fresh parsley
lemon wedges, to serve

1 Bring 600 ml /1 pt salted water to the boil in a large saucepan, add the turmeric, then dribble in the rice. Bring back to the boil, then reduce the heat and simmer gently, covered, for 15–20 minutes or until all the water is absorbed and the rice is tender but not mushy.

2 Meanwhile, melt 50 g /2 oz butter in a heavy-based frying-pan, add the onion and cook it gently for 15 minutes, until it is soft and golden.

3 Put the kippers in a tall jug, cover with boiling water and leave to stand for 10 minutes. Drain them carefully and remove the skin and bones. Flake the flesh coarsely with a fork.

4 When the rice is cooked, add the onions and any butter remaining in the pan, the flaked kippers and the hard-boiled eggs to it.

Mix gently but thoroughly, then season with cayenne pepper and freshly ground black pepper, and salt if necessary.

5 In a small pan, melt the remaining butter and stir it into the kedgeree. Heat the kedgeree through for 3–4 minutes, then pile it onto a warmed serving dish. Sprinkle with the parsley, garnish with the lemon and serve immediately.

● Kedgeree was originally an Indian dish — *khicharhi* — which included rice, onions, lentils, spices, fresh limes and fish.
● This kedgeree recipe can be made with either smoked haddock or canned tuna instead of the kippers.

Piquant kidneys, garnished with parsley and served on croûtons

Piquant kidneys

 50 minutes

Serves 4
450 g /1 lb lamb's kidneys
50 g /2 oz butter, melted
10 ml /2 tsp Worcestershire sauce
a dash of Tabasco
10 ml /2 tsp mushroom ketchup
15 ml /1 tbls Dijon mustard
15 ml /1 tbls lemon juice
1.5 ml /¼ tsp ground allspice
salt and ground white pepper
a pinch of cayenne pepper
45 ml /3 tbls thick cream
4 large croûtons, to serve
30 ml /2 tbls finely chopped fresh parsley, to garnish

1 Slice the kidneys in half through the centre and snip out the white core with scissors. Rinse thoroughly in cold water and pat dry on absorbent paper.
2 Put the melted butter in a bowl and stir in the Worcestershire and Tabasco sauces, mushroom ketchup, mustard, lemon juice, allspice, salt and white and cayenne peppers.
3 Pour the butter mixture into a large, heavy-based frying-pan and place over a moderate heat. When the butter mixture starts to bubble, lower the heat, then add the kidneys and cook for 15–20 minutes, turning once or twice.
4 Stir in the cream and adjust the seasoning. Place the croûtons on a warmed serving dish, pile the kidneys on top of them, sprinkle with the parsley and serve at once.

● Steps 1 to 3 can be done the night before and the dish can then be refrigerated overnight, covered.
● You can freeze the dish for up to 3

months: omit the salt and add 150 ml /5 fl oz chicken stock, home-made if possible, to the sauce, so that the kidneys are well covered. When reheating, remove the kidneys from the sauce, then reduce the sauce by fast boiling. Add the kidneys and reheat thoroughly.

Breakfast lamb cutlets

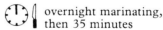 10 minutes, overnight chilling, then 10 minutes

Serves 4–6
90 ml /6 tbls redcurrant jelly
15 ml /1 tbls Dijon mustard
45 ml /3 tbls dry white breadcrumbs
salt and freshly ground black pepper
450 g /1 lb very thin 'breakfast' lamb cutlets (12–16 cutlets)
90 ml /6 tbls finely chopped fresh parsley
75 g /3 oz butter
lemon slices, to garnish
parsley sprigs, to garnish

1 Melt the redcurrant jelly in a small saucepan over a moderate heat. Combine it with the mustard and breadcrumbs and season with salt and pepper.
2 Coat the cutlets on both sides with this mixture. Roll them in parsley, then place them on a plate, cover loosely and refrigerate overnight.
3 Melt half the butter in a large, heavy-based frying-pan and, when sizzling, add as many cutlets as will fit in 1 layer. Sauté for 3 minutes each side, then remove to a warmed serving platter. Keep them warm while you cook the remaining cutlets, adding more butter if necessary.
4 Garnish the cutlets with slices of lemon, sprigs of parsley and an extra sprinkling of pepper and serve immediately.

A hearty breakfast of Apricot yoghurt muesli and Bacon coils, garnished with parsley and served with buttered toast and eggs

Bacon coils

 overnight marinating, then 35 minutes

Makes 16 coils
16 tiny button mushrooms
juice of 1 lemon
25 g /1 oz butter
16 thin slices of streaky bacon (about 450 g /1 lb)
45 ml /3 tbls finely chopped fresh parsley
225 g /8 oz sausage-meat
Dijon mustard, for spreading
freshly ground black pepper
poached or fried eggs, to serve
buttered toast, to serve
parsley sprigs, to garnish

1 Put the mushrooms in a small, deep bowl, pour the lemon juice over them, stir and leave to marinate overnight.
2 Melt the butter in a small saucepan over a moderate heat, then add the drained mushrooms and cook for 5–7 minutes, until brown and soft. Remove the mushrooms with a slotted spoon and reserve. Next, heat the grill to high.
3 Sprinkle each slice of bacon with parsley, then spread each one evenly with sausage-meat. Spread with mustard, then place a whole mushroom at one end. Season with pepper and roll up tightly.
4 Either spear each coil with a wooden cocktail stick or spear 8 coils onto each of 2 skewers. Put the coils under the grill, reduce the heat and grill them until they are crisp.
5 Remove the sticks or skewers and serve with poached or fried eggs, buttered toast and parsley sprigs to garnish.

BRUNCH

Replacing both breakfast and lunch, brunch combines delicious sweet and savoury dishes with, perhaps, the first cocktail of the day, in a splendidly leisurely way — ideal for a lazy weekend.

Sunday brunch is the ideal party for those who do not want to rise early, eat much before noon, or face cooking a big roast lunch with all the trimmings.

There is a powerful school of thought which maintains that guests should be offered a welcoming glass of something special as they arrive. Bloody Mary (see recipe) fits the bill admirably: it is invigorating and refreshing and can be used as a 'hair of the dog' hangover treatment.

Chilled orange juice is another suggestion. This can be drunk on its own; with the addition of vodka and cider, as in Chelsea reach (see recipe); with the addition of a sparkling white wine — or even champagne.

Start the meal with a melon salad which has a tangy lemon syrup and can be prepared the night before. Then offer your guests a selection of dishes which are both suitable for breakfast or for lunch, such as Smoked fish tarts or Ham and potato scallop (see recipes). Make sure that not all the dishes you choose to present involve last-minute cooking and that some, like the Devilled drumsticks (see recipe), can be kept warm in the oven for up to half an hour.

Scrambled eggs are an old favourite, but serve them in a new guise with olives and cones of crisp toast (see recipe). A savoury rice is always a good choice as an accompaniment to main courses, but pasta is equally easy to prepare, so think about the Pasta salad with herbed dressing (see recipe), as a tasty alternative.

Coconut-pineapple fingers will satisfy those of your guests who have a sweet tooth, and you could try the variation suggested in the recipe to make Coconut-cherry fingers at the same time.

While many people will only be drinking tea or coffee (so make sure that a supply of freshly brewed pots of both of these are readily available), others will be more adventurous. I have included a lovely Chilled Irish coffee which has the added 'lift' of Irish whiskey and liqueur to give it a splendidly rich taste. For other drink ideas see the chapter in the section on Cocktails (page 95).

Melon salad in lemon syrup

⟋⟍ 20 minutes,
plus chilling

Serves 8
1 small honeydew melon
1 Ogen, canteloupe or Charentais melon
a large wedge of water-melon

From left to right, Scrambled eggs with toast cones, Melon salad in lemon syrup, fresh orange juice and Ham and potato scallop

For the syrup
75 g /3 oz sugar
60 ml /4 tbls lemon juice
1.5 ml /¼ tsp ground ginger (optional)

1 For the syrup, put the sugar in a small pan with the lemon juice and 60 ml /4 tbls water. Heat gently until the sugar has dissolved. Add the ginger, if using, and bring to boiling point. Remove the pan from the heat immediately and let the syrup stand until warm.
2 Meanwhile, prepare the melons. Scoop out all the seeds from the melons, removing the black seeds from the water-melon with a small spoon. Slice the melon flesh away from the rind using a curved grapefruit knife. Cut the flesh into bite-sized pieces.
3 Put the melon pieces in a glass serving bowl, pour the warm syrup over them and

turn them gently until well coated with syrup. Cover and chill for at least 1 hour, then gently stir again before serving.

Smoked fish tarts

⟋⟍ making the pastry, plus chilling, then 40 minutes

Makes 16 tarts
450 g /1 lb smoked haddock fillet
8 canned smoked oysters, halved
2 medium-sized eggs
150 ml /5 fl oz milk
150 ml /5 fl oz thin cream
salt
freshly ground black pepper
For the shortcrust pastry
225 g /8 oz flour, plus a little extra for rolling
a pinch of salt
50 g /2 oz butter, diced small
75 g /3 oz hard margarine, diced small
30 ml /2 tbls cold water

1 Cover the smoked haddock fillet with water and poach it for 10 minutes, or until the fish flakes easily with a fork. Carefully

drain and then flake the fish, discarding any bones and skin.

2 Sift the flour and salt into a mixing bowl and add the butter and margarine.

3 Press out the lumps of fat using your thumb and fingertips, keeping your hands high in the bowl so that the crumbs shower back. Continue until the mixture resembles breadcrumbs.

4 Sprinkle the water over the surface and pull the dough together with a flat-bladed knife. Now use your fingers to continue the process.

5 Turn the dough out onto a lightly floured board and knead lightly. Pat into shape. Wrap and chill for 15 minutes.

6 Heat the oven to 190C /375F /gas 5 and grease 16 deep tart tins. Roll out the pastry and use it to line the tart tins.

7 Divide the fish equally among the tart cases and then put a halved smoked oyster in each tart.

8 Beat the eggs with the milk and cream; season with a little salt and freshly ground black pepper.

9 Spoon a little of the custard mixture into each tart. Bake until the filling is set, about 15 minutes, and the tarts are golden brown on top. Serve immediately.

Ham and potato scallop

 2 hours

Serves 8
8 medium-sized potatoes (about 1.1 kg /2½ lb)
750 g /1½ lb sweet-cured gammon joint
75 g /3 oz butter
1 small onion, finely chopped
5 ml /1 tsp mustard powder
40 g /1½ oz flour
400 ml /14 fl oz milk
1.5 ml /¼ tsp salt
1.5 ml /¼ tsp freshly ground white pepper
For the topping
100 g /4 oz butter
100 g /4 oz fresh white breadcrumbs

1 Peel the potatoes and cut them into 3 mm /⅛ in slices and reserve in a bowl of water. Cut the gammon joint into 20 mm /¾ in cubes and put them in a 2 L /3½ pt shallow ovenproof dish. Heat the oven to 180C /350F /gas 4.

2 Melt the butter in a large saucepan over a medium-low heat; add the onion and fry gently until it is soft but not coloured. Stir in the mustard and flour and, when blended, cook for 1 minute, stirring. Gradually add the milk and bring to the boil, stirring constantly, until the sauce is thick. Add the salt and pepper. Drain the reserved potato slices, then add them to the sauce and mix well.

3 Use this mixture to evenly cover the gammon cubes. Next, cover and cook in the oven for 1½ hours, or until the potatoes are tender.

4 Meanwhile, melt the butter for the topping in a large pan over a medium-high heat. Add the breadcrumbs and cook, stirring frequently, until the crumbs are a golden brown colour.

5 Take the dish from the oven and sprinkle the surface evenly with the crumbs.

6 Take the dish to the table to serve, or cover it and reduce the heat of the oven to the lowest setting and keep the scallop warm until needed.

Scrambled eggs with toast cones

Clever presentation lends a new look to scrambled eggs. This dish can be prepared in advance and kept hot for 30 minutes.

 40 minutes

Serves 8
8 medium-sized eggs
salt and freshly ground black pepper
40 g /1½ oz butter
16 stuffed green olives, halved
For the toast cones
16 large, thin slices of white bread
75 g /3 oz butter, melted, plus extra for greasing

1 First make the toast cones. Heat the oven to 190C /375F /gas 5. Trim the crusts from each slice of bread using scissors, then flatten each slice lightly with a rolling pin to make it more pliable.

2 Brush each piece of bread on one side with melted butter, then roll it up to form a cone with the buttered surface inside. Secure the overlapping edge with a wooden cocktail stick. Repeat with the other slices.

3 Arrange the cones on a greased baking sheet and brush them with the remaining butter. Bake for about 15 minutes, or until they are golden brown. Cool the cones on a wire rack.

4 Beat the eggs with seasoning to taste. Melt the butter in a pan over a medium heat, add the egg mixture and stir until it is thickened and creamy. Do not allow the eggs to overcook and become too firm.

5 Stir in the halved olives and transfer the mixture to a heatproof bowl and cover tightly. Place this over a pan of hot but not boiling water; the eggs will keep warm for 30 minutes without spoiling.

6 To serve, put the egg in a warm shallow bowl set in a larger bowl, piling the toast cones around the edge. Fill a few of the cones with egg to decorate the plate, if you wish.

175 g /6 oz pasta shells
For the sauce
20 ml /4 tsp dried basil
75 ml /3 fl oz olive oil
45 ml /3 tbls chopped fresh parsley
1 garlic clove, roughly chopped
5 ml /1 tsp salt
1.5 ml /¼ tsp ground nutmeg

1   Cook the pasta in plenty of boiling salted water until *al dente*.
2   Meanwhile, make the sauce. Soak the basil in 10 ml /2 tsp hot water for 5 minutes, then drain. Put all the ingredients for the sauce together in a blender and process until smooth.
3   Drain the pasta well and leave it for 5 minutes to cool a little. Stir the sauce into the pasta while it is still warm. Transfer the salad to a serving bowl, cover and chill it for at least 30 minutes to allow the flavour to develop fully.

Coconut-pineapple fingers

When making these finger cakes, it takes very little extra time to double up the quantities, and then use 300 ml /10 fl oz cherry pie filling for half the mixture and the crushed pineapple for the other half.

1 hour, plus cooling

Makes 16 fingers
75 g /3 oz soft margarine
75 g /3 oz caster sugar
5 ml /1 tsp salt
2 egg yolks
225 g /8 oz self-raising flour
butter or margarine, for greasing
For the topping
375 g /13 oz canned crushed pineapple
2 egg whites
175 g /6 oz caster sugar
175 g /6 oz desiccated coconut
50 g /2 oz soft margarine, melted

1   Heat the oven to 180C /350F /gas 4. Cream the margarine with the sugar and salt until soft, then add the egg yolks and beat until the mixture is blended.
2   Add the flour and stir with a fork until the mixture is evenly crumbly with no large lumps. Do not gather it into a ball. Turn the mixture into a greased baking tin 30 × 23 cm /12 × 9 in and press it flat.
3   Tip the canned pineapple into a sieve and leave it to drain for 1 minute, but do not press out any syrup. Spread the pineapple over the mixture in the tin.
4   Whisk the egg whites until stiff, add about a third of the sugar and whisk until the meringue is firm and glossy. Add the coconut, remaining sugar and melted fat and stir well.
5   Spread the mixture over the pineapple and bake for about 50 minutes, or until it is a deep golden brown on top.
6   Leave the cake to cool in the tin. When it is cold, cut it into 16 fingers.

Devilled drumsticks

10 minutes, plus 1 hour marinating, then 40 minutes

Serves 8–16
16 chicken drumsticks
1 large onion, finely chopped
90 ml /6 tbls lemon juice
90 ml /6 tbls soy sauce
2.5 ml /½ tsp salt
a pinch of freshly ground black pepper
7–8 drops of Tabasco
10 ml /2 tsp ground coriander
60 ml /4 tbls soft brown sugar
60 ml /4 tbls plum jam
60 ml /4 tbls vegetable oil
To garnish
lime slices
celery leaves

1   Make 2–3 slashes in each drumstick using a sharp knife. Put the drumsticks in a shallow ovenproof dish.
2   Mix together the remaining ingredients

Devilled drumsticks

and pour them over the drumsticks. Cover them and leave them to stand for at least 1 hour, turning them over occasionally.
3   Heat the oven to 180C /350F /gas 4. Uncover the dish and put it in the oven for 40 minutes, turning and basting the drumsticks with the sauce in the dish at least once.
4   Put the drumsticks on a serving plate, garnish with the lime slices and the celery leaves and serve, or cover the dish with foil and keep in a low oven for 30 minutes.

Pasta salad with herbed dressing

This dish can be prepared in advance. The pasta salad looks fresh and has a good tangy taste, especially when it is served with grilled pork or beef chipolata sausages.

20 minutes, plus chilling

Bloody Mary

5 minutes,
then 1 hour chilling

Makes 14 servings
150 ml /5 fl oz lemon juice
45 ml /3 tbls Worcestershire sauce
2.5 ml /½ tsp celery salt
a dash of cayenne pepper
1 L /1¾ pt tomato juice
½ × 70 cl bottle of vodka
ice cubes, to serve
lemon slices and celery sticks, to garnish

1 Place all the ingredients except the tomato juice and vodka in a bowl and stir.
2 Pour the tomato juice and vodka into a 2 L /3½ pt jug. Add the spicy mixture a little at a time, tasting and stirring after each addition. Add more vodka or tomato juice, if necessary. Stir well and refrigerate the jug until the first guests arrive.
3 Serve in individual glasses with ice, lemon slices and celery sticks.

Chelsea reach

3 minutes

Serves 1
50 ml /2 fl oz vodka
75 ml /3 fl oz unsweetened fresh orange juice
ice cubes
medium-dry cider
an orange slice, to garnish

1 Pour the vodka and the orange juice over ice cubes in a tall narrow glass. Top up with medium-dry cider, and then garnish the drink with an orange slice.

Chilled Irish coffee

making and cooling the coffee,
then 3 minutes

Serves 1
25 ml /1 fl oz Irish whiskey
15 ml /1 tbls Irish Mist liqueur (optional)
crushed ice
150 ml /5 fl oz strong, cold, black coffee
brown sugar, to taste
15 ml /1 tbls thick cream

1 Pour the whiskey and the liqueur, if using, over the ice in a goblet. Fill with coffee, sweetened to taste. Pour cream over the back of a spoon, to make a layer on top of the coffee. Serve with straws.

A glass of Chelsea reach, made with unsweetened fresh orange juice

COOK-AHEAD PARTY

Unexpected guests can always be accommodated if, at convenient times, you fill your freezer with some basics — pastry cases, sauces, fish fillets, garnishes, vegetables and fruit. Try these ideas for quick, stylish menus.

A well-stocked freezer can often come to the rescue in an emergency. Surprisingly, it isn't always the prepared dishes — the casseroles, the pâtés and the gateaux — that fit the bill. Unless you also own a microwave oven the large frozen dishes will take too long to defrost. Far more useful on these occasions are the component items and quick-thawing ingredients which you can assemble in a number of different ways. Here I look at starters and main courses and give you some recipes for both these, as well as a few dessert ideas and general tips that are helpful in an unexpected situation.

Quick meal ideas

These are a few suggestions for quick meals you can prepare.

White fish fillets such as cod and haddock, are among the most versatile of ingredients for quick meals. You can cut them into thin slices, dip them in egg and breadcrumbs or batter, deep-fry them and serve with tartare sauce. Or use them as a filling for quiches or, with a cheese sauce, in defrosted crêpes. Try the fillets steamed with vegetables in a sweet and sour sauce (see Cod in sweet and sour sauce) or combine them with tomatoes and garlic for Quayside soup (see recipe), a meal-in-a-bowl fish soup with a Mediterranean flavour which can be served in small quantities as a starter or in larger quantities for a main course. Or make a quick sauce for fried fish by puréeing gooseberries (canned or frozen) with lemon juice.

Prawns and shrimps can be used in similar ways to fish fillets. Mediterranean prawns (see recipe), prawns simmered with onions, mushrooms and herbs in garlic butter, is a dish that can be served as a first course or as a main course with rice or noodles.

Pork fillet is far more useful than even chops when speed is of the essence. It can be sliced frozen and it thaws as it fries. Combined with a gin and orange sauce (see recipe) it becomes a real party dish; you can make other sauces, too — lemon juice and soured cream, cream and calvados, orange juice and ginger syrup — all are delicious.

Liver can be sliced into ribbon-thin slices while it is frozen and it will then cook almost instantly. Try it with the sauces suggested for pork. If you need to stretch the dish, serve it with tiny forcemeat balls, fried straight from the freezer. Forcemeat balls served with a dipping sauce — say, Herby mustard sauce (page 51), or a sweet and sour sauce — also make a good first course.

Sausages from the freezer can be used in many ways. Fry them first to brown the outside, then simmer them in a tasty sauce — try Fondue tomato sauce (page 51) — to cook them through or alternatively, for a more tangy flavour, try a barbecue sauce. You can also split the sausages lengthways and arrange them in a wheel pattern on a pizza base topped with tomatoes, herbs, olives, cheese, salami, mushrooms and green pepper for an extra-special pizza.

Savoury sauces

A good selection of savoury sauces frozen in 300 ml /10 fl oz quantities for quick thawing, will help you to be more versatile with other frozen foods. Make your own tomato, bolognese, barbecue and sweet and sour sauces. Sweet and sour sauce can be served with shallow or deep-fried prawns or fish slices, grilled sausages, pork chops or thinly sliced chicken or turkey breast. Cook rice or noodles to complete the meal.

Use a bechamel sauce (page 43) with added egg yolks for a rich, savoury flan filling — see Broccoli quiche (another possible for a starter as well as a main course). Or add chopped herbs, mushrooms or potted shrimps to make it into a sauce for serving with steamed or poached fish. Bechamel can also be combined with bolognese sauce and quick-cook lasagne for a one-pot meal.

Frozen cheese sauce with chopped asparagus or broccoli stirred in makes a tasty crêpe or flan filling — or it can be used to fill small individual tartlet cases for a first course.

Enlivening frozen vegetables

Frozen vegetables are a life-saver when time is short but served plain they are rather dull. Try some of these ideas to brighten them up.
● Simmer broad beans in a sauce made with 15 g /½ oz butter, 15 g /½ oz flour and 150 ml /5 fl oz sweet cider. Add 10 ml /2 tsp freshly chopped summer savory or parsley.
● Toss cooked spinach in butter, then in thick cream. Season well with pepper and sprinkle with chopped hard-boiled egg.
● Toss florets of cauliflower and broccoli, slices of carrot or courgette in beaten egg then breadcrumbs. Deep fry them in hot oil and serve with tartare sauce.
● Toss cooked vegetables with cooked, drained pasta and butter or thick cream. Sprinkle with herbs and Parmesan cheese.
● Simmer French beans, broad beans or frozen vegetables in any left-over white wine you may have, with plenty of fresh herbs, for a quick à la grecque first course. Serve it warm with hot, crusty bread.
● Cook Brussels sprouts, cauliflower or broccoli florets for 3 minutes. Drain, refresh under cold water, then sauté in hot butter with chopped almonds or walnuts.
● Serve peas French-style with lettuce, tiny onions and strips of ham.
● Sauté courgette or aubergine slices in butter with chopped onion and garlic, add 3 or 4 skinned and chopped tomatoes and season well. Cook until the tomatoes are soft.

Desserts

Ice creams and mousses are the ideal frozen desserts for last-minute emergency meals.

Nine emergency basics
Pizza bases will cope with many children's meals. Let them rise, but freeze untopped.
Half-baked pastry cases (in rigid containers) will help you to make a quick quiche or fruit tart. Tarlet cases are equally useful.
Crêpes: freeze them, layered with grease-proof paper, so that they can be separated for quick thawing.
Cooked chicken in stock: cook a whole chicken in stock and then remove bones and skin. Divide the flesh between 300 ml /10 fl oz containers and fill spaces with the reduced stock. Thaw in a saucepan over a low heat for a flan or omelette filling.
Chopped vegetables do save time. Ready-chopped onions, mushrooms, red and green peppers are most useful.

Take them out of the freezer and put them in the refrigerator half an hour or so before the meal starts and they will be ready to eat when needed.

Some fruit freezes far better than others: plums, cherries, blackberries, gooseberries, raspberries and rhubarb freeze well, strawberries less so. These fruit defrost quite quickly so you can serve them simply, with cream, yoghurt or custard. Alternatively cook them with a crumble or pastry topping, which you can also have ready-frozen. Another possibility is a quick trifle with boudoir biscuits, custard, cream and fruit. Strawberries can be puréed (see page 60) and served in individual glasses with a twirl of whipped cream.

Herb butter

This clever garnish will enhance fish, soups, vegetables and steaks.

softening the butter,
then 15 minutes

Makes 450 g /1 lb

450 g /1 lb butter, unsalted
90 ml /6 tbls very finely chopped fresh parsley
30 ml /2 tbls finely chopped fresh tarragon
30 ml /2 tbls finely snipped fresh chives
juice of 1 lemon
salt and freshly ground black pepper

1 Bring the butter to room temperature and then soften it slightly.
2 Put the butter into a large bowl with the herbs and mix everything very thoroughly with a fork. Make sure the herbs are well distributed.
3 Season to taste with the lemon juice and salt and freshly ground black pepper.
4 Divide the mixture into 2 and shape into rolls about 4 cm /1½ in in diameter. Chill until firm, then wrap in foil and freeze for up to 3 months. Slice from the pats as needed and return the remainder to the freezer.

Tomato mint cooler

20 minutes, 4½ hours freezing,
then 10 minutes

Purées of unusual vegetables will make interesting side dishes, or can be diluted for soup. Freeze them in 300 ml /10 fl oz quantities for quick thawing and then reheat with plenty of butter and seasoning. Jerusalem artichokes and celeriac are good choices.

Tomato purée is useful: chop tomatoes and simmer them until reduced to a thick pulp. Cool and rub through a sieve to remove the seeds. Frozen in cartons, the purée will keep for 9 months.

Duchesse potatoes (potato, puréed with butter, egg yolks and nutmeg to season) are one of the best ways of freezing potatoes. They quickly thaw and reheat in the oven.

Concentrated stock, frozen in an ice cube tray, gives you individual home-made cubes for the base to a sauce or soup.

Quick freezer garnishes

Lemon slices (or orange and lime) can be kept in a bag in the freezer. Use them to garnish drinks, or to float on cold soups. Cut halfway across a slice and pull the corners in opposite directions to make lemon twists for garnishing fish, sweet or savoury salads and also dips.

Herbs, for example parsley or thyme, can be frozen, finely chopped and mixed with a little water, in ice cube trays. Add them to soups in the frozen cube, or turn the cubes into a sieve and run hot water through to defrost. Pat the herbs dry and use. Do not keep for more than three months.

Herb butter (see recipe) is useful. Frozen as a roll, you can slice off pats as needed and return the rest to the freezer. Use parsley on its own for parsley butter, with 15 ml /1 tbls finely chopped freshly parsley per 25 g /1 oz of softened butter. Pound the parsley and work it into the butter. Season to taste with lemon juice and black pepper, then freeze.

Croûtons, especially in pretty shapes, are invaluable for added texture and glamour. Buy thick-sliced bread and remove the crusts. Cut shapes, freeze, then when needed thaw for 5 minutes before frying. Alternatively freeze them cooked — they will need 3–4 minutes in a hot oven before serving.

Tiny croûton cubes can be sprinkled onto soups, and anything with a soft texture is delicious served on croûtons. They will add crunch to an omelette filling, while a vegetable purée, such as spinach, looks pretty with heart-shaped croûtons on top.

Serves 6

500 g /1 lb canned tomatoes
5 ml /1 tsp Worcestershire sauce
5 ml /1 tsp lemon juice
60 ml /4 tbls vodka
60 ml /4 tbls mint leaves
salt and freshly ground black pepper
6 sprigs of mint, to garnish
Cheese straws (page 45), to serve
1 green pepper, thinly sliced, to serve
6 celery sticks, sliced into strips, to serve

1 Put the canned tomatoes in a blender with the Worcestershire sauce, lemon juice, vodka, mint leaves, salt and freshly ground black pepper, and blend together until the mixture is smooth.

2 Put into a container, cover and freeze for 1½ hours or until the mixture is set firmly at the sides.

3 Turn the mixture into a chilled bowl and beat it vigorously. Then return it to the container, cover and freeze again for a minimum

Pork in gin and orange (page 43)

of 3 hours. (It will keep for 3–4 months.)

4 After freezing, transfer the container to the main part of the refrigerator 10–20 minutes before serving. Spoon the tomato mint cooler into chilled glasses and garnish each one with the sprigs of mint. Serve with plenty of crispy cheese straws, warm or cold, sliced green pepper and celery sliced into fine matchstick strips.

Mediterranean prawns

Flavoured butters, perfect for garnishing food, can be used for cooking, too. Here they impart flavour to a prawn starter.

🔪 25 minutes

Serves 4
350 g /12 oz frozen peeled prawns
50 g /2 oz frozen Herb butter (see recipe)
225 g /8 oz frozen finely chopped onion
1 small garlic clove, chopped
125 g /4 oz frozen chopped or sliced mushrooms
5 ml /1 tsp cornflour
10 ml /2 tsp lemon juice
5 ml /1 tsp grated lemon juice
salt
freshly ground black pepper
a large pinch of cayenne pepper
25 g /1 oz frozen Parsley butter (see box, page 41)
flat-leaved parsley, to garnish

1   Thaw the prawns by immersing them, in their bag, in cold water. Remove the bag, drain them and pat dry on absorbent paper.
2   Melt the herb butter in a pan and fry the prawns over a moderate heat for 5 minutes, turning them frequently. Remove the prawns with a slotted spoon and keep them warm. Add the onion and garlic to the pan and fry, stirring constantly, for 4 minutes. Add the mushrooms and cook for a further 3 minutes.
3   Blend the cornflour with 15 ml /1 tbls of cold water and stir it into the pan. Add the lemon juice and the zest and return the prawns to the pan. Season well with salt, freshly ground black pepper and cayenne pepper and simmer for 4 minutes.
4   Stir in the parsley butter, cut into small pieces. Spoon the prawns onto heated, individual plates and then serve them garnished with flat-leaved parsley.

● Served with rice (allow 50 g /2 oz uncooked rice per person), this dish will make a main course.

Quayside soup

🔪 45 minutes

Serves 6
500 g /1 lb frozen cod fillets
500 g /1 lb frozen haddock fillets (or use other combinations of white fish)
1 L /1¾ pt frozen tomato purée (see box, page 41) or canned thick cream of tomato soup
60 ml /4 tbls oil
225 g /8 oz sliced onion
5–10 ml /1–2 tsp chopped garlic
4 celery sticks, finely chopped
grated zest and juice of 1 orange
4 ice cubes of chopped parsley (see box, page 41)
salt and freshly ground black pepper
90 ml /6 tbls plain or garlic-flavoured croûtons, to garnish (see box, page 41)

1   Immerse the fish, in its wrapping, in cold water to thaw it. Put the tomato purée into a pan, if using, and thaw it over a moderate heat; or gently heat the can of soup.
2   Heat the oil in a large pan and fry the onion, garlic and celery over a moderate heat for 5 minutes, stirring occasionally.
3   Add the warmed tomato purée or soup, orange zest and juice and the herb cubes and bring to the boil. Chop the unwrapped fish fillets into equal sized pieces and add to the pan. Season with salt and black pepper. Cover the pan and simmer for 15 minutes.
4   Serve garnished with croûtons.

Cod in sweet and sour sauce

🔪 45 minutes

Serves 4
750 g /1½ lb frozen cod fillet (or another white fish)
225 ml /8 fl oz sweet and sour sauce, frozen or canned
oil, for greasing
125 g /4 oz frozen sliced green pepper
125 g /4 oz frozen sliced red pepper
125 g /4 oz button mushrooms, thinly sliced
30 ml /2 tbls cashew nuts
1 orange, thinly sliced, to garnish (optional)
green salad, to serve

1   Thaw the fish in its wrapping by immersing it in cold water for at least 10 minutes. Turn the sweet and sour sauce into a small pan and heat it very gently.
2   Brush a shallow baking dish with oil. Unwrap the fish, pat it with absorbent paper and arrange it in a single layer in the dish. Scatter the frozen pepper slices, the mushrooms and cashews over the fish and pour on the warmed sauce. Cover the dish tightly with foil.
3   Choose a pan with a tight fitting lid into which the dish fits and arrange the dish in it on a trivet. Pour boiling water into the saucepan under the dish and steam for 20–25 minutes, until the fish is cooked and firm. Transfer the fish, vegetables and sauce to a warmed serving dish. Garnish with thinly sliced orange if you wish and serve with a green salad — lettuce, cucumber, avocado and spring onion are a good combination.

Cod in sweet and sour sauce served with a green salad

Broccoli quiche

making the pastry case and
sauce, then 50 minutes

Serves 6
For the shortcrust pastry
250 g /8 oz plain flour
5 ml /1 tsp icing sugar
2.5 ml /½ tsp salt
150 g /5 oz butter, chilled, plus extra
for greasing
1 medium-sized egg yolk
5 ml /1 tsp lemon juice
30 ml /2 tbls iced water
For 275 ml /10 fl oz bechamel sauce
40 g /1½ oz butter
30 ml /2 tbls onion, finely chopped
30 ml /2 tbls ham or veal, finely chopped
30 ml /2 tbls flour
425 ml /15 fl oz milk
¼ chicken stock cube, crumbled
½ bay leaf
6 white peppercorns
a good pinch of freshly grated nutmeg
60 ml /4 tbls dry white wine
60 ml /4 tbls chicken stock
salt and white pepper
15 ml /1 tbls lemon juice or 5–10 ml /1–2 tsp
Madeira, plus a pinch of sugar
For the filling:
1 kg /2 lb frozen broccoli spears
3 medium-sized egg yolks
90 ml /6 tbls thick cream
45 ml /3 tbls Parmesan cheese, grated
salt and freshly ground black pepper
a pinch of grated nutmeg

1 Make the pastry case in advance: sift the
flour, icing sugar and salt into a large bowl.
Cut the cold butter into 5 ml /¼ in dice and
add to the bowl.
2 Cut the butter into the flour mixture
until it resembles coarse breadcrumbs.
3 Holding your hands just above the bowl
rim, scoop up some of the mixture in the
fingers of both hands and lightly press out
the lumps of fat between your thumbs and
fingertips. Do this 6–7 times until the
mixture resembles fine breadcrumbs.
4 Beat the egg yolk. Add the lemon juice
and 15 ml /1 tbls iced water and beat lightly.
5 Sprinkle the flour mixture with the egg
and lemon mixture, tossing and mixing with
a fork. Mix in another 15 ml /1 tbls iced
water. Continue tossing until the pastry
holds together, then press it into a ball.
6 First wrap the pastry in greaseproof
paper, then a dampened tea-towel and chill it
for at least 1 hour, or up to 24 hours.
7 Grease a 20 cm /8 in flan tin. Roll out
the pastry, fill the flan tin and prick the base.
Cover with foil and fill the foil with beans.
Bake blind for 10 minutes at 200C /400F /
gas 6. Turn down the oven to 180C /350F /
gas 4, remove the foil and beans and cook it
for a further 8–10 minutes. Cool and then
freeze.
8 Make the bechamel sauce in advance:
melt the butter over a low heat, add the
onions and sauté them gently until soft but
not coloured. Stir in the ham (or veal) and
the flour and cook for 2–3 minutes, stirring
constantly with a wooden spoon.

9 In another pan, bring the milk almost to
the boil and stir one quarter of it into the
flour and butter, off the heat. Return to a low
heat and bring to the boil, stirring.
10 As the sauce begins to thicken, add the
remainder of the milk, a little at a time,
stirring briskly between additions. Continue
stirring until the sauce bubbles.
11 Transfer it to the top pan of a double
boiler, over simmering water. Add the stock
cube, bay leaf, peppercorns and nutmeg.
12 Boil 60 ml /4 tbls wine until reduced to
15 ml /1 tbls. Stir this into the sauce. Then
boil 60 ml /4 tbls chicken stock until reduced
to 15 ml /1 tbls; add this to the sauce too.
13 Taste the sauce and either sharpen it
with salt and pepper and lemon juice or
soften it with Madeira and sugar.
14 Cook for 30 minutes. Cool and freeze.
15 For the broccoli quiche: leave the flan
case to thaw at room temperature while you
prepare the filling. Thaw the bechamel sauce
over a gentle heat.
16 Steam the frozen broccoli over rapidly
boiling water for 10 minutes then plunge it
into cold water. Drain it and toss it on
crumpled kitchen paper to dry.
17 Arrange the broccoli in the flan case.
Heat the oven to 180C /350F /gas 4.
18 Beat the egg yolks and cream together
in the top pan of a double boiler and stir in
the warmed bechamel sauce. Stir until the
sauce thickens, then add the cheese and
season the sauce with salt, black pepper and
nutmeg. Pour the sauce over the broccoli.
19 Bake the flan in the oven for 30–35
minutes, or until golden brown. Serve with a
tomato salad and crusty bread.

Pork in gin and orange

45 minutes

Broccoli quiche

Serves 4
100 ml /4 fl oz frozen, concentrated orange
juice
2 ice cubes of chopped thyme (see box, page 41)
750 g /1½ lb frozen pork fillet
25 g /1 oz butter
125 g /4 oz frozen finely chopped onion
15 ml /1 tbls flour
60 ml /4 tbls gin
salt and freshly ground black pepper
90 ml /6 tbls thick cream
orange slices, to garnish
buttered green noodles or rice, to serve

1 Immerse the can of orange juice in water
to thaw it. Place the ice cubes in a sieve and
pour hot water on them to release the herb.
2 Cut the pork fillets into 20 mm /¾ in
thick slices. Melt the butter in a frying-pan
and fry the meat over a moderately high heat,
turning it, so that it is evenly browned on
both sides. Remove the meat from the pan
with a slotted spoon and keep warm.
3 Add the finely chopped frozen onion to
the pan, fry over a moderate heat, stirring,
for 4–5 minutes. Stir in the flour and cook for
2–3 minutes to form a pale roux. Gradually
pour in the thawed orange juice and continue
stirring until the sauce thickens, then stir
in the thyme and the gin. Season with salt
and freshly ground black pepper.
4 Return the reserved pork fillets to the
pan. Cover the pan and simmer gently for 25
minutes until you are sure that the pork is
thoroughly cooked.
5 Stir in 60 ml /4 tbls of the cream. Taste
the sauce and adjust the seasoning if necessary. Spoon the pork into a heated serving
dish and swirl the remaining cream on top.
Garnish with orange slices and serve with
buttered green noodles or rice.

● You can substitute pork chops for the
pork fillet in this recipe.

WINE & CHEESE PARTIES

The range of wine and cheese available today is enormous, so treat your guests to both traditional favourites and adventurous new buys. My delicious cheese receipes will create a superb buffet spread.

Wine and cheese parties provide great scope for imagination and creativity. In this chapter I offer advice on which wines to serve and I suggest that you have several bottles each of two or three different wines so that your guests can compare the tastes. Also included are an enticing range of cheese recipes to help make your party a really splendid and memorable occasion.

Choose recipes to suit the number of guests you are inviting. For instance, if there are to be about a dozen people you can prepare special, individual dishes like Roquefort soufflés (see recipe).

For an impressive and delicious centrepiece, try my Spectacular cheese 'pineapple' — three cheeses, mixed with cognac and various other flavourings, are then rolled into the shape of the fruit. Scored in a diamond pattern and studded with stuffed olives, this lovely, unusual creation really does resemble a pineapple.

If, on the other hand, you are having a larger gathering, plan to serve a wide selection of nibbles to hand round throughout the party. Cheese straws, Celery boats, Prawn and cheese balls and Stilton mousse mould served with Melba toast (see recipes) are all ideal. Whatever style of party you decide to hold, do remember that quality is important and that good cheese complements the flavour of good wine.

Wines

Start with something fairly light and then move onto a good bordeaux or burgundy. Or you could compare two wines from the same district. For instance, serve a Crozes-Hermitage and a Gigondas; both are from the Rhône, the first from the north and the second from the south.

Another idea is to serve wines from different countries — a Rioja from Spain, a St Emilion from France and a Barolo from Italy. Your choice need not be confined to Europe, however. The United States, Australia and New Zealand also produce some fine wines which are becoming more easily available.

Finish your wine-tasting with a good dessert wine. Try a delicious Frontignan from the Languedoc, or the heady Muscat de Beaumes de Venise from the Rhône.

If you are having a large party, it is a good idea to stick to a couple of wines only, or simply serve one type of red and one of white. Remember to chill the white wines and open at least half the red wines ahead of time to let their flavour develop. White wines can go well with cheese. A Franken wine from Germany is perfect with delicate cream cheese and so are many of the other flowery German wines, such as Niersteiner Gutes Domtal or a light Gewürztraminer from Alsace.

Serve a red wine with blue cheeses, hard cheese and the stronger goats' cheeses. Try Spanish Riojas and Portuguese Daos which are good value for money. Many of the Italian Chiantis or Valpolicellas are sold in large, reasonably priced 2-litre bottles, and some of the French *vin du pays* sold in 7-litre plastic barrels are very good value indeed. Make sure, though, that you try them yourself first in case they do not suit your taste or the food that you have prepared.

Cheeses

Choose a selection of cheeses, making sure they are in prime condition. A whole Brie, Cheddar or Stilton looks and tastes much better than a lot of small pieces which tend to dry up and lose their flavour. For a change, try some of the less well-known cheeses like Explorateur, St André, mild or strong goats' cheeses, Boursault and the creamy, delicate blue Italian San Gaudenzio.

Many of the German cheeses are delicious, too, while a good, mature Cheddar is still very hard to beat. Aim to provide at least one creamy white cheese, one blue cheese and one hard cheese for your guests to have contrasting flavours and textures to sample during the party.

In addition to the tasty bite-sized cheese recipes in this chapter, try fried Camembert for something a little different. The following recipe uses one Camembert which serves eight people:

Cut 1 fairly firm Camembert cheese into portions (or use 8 × 25 g /1 oz ready-cut portions) and freeze them for 1 hour. Mix a pinch of cayenne pepper with 30 ml /2 tbls flour, then roll each Camembert portion first in this flour mixture, then in 2 medium-sized beaten eggs, and then in 50 g /2 oz breadcrumbs, fresh or dried, or crumbled cream crackers. Heat oil in a deep-frier to 180C /350F or until a bread cube browns in 60 seconds. Fry the portions of Camembert for 30 seconds or until they are golden brown. Drain them carefully on absorbent paper, and garnish them with dessert apple wedges. Serve them immediately.

Other food

Platters of fresh celery, cucumber and carrot sticks, or cauliflower sprigs, are easier to manage than large bowls of salads. They also provide a refreshing contrast to some of the richer cheeses. Melba toast, French bread and cheese-flavoured biscuits are all good accompaniments.

Finish off the party with big bunches of black and white grapes or a wine jelly. My delicate, peach-coloured Muscat jelly (see recipe) is made from Muscat de Beaumes de Venise. Although this dessert wine is expensive, it really is worth buying — your guests will be sure to appreciate this lovely dish. Round off the party by serving jugs of piping hot, fresh coffee.

A selection of wine and cheese with Prawn and cream cheese balls (page 47)

Celery boats

Choose sticks with large cavities to make these tasty hors d'oeuvres.

 20 minutes

Makes 12 boats
6 celery sticks, trimmed and washed
175 g /6 oz cream cheese
45 ml /3 tbls soured cream
a pinch of cayenne pepper
45 ml /3 tbls red caviar-style lumpfish roe

1 Neaten the ends of each stick and remove any fibrous strings. Cut the sticks in half, each about 7–9 cm /3–3½ in long.
2 Beat together the cream cheese and soured cream until they are smoothly blended. Beat in the cayenne pepper.
3 Divide the cream cheese mixture equally among the celery boats and pack it into the cavities. Smooth the surface and sprinkle the lumpfish roe over the top.

Olive and cheese pâté

🕙 15 minutes,
plus chilling

Serves 6
225 g /8 oz ricotta cheese
100 g /4 oz San Gaudenzio or mild Gorgonzola
100 g /4 oz butter, softened
1 garlic clove, crushed
10 ml /2 tsp chopped fresh parsley
100 g /4 oz large green olives, stoned
hot buttered toast, to serve

1 Mash the cheeses, softened butter, garlic and parsley to form a paste.
2 Reserve a few olives for decoration and finely chop the rest. Stir them into the cheese mixture and put this into an earthenware terrine, pressing it down well. Chill in the refrigerator for at least 30 minutes.
3 Garnish it with the reserved olives, cut in half, and serve it with hot buttered toast.

● If wished, roll the pâté into small balls and put them on cocktail sticks.

Cheese straws

Delicious served with wine, these cheese straws can be made **1–2 days in advance, stored in an airtight tin and then quickly refreshed in a hot oven.**

🕙 35 minutes,
plus chilling

Makes about 200
225 g /8 oz flour
salt
a pinch of cayenne pepper
125 g /4 oz butter
125 g /4 oz mature Cheddar, grated
2 egg yolks
beaten egg, to glaze
15 ml /1 tbls poppy seeds
15 ml /1 tbls sesame seeds

1 Heat the oven to 200C /400F /gas 6. Sift the flour with a good shake of salt and cayenne pepper into a large mixing bowl. Cut the butter into the flour and rub it in until the mixture resembles breadcrumbs.
2 Stir in the cheese. Beat the egg yolks with 30 ml /2 tbls water and add them to the rubbed-in mixture. Blend the mixture together. Add a further 15 ml /1 tbls water, if needed, to form a ball.
3 Turn it onto a lightly floured board and knead it quickly until it is smooth. Wrap it in cling film and chill it for 30 minutes.
4 Thinly roll the pastry to a rectangle. Trim the edges, then brush it with the beaten egg and sprinkle half with poppy seeds and half with sesame seeds.
5 Cut the pastry into thin strips, about 5 mm /¼ in wide. Then cut each strip into 6.5 cm /2½ in lengths. Twist the two ends of each straw in opposite directions and place them on greased baking sheets, spacing them 6 mm /¼ in apart.
6 Bake them for 10–12 minutes, until they are golden brown. Cool them on a wire rack before serving or storing them.
7 If you want to serve them hot, refresh the straws for 1–2 minutes in an oven heated to 200C /400F /gas 6.

● Try adding mustard powder to the dry ingredients of this recipe to heighten the cheese flavour.
● If you cook these straws flat, without the twist, you can sandwich two together with a creamy cheese mixture.

Roquefort soufflés

Prepare the bechamel sauce and the dishes in advance; a piece of buttered paper placed on the top of the sauce prevents a thick skin from forming. Whisk the egg whites and bake the soufflés when the guests arrive and are ready to eat.

making the sauce,
then 25 minutes

Serves 12
600 ml /1 pt Bechamel sauce (see page 43)
5 eggs, separated
125 g /4 oz Roquefort cheese
salt
freshly ground black pepper

1 Make the bechamel sauce and beat in the egg yolks.
2 Crumble the Roquefort, then mash it with a fork, adding a little of the sauce to make a smooth paste. Stir in the sauce. Check the seasoning and add salt and pepper if necessary.
3 Lightly grease 12 ramekins 6.5 cm /2½ in in diameter, and tie greaseproof paper around the rims to form collars.
4 Heat the oven to 200C /400F /gas 6.
5 Whisk the egg whites with a pinch of salt until they are stiff but not dry. Fold the whites into the sauce with a metal spoon.
6 Pour the mixture into the prepared ramekins and place them in a large roasting pan one-third full with boiling water.
7 Turn down the oven to 170C /325F /gas 3 and bake the soufflés for 14 minutes, then raise the heat to 200C /400F /gas 6 and bake them for a further 4 minutes. The tops should be golden and well risen with the insides still a bit creamy. Serve them immediately.

Stilton mousse mould

Although it is made like a mousse and is very light in texture, this mould cuts easily into slices and should be served with Melba toast to offset its richness.

making the sauce, then 15
minutes, plus setting

Serves 12–16
600 ml /1 pt Bechamel sauce (see page 43)
5 eggs, separated
225 g /8 oz Stilton cheese
25 g /1 oz gelatine
chopped watercress, to garnish
Melba toast, to serve (see note)

1 Make the bechamel sauce, then beat in the egg yolks.
2 Mash the Stilton with a fork in a large bowl and add a little of the sauce to make a thick paste. Beat it thoroughly to eliminate all lumps. Gradually add the remaining sauce, stirring constantly.
3 Sprinkle the gelatine over 75 ml /5 tbls water in a small bowl. Put the bowl into a pan of simmering water until the gelatine has

dissolved, then add it to the cheese sauce.
4 In a large bowl, whisk the egg whites until they are stiff but not dry, then fold them into the sauce with a metal spoon.
5 Pour the mousse into a wetted 1.4 L /2½ pt mould and put it in the refrigerator for 4–5 hours to set.
6 About 1 hour before serving, turn out the mould by dipping the bottom in very hot water for 2–3 seconds, then put a plate on top, invert the two and the mould should slip out onto the plate. Let the mousse come to room temperature, then surround it with the chopped watercress and serve with Melba toast slices.

● For the melba toast, cut slices of white bread which are 6 mm /¼ in thick and toast them on both sides, under a hot grill. Then, with a sharp knife, split each slice in half and return them to the grill to brown the uncooked sides. Alternatively, the last stage can be done in a moderate oven.

Spectacular cheese 'pineapple'

This lovely cheese creation is an ideal centrepiece for a buffet table.

20 minutes, plus chilling,
10 minutes to decorate

Serves 12
500 g /1 lb Cheddar cheese, grated
250 g /8 oz Roquefort cheese, sieved
250 g /8 oz cream cheese
the juice of 1 lemon
60 ml /4 tbls cognac
30 ml /2 tbls Worcestershire sauce
60 ml /4 tbls warm milk
60 ml /4 tbls mayonnaise
30 ml /2 tbls finely chopped fresh parsley
2 pinches of cayenne pepper
a dusting of paprika
12 stuffed olives, sliced
For the garnish
pineapple top (use the fruit for another recipe)
Roquefort cheese
finely chopped fresh parsley
red and green dessert apples
lemon juice, for brushing

1 Mix together the first 10 ingredients until they are completely smooth. Shape the mixture into the form of a pineapple using a spatula dipped in hot water. Chill the 'pineapple' for at least 3 hours.
2 When ready to serve, sprinkle paprika over the 'pineapple', score it with a knife into regular diamond patterns and stud it with the sliced stuffed olives. Top with the pineapple leaves.
3 Make cheese balls from the Roquefort and roll them in finely chopped parsley until they are completely coated. Core some of the apples, cut them in sections almost to the bottom to make apple 'flowers', brush lightly with lemon juice to stop them going brown then top them with the cheese balls. Cut the other apples into wedges. Surround the cheese 'pineapple' with the apples and serve immediately.

Prawn and cream cheese balls

 25 minutes

Makes 30 balls
450 g /1 lb ricotta cheese
45 ml /3 tbls thick cream
2–3 drops of Tabasco
salt
freshly ground black pepper
30 boiled peeled prawns (about 350g /12 oz)
150 ml /10 tbls finely chopped fresh tarragon

1 Put the ricotta in a large bowl, add the cream and Tabasco and season with salt and pepper. Mash the cheese thoroughly so that it forms a thick paste.
2 Using 15 ml /1 tbls of the cheese mixture at a time, form it into balls and push a prawn into the middle of each ball. Smooth over the edges. Put the balls on a large plate in the refrigerator for 10 minutes to firm up.
3 Sprinkle the tarragon onto a large plate, spreading it out well.
4 Push a cocktail stick through the top of each ball, then roll them, one by one, in the chopped tarragon. Sprinkle a little tarragon over the top of each ball near the stick to cover them completely and serve.

Muscat jelly

10 minutes, plus cooling and setting

Serves 12–16
200 g /7 oz sugar
300 ml /10 fl oz lemon juice
the grated zest of 2 lemons
75 cl bottle Muscat de Beaumes de Venise
50 g /2 oz gelatine
300 ml /10 fl oz thick cream
30 ml /2 tbls icing sugar
seedless white grapes, to garnish

1 Put the sugar, lemon juice and zest into a saucepan with 700 ml /1¼ pt water. Bring to the boil and then simmer for 10 minutes to dissolve the sugar. Cool. Add the wine.
2 In a small bowl, sprinkle the gelatine over 75 ml /5 tbls cold water. Put the bowl into a pan of simmering water until the gelatine has dissolved. Stir the gelatine into the wine mixture and mix well.
3 Pour the liquid into a wetted 2 L /3½ pt ring mould and put it in the refrigerator to set for 5–6 hours or overnight.
4 About 20 minutes before serving, turn out the jelly by putting a cloth dipped in very hot water over the bottom of the mould. Put a plate over the mould, invert the two, tap the mould sharply and the jelly should slip out onto the plate.
5 Whip the cream with the icing sugar until soft peaks form. Pile some in the centre of the jelly and, using a small rose nozzle, pipe the rest around the edge. Garnish with the seedless grapes and serve.

Spectacular cheese 'pineapple'

FONDUES

For an informal party, try one of my four glamorous fondues. Since the preparations are done in advance and the guests cook for themselves, you can enjoy the occasion without too much work on the night.

Dip-in dinners come in many shapes and sizes! The best known is probably the traditional Swiss cheese fondue. The story goes that it was invented by thrifty Swiss villagers as a way of using up hard, stale cheese during the long winters when food was scarce. They melted the cheese in a pot with local white wine and dipped pieces of bread into it for a hearty feast. The melting process gave its name to the dish — *fondre* is the French verb meaning to melt.

My four dip-in meals are ideal for those occasions when you want to present a meal with a difference. The ingredients can be prepared and kept in the refrigerator ready for your guests to cook the meal themselves in a central pot of simmering oil. Using a special long-handled fondue fork, they dip each piece of food into the oil to cook it, but do warn them that the food will stick if it touches the bottom of the pot. Also, remind your guests that they should not eat their food straight from the fondue fork since it will be extremely hot.

Should you serve any other courses? I think so, but do keep them simple. Try an appetizing salad to start with, such as my Italian pepper salad (see page 16), Salade provencale (see page 21), a green salad or a mixed salad. Or you could try a rice-based salad (see Mexican rice, page 24).

For dessert serve an ice cream like my attractive Strawberry ice-cream rolls (page 30) or even the Red berry sorbet (see page 21), which will need very little attention at the last minute.

Fondue bourguignonne
Despite its name, Fondue bourguignonne does not come from Burgundy, but originated across the border in Switzerland. This ideal and delicious do-it-yourself dish provides each guest with a bowl of marinated steak cubes and a variety of piquant sauces in which to dip the meat after it has been cooked.

Sukiyaki
Perhaps the best-known Japanese dish — and the one that most appeals to Western palates — is Sukiyaki. In this dish the attractively arranged bites of beef and vegetables are quickly stir-fried, then dipped in raw egg yolk to cool them before being dipped in one of the three tasty sauces that complement the meal so well.

Fisherman's fondue
As the name suggests, this menu uses seafood as its basis. Prawns, cuttlefish or squid for the more adventurous, and a selection of other white fish are marinated in lemon juice, crumbled chicken stock cube, cayenne and thin slices of spring onion. Again, the prepared bits of fish are cooked in simmering oil and dipped in a choice of savoury sauces before being eaten.

Mongolian hot-pot
Last, but by no means least, of my fondues is the Mongolian hot-pot. It uses simmering chicken stock as the cooking agent instead of oil. The food is traditionally cooked on a table-top burner, with a built-in charcoal chimney in the centre. The funnel going through the bowl keeps the stock evenly hot, but a large flameproof casserole on a burner makes a very good substitute.

As the pieces of food are cooked in the stock it becomes richer, subtly changing its flavour throughout the course of the meal. Plain, steamed rice is an ideal accompaniment for this hot-pot, and the stock can be served as a delicious soup at the end of the meal. Unlike the previous fondues, the Mongolian hot-pot relies on only the raw egg yolk to cool the food and a tiny taste of soy sauce to enhance the flavour.

Drinks
Fondue parties tend to make people particularly thirsty, and since not everyone can cook food at the same time, there are long pauses between mouthfuls. Try serving a robust, fruity red wine with the Fondue bourguignonne; dryish white wine or a pot of China tea with the Sukiyaki or the Fisherman's fondue; while it may be worth experimenting with a bottle of sake to go with the Mongolian hot-pot. Sake is the traditional Japanese rice wine which should be served warm in tiny cups, but if you find that it does not suit your guests, a dry sherry is a very good alternative.

Equipment
Swiss-type fondues are usually cooked in special fireproof pots known as *caquelons*, made of cast iron, copper, stainless steel or earthenware. They are traditional, but they are not the only kind of pot you can use. If you don't want to go to the expense of buying a special fondue pot straight away, don't worry. A flameproof casserole on an electric hot plate or an efficient burner (night lights are not hot enough), a chafing dish or an electric frying-pan can be used. It is worth buying long-handled fondue forks. They are sold in sets of 4 or 6, with different coloured handles, so that guests can recognize their own forks.

Much more important than fancy equipment are truly first-class ingredients that look appetizing raw, cook quickly and taste wonderful: tender, lean meat cut into bite-sized pieces, fresh chopped vegetables and seafood. The chances are, your guests will become hooked on these do-it-yourself meals, and there may well be another fondue party given in the very near future.

Fondue bourguignonne

When you start cooking the fondue, serve an attractive rice dish, made with long-grain rice, peas, peanuts and raisins, or a seasonal salad. It will give your guests something to eat while they are waiting for their next piece of meat to cook. Remind everyone not to eat with the long-handled forks, as the prongs will be dangerously hot!

2 hours marinating, then table cooking

Serves 6
1 kg /2 lb fillet steak
300 ml /10 fl oz oil, for deep frying
For the dry marinade
1 beef stock cube, crumbled
45 ml /3 tbls lemon juice
5 ml /1 tsp cayenne pepper
To serve
Steak sauce (see recipe)
Herby mustard sauce (see recipe)
Fondue tomato sauce (see recipe)

1 Trim any fat or gristle from the steak and cut the meat into 20 mm /¾ in cubes.
2 Prepare the marinade. In a small bowl, mash the crumbled beef stock cube with the lemon juice, then season to taste with cayenne pepper.
3 Put the meat cubes in a large, shallow bowl. Add the marinade mixture and toss until the meat cubes are well coated. Cover the bowl and leave the meat to marinate for at least 2 hours.
4 In a fondue pot, or a flameproof casserole, heat the oil to 180C /350F on the stove, then very carefully transfer it to a table-top burner.
5 When ready to eat, divide the beef among individual plates and give each guest a portion of beef, a long-handled fondue fork and a table fork. Serve the 3 sauces in separate bowls.
6 Each guest then cooks his own meat on a fondue fork, dipping it in the hot oil.
7 When the meat is done to taste, it is dipped in one of the sauces, then transferred to the table fork for eating.

A few safety hints
● Choose a pot large enough to take at least 750 ml /1¼ pt oil. It should never be more than two-thirds full.
● Take care not to overheat the oil. Heat it on the stove in the fondue pot until it reaches about 180C /350F. At this temperature, a 15 mm /½ in cube of day-old bread will take 1 minute to become brown. Carefully transfer the hot oil to the burner. Keep it at the same temperature during the cooking.
● Be extremely careful when transferring the pot with hot oil to the table. Wear thick oven gloves, walk at a slow, steady pace and make sure that people keep out of your way.
● Protect your table with mats so that it doesn't get marked.
● Make sure the burner is secure so no one can knock over the pot by accident.
● Do not put too much food in the oil at the same time — the oil will froth up and the temperature will drop.
● Remind your guests that the meat should not touch the bottom of the pot, as it will immediately stick.

Steak sauce

5 minutes

Fondue bourguignonne

Makes 200 ml /7 fl oz

150 ml /5 fl oz soured cream
45 ml /3 tbls tomato ketchup
1.5 ml /¼ tsp cayenne pepper
5 ml /1 tsp soy sauce
5 ml /1 tsp Worcestershire sauce
10 ml /2 tsp grainy mustard
juice of ½ lemon

1   Put the soured cream, tomato ketchup, cayenne pepper, soy sauce, Worcestershire sauce, grainy mustard and lemon juice in a small serving bowl and mix until well blended.
2   Cover with cling film and chill in the refrigerator until needed.

Herby mustard sauce

25 minutes

Makes 150 ml /5 fl oz

lemon juice
2 egg yolks
salt and freshly ground black pepper
100 g /4 oz unsalted butter
10 ml /2 tsp Dijon mustard
25 ml /1½ tbls tomato purée
10 ml /2 tsp finely chopped fresh parsley
10 ml /2 tsp finely chopped fresh chives

1   In the top pan of a double boiler, put 2.5 ml /½ tsp lemon juice, 10 ml /2 tsp cold water, the egg yolks and the salt and the freshly ground black pepper to taste. Mix thoroughly.
2   Divide the butter into 4 equal pieces and add one to the saucepan. Place the top of the double boiler over hot but not boiling water and stir constantly with a wire whisk until the butter is melted and the mixture begins to thicken.
3   Add the second piece of butter and continue whisking. When the butter has melted and the sauce has thickened, add another piece of butter, stirring from the bottom of the pan until it has melted. Add the remaining butter, whisking until it melts and is fully incorporated into the sauce.
4   Remove the top pan from the hot water and continue to beat for 2–3 minutes. Replace the pan over the hot water and cook for a further 2 minutes, beating constantly until an emulsion forms and the sauce becomes rich and creamy.
5   Add the Dijon mustard and the tomato purée, and blend well. Add more lemon juice if necessary, and salt and freshly ground black pepper to taste. Strain the sauce through a fine sieve into a clean bowl and keep warm over warm water.
6   Just before serving, stir in the chopped parsley and chives, then pour the sauce into a small, heated serving bowl.

Fondue tomato sauce

20 minutes

Makes 300 ml /10 fl oz

225 g /8 oz fresh, ripe tomatoes
15 ml /1 tbls finely chopped fresh parsley
15 ml /1 tbls Dijon mustard
45 ml /3 tbls olive oil
5 ml /1 tsp lemon juice
15 ml /1 tbls chopped black olives
30 ml /2 tbls chopped gherkins
15 ml /1 tbls finely chopped onion
5 ml /1 tsp finely chopped fresh basil
5 ml /1 tsp tomato purée
salt
freshly ground black pepper

1   Make a tiny cut in the top of each tomato. Place them in a bowl, cover them with boiling water and leave for 10 seconds. Remove the tomatoes from the water, slip off the skins and cut the skinned tomatoes in half. Remove the seeds and juice and reserve for another recipe. Next, finely dice the tomato flesh.
2   In the top pan of a double boiler, combine the diced tomato flesh with the chopped fresh parsley, the Dijon mustard, the olive oil, the lemon juice, the chopped black olives, the chopped gherkins, the chopped onion, the finely chopped fresh basil and the tomato purée, and season to taste with salt and freshly ground black pepper.
3   Place the sauce over simmering water and let it heat through gently, stirring it occasionally with a wooden spoon.
4   Turn the sauce into a small, heated serving bowl.

Fondue tomato sauce, Steak sauce and Herby mustard sauce

Sukiyaki

 55 minutes

Serves 4

600 g /1¼ lb beef fillet, sliced thinly across the
*   grain*
1 medium-sized onion, sliced into very thin
*   rings*
2 large spring onions, cut into 25 mm /1 in
*   lengths*
50 g /2 oz mushrooms, wiped and sliced
125–175 g /4–6 oz raw spinach, washed, dried,
*   trimmed and cut into strips*
2 medium-sized firm tomatoes, blanched,
*   skinned, seeded and diced*
1 small bunch watercress, washed and trimmed
200 g /7 oz canned bamboo shoots, drained and
*   thinly sliced*
175 g /6 oz soybean curd (tofu), cut into 4 cm ×
*   1.2 cm /1½ × ½ in cubes*
60 ml /4 tbls corn oil

For the cooking sauce

60 ml /4 tbls sake
15 ml /1 tbls soft brown sugar
15 ml /1 tbls corn oil
150 ml /5 fl oz Japanese soy sauce

To serve

225 g /8 oz long-grain rice, cooked (see
*   page 55)*
4 egg yolks
Sansho sauce (see recipe)
Japanese ginger sauce (see recipe)
Teriyaki sauce (see recipe)

1   Cut the thin beef slices into 4 cm /1½ in
squares.
2   Attractively arrange the squares of raw
meat, the prepared vegetables and the cubed
bean curd on a large platter or wooden board.
3   Place a Japanese chafing dish or an
electric frying-pan in the centre of the table.
Alternatively, use a large frying-pan, preferably cast iron, on a table-top burner.
4   For each guest, set a plate, a bowl of
cooked rice and a pair of chopsticks. Beside
each place, set 4 Japanese sake cups, or tiny
glasses, coffee saucers or ramekin dishes. Put
a lightly beaten whole raw egg yolk in one of
the cups, and a portion of each of the serving
sauces in the other 3 cups.
5   In a small bowl, mix the ingredients for
the cooking sauce.
6   Start cooking once your guests are seated
at the table. Put 15 ml /1 tbls corn oil in the
chafing dish, electric frying-pan or ordinary
frying-pan. If using an electric frying-pan,
start it at 200C /400F, then reduce the heat
to 130C /250F to cook the meat and
vegetables. Otherwise, heat the oil over a
moderate heat. Add enough cooking sauce to
cover the base of the hot pan.
7   Place 1 portion of the meat pieces in the
sauce and cook for 1 minute. Add a portion
of the vegetables and bean curd, and cook for
2 more minutes.
8   At this point, turn the ingredients over,
so that the vegetables are at the bottom and
the meat pieces on top. Add a little more
sauce, if necessary, and continue cooking for
another 3 minutes over a moderate heat, until
the vegetables are tender but still crisp.
9   Serve the food as soon as it is cooked,
then repeat the procedure with the other
portions.
10   The raw egg yolk helps to cool the hot
food. Each guest dips a morsel of food in the
egg yolk, then in a sauce before eating.

Sansho sauce

**Sansho is Japanese pepper. Ground sansho
can be bought from Japanese shops.**

15 minutes,
plus cooling

Makes 150 ml /5 fl oz

2 spring onion stalks
90 ml /6 tbls soy sauce
90 ml /6 tbls sake
30 ml /2 tbls soft brown sugar
1.5 ml /¼ tsp ground sansho, or a pinch each
*   of cracked black peppercorns and allspice*

1   Cut the spring onion stalks across the
width into very thin slices.
2   In a small saucepan, combine the soy
sauce, sake, soft brown sugar, sliced spring
onion stalks and ground sansho or peppercorn and allspice mixture.
3   Simmer the mixture over a low heat,
stirring continuously with a wooden spoon,
until the sauce begins to thicken slightly.
Leave to get cold.
4   For serving, divide the sauce among tiny
individual bowls.

Japanese ginger sauce

15 minutes,
plus cooling

Makes 90 ml /6 tbls

10 ml /2 tsp Japanese soy sauce (shoyu)
¼ chicken stock cube
30 ml /2 tbls mirin (Japanese sweet sake)
5 ml /1 tsp soft brown sugar
10 ml /2 tsp grated fresh ginger root
20 ml /4 tsp finely chopped spring onion

1   In a small saucepan, combine all the
ingredients with 60 ml /4 tbls water.
2   Simmer the ingredients gently until the
sugar has melted, stirring occasionally. Leave
the sauce to get cold and then serve it in tiny
individual bowls.

Teriyaki sauce

10 minutes,
plus cooling

Makes 150 ml /5 fl oz

45 ml /3 tbls Japanese soy sauce (shoyu)
90 ml /6 tbls mirin (Japanese sweet sake)
30 ml /2 tbls sugar

1   In a small saucepan, combine the
Japanese soy sauce, mirin and sugar.
2   Simmer over a low heat, stirring constantly with a wooden spoon, until the sauce
begins to thicken slightly. Remove from the
heat and leave to get cold.
3   Divide among tiny individual bowls, one
for each person, for serving.

*Left, Sukiyaki and, right, ingredients for some
of the sauces*

Fisherman's fondue

30 minutes, plus 2 hours marinating, then 15 minutes, plus table cooking

Serves 6
225 g /8 oz halibut fillet
225 g /8 oz monkfish fillet
225 g /8 oz salmon steak, filleted and skinned
225 g /8 oz cuttlefish or squid, cleaned and sliced
225 g /8 oz boiled, peeled prawns
300 ml /10 fl oz oil, for deep frying
For the dry marinade
2 spring onion stalks, thinly sliced
1 chicken stock cube, crumbled
90 ml /6 tbls lemon juice
1.5 ml /¼ tsp cayenne pepper
To serve
Quick dry mustard sauce (see recipe)
Plum sauce (see recipe)
Ginger and soy sauce (see recipe)

1 Cut the halibut, monkfish and salmon into thin strips and place them in separate bowls. Place the prepared cuttlefish or squid in another bowl and then put the prawns in a fifth bowl.
2 Prepare the marinade. In a small bowl, combine the crumbled chicken stock cube, lemon juice, cayenne pepper and thinly-sliced spring onion stalks. Mix until well blended.
3 Divide the marinade among the 5 bowls and toss until the fish, cuttlefish or squid, and prawns are well coated. Cover the ingredients and leave them to marinate for at least 2 hours.
4 A few minutes before serving, heat the oil

on the stove in a fondue pot or flameproof casserole to about 180C /350F.
5 Place the table-top burner in the centre of a large round tray and carefully transfer the pot of hot oil to the burner to keep hot. Arrange the marinated fish, cuttlefish or squid, and prawns on the tray. Alternatively, place them in separate dishes and arrange them around the pot.
6 Give each guest a fondue fork and a separate table fork for eating, and serve the accompanying sauces in bowls, or in separate individual small bowls for each guest.
7 Each guest cooks his own fish, cuttlefish or squid, and prawns, spearing 1 piece at a time on the fondue fork and dipping it into the hot fat to cook. When done to taste, each piece is dipped into one of the sauces and then it should be transferred onto the other fork for eating.

Quick dry mustard sauce

5 minutes

Serves 6
30 ml /2 tbls mustard powder
45 ml /3 tbls lemon juice
1.5 ml /¼ tsp chicken stock cube, crumbled

1 In a small bowl, combine the mustard powder, lemon juice and chicken stock cube. Blend the ingredients to a smooth paste, using a fork.
2 Transfer to a serving bowl or divide among 6 tiny individual bowls to serve.

Fisherman's fondue

Plum sauce

5 minutes

Serves 6
5 ml /1 tsp tomato purée
90 ml /6 tbls Chinese plum sauce

1 Combine the tomato purée and the Chinese plum sauce in a bowl; mix until well blended.
2 Transfer the mixture to a small serving bowl or to 6 tiny individual bowls.

● Chinese plum sauce is made from plums, apricots, chillies, vinegar and sugar. It is sold canned or bottled in Oriental food shops or specialist sections of supermarkets.

Ginger and soy sauce

5 minutes

Serves 6
8 thin slices fresh ginger root, cut into threads
90 ml /6 tbls soy sauce
45 ml /3 tbls lemon juice
a pinch of cayenne pepper

1 In a small bowl, combine the ginger, soy sauce and lemon juice. Season to taste with a pinch of cayenne pepper and mix well.
2 Transfer to a serving bowl or divide among 6 tiny individual bowls.

Mongolian hot-pot

♨ 40 minutes,
then table cooking

Serves 6
1.1–1.7 L /2–3 pt lightly flavoured chicken stock, home-made from cubes or diluted canned consommé
225 g /8 oz boiled, pceled prawns
6 large mushrooms, sliced
350 g /12 oz boned chicken breasts, skinned and thinly sliced
350 g /12 oz pork fillet, thinly sliced
350 g /12 oz shelled scallops, cleaned and thinly sliced
175 g /6 oz spinach leaves, washed and dried
12 chicory leaves
spring onion tassels
To serve
350 g /12 oz long-grain rice
6 egg yolks
soy sauce
1 spring onion, thinly sliced

1   Start by putting the rice on to steam (see notes below).
2   Fill the pot or casserole with the stock. Place it on top of the burner and heat it until it is bubbling.
3   Arrange the prawns, mushrooms, chicken, pork, scallops, spinach, chicory and onion tassels on a large platter, or platters.
4   For each guest, set a bowl of cooked rice, chopsticks, a spoon, a porcelain bowl for the soup and 2 small bowls. Put a lightly beaten raw egg yolk in one of the bowls and some soy sauce in the other bowl.
5   When ready to eat, each guest selects a raw ingredient using chopsticks, then drops the item into the stock for 1–2 minutes.
6   When the food is done to taste, it is fished out with the chopsticks, dipped into the raw egg yolk to cool, then in soy sauce to flavour.
7   To eat the rice, each guest flavours it with a little hot stock and soy sauce.
8   When all the raw ingredients have been cooked and eaten, spoon the reduced, highly flavoured broth into the individual procelain bowls and sprinkle with thinly sliced spring onion. Flavour to taste with soy sauce and drink as a soup.

● To steam rice: place a heat-proof soufflé dish 18 cm /7 in in diameter on a trivet in a large, heavy-based casserole or saucepan. Spread the rice over the dish to a depth of 3 cm /1¼ in, cover with the same depth of boiling water. Pour more boiling water into the casserole or saucepan to come up to the base of the soufflé dish. Bring this water back to the boil, cover tightly and steam over a low heat for exactly 30 minutes.
● An alternative way to steam rice: wash the rice under cold running water until the water runs clear. Put the rice in a large saucepan with 2.3 L /4 pt boiling water. Bring it back to the boil, and boil for 10 minutes. Drain, then put the rice in a wet tea-towel in a steamer basket and steam over rapidly boiling water for 30 minutes.

Mongolian hot-pot

FEEDING THE FAMILY

These recipes are ideal for family occasions, large and small, where the accent is on informality and you want something tasty but simple to prepare — leaving you free to relax and enjoy the company.

The advantage of the recipes in this chapter is that they can be made in advance, and require the minimum of last-minute preparations and no elaborate table settings. They are perfect for occasions when you've been out all day and want to produce an evening meal as effortlessly as possible. Also, when you have a large family gathering during, say, a bank holiday weekend, and prefer to spend your time catching up on all the news rather than in the kitchen.

In the main, these dishes are neither extravagant nor complicated and will appeal to all ages.

Main course dishes

Casseroles are an excellent choice if you have a relaxed weekend ahead, since their timing is not critical. Try Mexican chicken casserole (see page 22), or Beef curry with fennel, served with a bowl of rice (see page 65).

Pasta dishes are popular with all ages. Serve Lasagne bolognese (see page 17), or Pastitsio (see recipe); this is my version of a Greek dish of pasta with a vegetable sauce, topped with a lovely yoghurt sauce. Make it the day before, then simply put it in the oven for 50 minutes to cook before the meal. This dish is also ideal for vegetarians.

In the summer, when the children are at home on their long school holidays, a buffet lunch or supper out of doors is a treat everyone will enjoy. Ham and egg pasties (see recipe) will be very popular, as will Kebabs and pitta (see recipe): marinated meat and vegetables are threaded onto skewers then cooked, ready to be packed into hot pitta bread. Remember to provide plenty of napkins for this dish.

Guy Fawkes' night is an excellent opportunity to join forces with other families in the neighbourhood and have a big party, with properly supervised fireworks. Ranchburgers (see page 26) and Party jacket potatoes (see recipe) are tasty and filling and will be popular with all age groups. Devilled chicken drumsticks with lemon juice and soy sauce (see page 38) will add a piquant flavour to your buffet.

For the adults, hot Mulled spiced wine (see page 93) will help to successfully ward off the November chill as well as making the party go with a swing.

Salads

Salads are marvellous for a buffet spread. Both my Circles salad and Fruity cabbage salad (see recipes) are delicious and unusual — serve them with a choice of two dressings, Cheese or Peanut (see recipes). Cabbage and pepper slaw (see page 29) looks impressive as it's served in a hollowed-out cabbage and has a really crispy texture.

You may like to have a 'pick-and-choose' salad table. Provide separate bowls of chicory leaves, sliced celery, sliced leeks, radishes, shredded red cabbage, sliced cucumber, green or black seedless grapes, raisins, sunflower seeds and croûtons, plus a choice of dressings. Let your guests select their own mixed salad.

Another good idea is to assemble platters of raw vegetable sticks, crackers and tortilla chips and serve them with a tangy dip. Try my Tomato dip, which serves 8–12: blend together 450 g /1 lb cream cheese, 30 ml /2 tbls tomato purée, 30 ml /2 tbls Worcestershire sauce and 5 ml /1 tsp lemon juice. Add

celery salt and black pepper to taste. If wished, fold in 50 g /2 oz each green olives (stoned and chopped) and cocktail gherkins (chopped). Spoon the mixture into a bowl, cover and chill it for at least 2 hours and up to 24, if you wish.

Desserts

My fresh fruit dip (see recipe) is great fun to eat — guests select their own pieces of fruit, marshmallows and sponge fingers and then dip them into a marshmallow and chocolate sauce. My Sweet choux puffs (see recipe) are irresistible: pile the delicate choux puffs into a mound, then serve them accompanied by two bowls of fillings, one chocolate and one strawberry, so that the guests are able to choose for themselves.

Other suitable desserts are Red berry sorbet (see page 21), and Strawberry ice-cream rolls (see page 30), both of which look stunning on the buffet table. For the very sweet-toothed, serve spicy Shoo-fly pies (see page 30) or Coconut-pineapple fingers (see page 38).

If the main course has been very hearty, a fresh fruit salad might be all that your guests have room for, while any weight-watchers will appreciate a selection of seasonal fruits such as apples, bananas and satsumas.

Preparing Kebabs and pitta

Ham and egg pasties

Kebabs and pitta

45 minutes, marinating, then 30 minutes

Serves 12

1.4 kg /3 lb boneless lamb, trimmed of excess fat
12 lambs' kidneys, skinned, halved and cored
oil, for greasing
12 small onions, halved or quartered
3 large oranges, segmented
750 g /1 lb 10 oz small courgettes, in 4 cm / 1½ in slices
450 g /1 lb small button mushrooms
450 g /1 lb small tomatoes, halved
12 small onions, halved or quartered
12–24 bay leaves
salt

For the meat marinade

150 ml /5 fl oz olive oil
30 ml /2 tbls orange juice
5 ml /1 tsp grated orange zest
15 ml /1 tbls red wine vinegar
2 bay leaves, crushed
10 ml /2 tsp dried thyme
freshly ground black pepper

For the vegetable marinade

150 ml /5 fl oz olive oil
2 small onions, finely chopped
2 garlic cloves, crushed
45 ml /3 tbls fresh parsley, chopped
2.5 ml /½ tsp ground coriander
30 ml /2 tbls cider vinegar
15 ml /1 tbls lemon juice

To serve

2 boxes salad cress, trimmed
3 Spanish onions, sliced into rings
24 pieces pitta bread, slit

1 Cut the lamb into 25 mm /1 in cubes. Cut each halved kidney into 2 pieces. Brush 12 flat skewers with oil and thread the lamb, kidneys, onions and oranges alternately onto the skewers.

2 Stir together all the ingredients for the meat marinade and pour them into a roasting tin. Place the kebabs in a single layer in the marinade and leave them at room temperature for 3–6 hours, turning once.

3 To make the vegetable kebabs, brush 12 flat skewers with oil and thread them with the vegetables and bay leaves, alternating the colours.

4 Stir together the ingredients for the vegetable marinade and pour them into a roasting tin. Place the kebabs in a single layer in the marinade and leave them at room temperature for 3–6 hours, turning once.

5 Toss together the cress and onion rings for the garnish. Cover and refrigerate them until ready to serve.

6 When ready to cook, heat the oven to 220C /425F /gas 7. Put the pittas into a baking dish and cover them with foil. Place the dish on the top shelf of the oven for 10 minutes.

7 Meanwhile, baste all the kebabs with the marinade and sprinkle the lamb kebabs with salt. Arrange the kebabs on 2 wire cooling trays and stand each in a roasting tin.

8 Move the dish of pittas to the floor of the oven, then place the lamb kebabs on the top shelf and the vegetable kebabs on the lower shelf and cook them for 15 minutes, turning them once.

9 Arrange the lamb and vegetable kebabs alternately on a heated serving dish and then pile the cress and onion rings in the centre. Arrange the pittas in a napkin-lined basket and cover them with another napkin to keep them warm. Serve the kebabs and pittas at once while they are still hot.

Ham and egg pasties

1 hour,
plus 20 minutes baking

Makes 12 pasties
3 × 375 g /13 oz packs frozen puff pastry,
  defrosted
flour, for dredging
1 medium-sized egg, beaten
For the filling
2 carrots
225 g /8 oz frozen peas
225 g /8 oz broccoli spears
175 g /6 oz cream cheese
salt and freshly ground black pepper
2.5 ml /½ tsp curry powder
200 g /7 oz canned sweetcorn kernels, drained
450 g /1 lb lean ham, finely diced
2 medium-sized hard-boiled eggs, chopped

1   To make the filling, cook the carrots,
peas and broccoli spears separately in boiling
salted water until they are just tender, then
drain them. Finely dice the carrots, chop the
broccoli spears and leave all the vegetables
to cool.
2   In a bowl, beat the cream cheese with a
wooden spoon until it is light and fluffy.
Season with salt, pepper and curry powder.
Add the carrots, broccoli, peas, sweetcorn,
ham and chopped eggs and stir gently to
combine them.
3   Roll out each pack of pastry on a lightly
floured board. From each piece, cut 4 × 20
cm /8 in circles. Re-roll the trimmings and
then cut out leaf or heart shapes to make
decorations.
4   Spoon the filling mixture into the centre
of the pastry circles. Dampen the edges of
the pastry with water. Draw 2 sides over to
meet and enclose the filling, then press the
edges together to join. Place the pasties on 2
baking sheets.
5   Brush the pasties with the beaten egg.
Arrange the decorative shapes on the pasties
and brush them with egg to glaze.
6   Heat the oven to 200C /400F /gas 6. Bake
the pasties for 20 minutes, until they are
golden brown, reversing the baking sheets
after 15 minutes. Serve them hot.

Party jacket potatoes

15 minutes, overnight setting,
20 minutes, plus baking

Serves 12
12 large potatoes, scrubbed, halved lengthways
For the tuna dressing
400 g /14 oz canned tuna, drained and flaked
4 spring onions, finely chopped
a large pinch of cayenne pepper
350 g /12 oz butter, clarified (see note)
salt and freshly ground black pepper
2 bay leaves, to garnish
For the ham dressing
3 medium-sized eggs, hard-boiled
3 bunches of watercress, trimmed and chopped
350 g /12 oz lean ham, finely diced
salt
freshly ground black pepper
575 ml /1 pt soured cream

Pastitsio served with a salad and brown bread

1   The day before, make the tuna dressing:
combine the tuna, onions and cayenne
pepper in a bowl. Pour on the clarified butter
and stir, without mashing the fish, until it is
evenly distributed. Adjust the seasoning, turn
it into a serving bowl, cover and refrigerate
overnight.
2   To make the ham dressing, chop 2 eggs
and stir them with the watercress, ham and
seasoning into the soured cream. Turn the
mixture into a serving bowl, cover and
refrigerate for up to 8 hours.
3   When ready, heat the oven to 200C /
400F /gas 6. Season the potatoes well and
arrange them, cut sides up, on baking sheets.
Bake them for 1–1¼ hours, until soft.
4   Meanwhile, slice the remaining egg and
garnish the ham dressing. Garnish the tuna
dressing with the bay leaves. Serve the
potatoes piping hot, accompanied by the 2
dressings.

● To clarify butter, in a heavy-bottomed
pan, melt butter over a very low heat. It will
foam, and then the foam will sink, leaving
the butter clear like oil. Pour off the clarified
butter, leaving the sediment in the pan.

Pastitsio

1 hour 45 minutes,
then 50 minutes baking

Serves 10–12
750 g /1 lb 10 oz green noodles
salt
butter, for greasing
50 g /2 oz freshly grated Parmesan cheese
For the sauce
225 g /8 oz brown lentils, washed and drained
2–3 parsley stalks
1 bouquet garni
25 g /1 oz butter
90 ml /6 tbls olive oil
3 medium-sized onions, chopped
2 garlic cloves, crushed
225 g /8 oz carrots, finely diced
1 large aubergine, finely diced
350 g /12 oz courgettes, thinly sliced
800 g /1 lb 12 oz canned peeled tomatoes
100 g /4 oz mushrooms, thinly sliced
60 ml /4 tbls tomato purée
30 ml /2 tbls freshly chopped parsley
5 ml /1 tsp dried oregano
salt
freshly ground black pepper

To garnish and serve
lettuce leaves
1 orange, thinly sliced
Peanut dressing or Cheese dressing (see recipes below)

1 In a bowl, toss the leeks, onions, chicory, radishes, grapes and watercress.
2 Line a bowl with lettuce. Pile the salad onto the lettuce. Garnish with orange. Cover and chill for at least an hour. Serve with a choice of dressings.

Fruit cabbage salad

 30 minutes,
plus chilling

Serves 10–12
450 g /1 lb red cabbage, shredded
1 large cucumber, finely diced
1 head celery, thinly sliced
225 g /8 oz stoned dates, chopped
350 g /12 oz canned mandarin oranges, drained
75 ml /5 tbls orange juice
45 ml /3 tbls oil
Peanut dressing or Cheese dressing, to serve (see recipes below)

1 In a large bowl, combine the cabbage, cucumber, celery, dates and oranges. Mix together the orange juice and oil and stir in.
2 Cover and chill the salad for 1 hour or more, then serve with a choice of dressings.

Cheese dressing

 10 minutes

Makes about 425 ml /15 fl oz
150 ml /5 fl oz mayonnaise
150 ml /5 fl oz soured cream
75 g /3 oz cream cheese
30 ml /2 tbls freshly grated Parmesan cheese
30 ml /2 tbls freshly chopped parsley
30 ml /2 tbls chopped stuffed olives
salt and freshly ground black pepper

1 Beat together the mayonnaise, soured cream and cheeses. Stir in the parsley, olives and seasoning. Turn the mixture into a serving bowl, cover and chill until needed.

Peanut dressing

10 minutes

Makes about 275 ml /10 fl oz
150 ml /5 fl oz olive oil
5 ml /1 tsp caster sugar
5 ml /1 tsp mustard powder
1 garlic clove, crushed
60 ml /4 tbls cider vinegar
45 ml /3 tbls crunchy peanut butter
salt and freshly ground black pepper
75 g /3 oz unsalted peanuts, skins rubbed off

1 Combine all the ingredients except the peanuts and shake vigorously. Stir in the peanuts, then adjust the seasoning if necessary.

For the topping
4 medium-sized eggs
150 ml /5 fl oz milk
275 ml /10 fl oz yoghurt
a large pinch of freshly grated nutmeg
salt and freshly ground black pepper

1 Put the lentils, parsley stalks and bouquet garni into a pan. Cover them generously with water and bring to the boil, then lower the heat, cover the pan and simmer for 45–60 minutes, until the lentils are just tender. Drain them, discarding the herbs.
2 Meanwhile, heat the butter and oil in a large pan and fry the onions, garlic, carrots, aubergine and courgettes over a medium heat for 5 minutes, stirring frequently. Lower the heat, cover and simmer for 10 minutes.
3 Add the tomatoes and their juice and the mushrooms, and stir well. Stir in the tomato purée, parsley and oregano and season well with salt and pepper.
4 Simmer the sauce for 20 minutes or until it is thick, then stir in the lentils and adjust the seasoning if necessary.
5 Cook the noodles in a large pan of boiling salted water for 10 minutes or until they are just tender, then drain.
6 Grease a very large, shallow baking dish.

Pour in one-third of the sauce, then add half the noodles. Sprinkle with half the cheese. Add more sauce, the remaining noodles, the remaining cheese and the rest of the sauce.
7 To make the topping, beat the eggs, then gradually beat in the milk and yoghurt. Season with nutmeg, salt and pepper. Pour the topping over the dish and stand it on a baking sheet. At this point you can cover the dish and refrigerate it for up to 24 hours, then bring it up to room temperature before cooking it.
8 Heat the oven to 200C /400F /gas 6. Cook the pastitsio for 50 minutes, until it is deep brown. Serve at once.

Circles salad

30 minutes,
plus chilling

Serves 10–12
4 medium-sized leeks, in 5 mm /¼ in rings
2 small onions, sliced into rings
3 heads chicory, thinly sliced
12 large radishes, thinly sliced
225 g /8 oz seedless green grapes
2 bunches watercress, trimmed

Fresh fruit dip

Provide bright plastic cocktail sticks and lots of paper napkins for this dish! Children will particularly enjoy this dessert which is colourful to look at and fun to eat.

40 minutes,
plus cooling

Serves 10–12
6 small bananas
about 60 ml /4 tbls lemon juice
4 dessert apples
4 large oranges, peeled and segmented
1 small pineapple, peeled, cored and cut into
*   20 mm /¾ in chunks*
100 g /4 oz pink marshmallows
sponge finger biscuits, to serve
For the sauce
100 g /4 oz sugar
175 g /6 oz plain chocolate, melted
100 g /4 oz white marshmallows, cut into
*   small pieces*

1   To make the sauce, put the sugar in a saucepan with 575 ml /1 pt water. Stir over a low heat to dissolve the sugar, bring to the boil and boil for 7 minutes.
2   Pour the hot syrup over the chocolate in a large bowl, stir to blend thoroughly, then return the mixture to the pan. Add the marshmallows, stir over a low heat until they melt, then simmer for 10 minutes.
3   Pour the sauce into a serving bowl and leave it to cool. (The sauce may be made up to 8 hours in advance and left to chill in the refrigerator until needed.)
4   As near to the mealtime as possible, cut the bananas into 20 mm /¾ in slices and toss them in the lemon juice. Place them in a serving bowl. Core and thinly slice the apples, toss them in the lemon juice and place them in a serving bowl. Arrange the orange segments, pineapple chunks and pink marshmallows each in separate bowls.
5   To serve, arrange the bowls of fruit and marshmallows around the sauce. Provide coloured plastic cocktail sticks for spearing the fruit pieces and the marshmallows, and sponge finger biscuits for dipping into the chocolate and marshmallow sauce.

Sweet choux puffs

1 hour 45 minutes,
plus cooling

Sweet choux puffs, served with a choice of fillings, either chocolate or strawberry

Makes 24 puffs
150 g /5 oz flour
a large pinch of salt
100 g /4 oz butter
4 medium-sized eggs, lightly beaten
icing sugar, for dredging
For the fillings
50 g /2 oz flour
30 ml /2 tbls cornflour
575 ml /1 pt milk
4 medium-sized eggs, separated
100 g /4 oz caster sugar
100 g /4 oz plain chocolate, melted
a few drops of vanilla essence
225 ml /8 fl oz thick strawberry purée
*   (see note below)*
For the decorations
1 chocolate flake bar, crumbled
fresh strawberries (optional)

1   First make the fillings: sift together the flour and cornflour and pour on enough milk to make a smooth paste. Beat in the egg yolks and sugar.
2   Bring the remainder of the milk to the boil in a small pan, then pour it, stirring constantly, onto the egg mixture. Pour the custard into the top pan of a double boiler or a bowl fitted over a pan of simmering water.
3   Cook the custard, stirring, for about 10 minutes, or until it is thick enough to coat the back of a spoon. Place the pan or bowl in cold water and beat the custard until it cools and thickens further.
4   Divide the mixture in half. Beat the chocolate and vanilla essence into one half, and the strawberry purée into the other.
5   In a large bowl, whisk the egg whites until they are stiff, then fold half into each of the fillings. Place the fillings in bowls, cover and refrigerate them for 24 hours, if wished.
6   Make the choux puffs. Heat the oven to 200C /400F /gas 6. Sift together the flour and salt. Put the butter in a saucepan with 275 ml /10 fl oz water and bring slowly to the boil. Stir, remove the pan from the heat and tip in the flour. Beat quickly until smooth, then leave to cool for 5 minutes.
7   Beat in the eggs, a little at a time, until the mixture is smooth and glossy.
8   Place tablespoons of the mixture, well apart, on lightly dampened baking sheets and cover them with inverted roasting pans.
9   Bake the puffs on the top shelf of the oven for 30 minutes, or until they are well risen and crisp. Immediately slit them horizontally and leave to cool on a wire rack.
10   To serve, pile the choux puffs in a bowl to form a pyramid. Sift icing sugar over them. Decorate the chocolate filling with the flake bar and the strawberry filling with the strawberries, if wished. Provide spoons and let your guests help themselves.

● To make thick strawberry purée, either crush the fresh or frozen fruit with a wooden spoon and press it through a nylon sieve, or use a blender. As a guide, 300 g /11 oz fresh berries will give 225 ml /8 fl oz purée. Add 10 ml /2 tsp arrowroot (or cornflour) to 30 ml / 2 tbls purée. Blend to a smooth paste. Add the mixture to the remaining purée and bring it to the boil, stirring continuously. Remove it from the heat. Add icing sugar to taste and allow the purée to cool.

Food for Crowds

EASY ENTERTAINING

A marvellously simple way to entertain is to give a drinks party. To help ensure that the food will be as varied and appealing as the liquid refreshment, follow my suggestions here for mouthwatering nibbles and dips.

At a truly successful drinks party there should always be plenty of food from which to pick and nibble. Ready-made snack food is popular and very varied, so do not hesitate to buy it and make liberal use of it to save yourself time and energy.

Buy your nibbles on the day before the event, so that you have no last-minute panics, and so that you can spend the day of the party organizing the room, the drinks, the dips and setting the food out on individual serving plates.

Make sure all your guests are aware of the time the party begins. Telephone or send written invitations, with maps for those who may have difficulty finding the address. The invitations should make it quite clear that it is a drinks party and not a meal, so that everyone knows what to expect.

Something to drink

Make a large bowlful of punch, choose one from those on pages 90–94, and, for drivers, make my special non-alcoholic punch, Fruit of the vine. Put the juice of 1 lemon and 1 orange into a small bowl with 60 ml /4 tbls caster sugar, and stir until the sugar dissolves. Put a block of ice in a serving bowl and pour the citrus sugar mixture over it. Pour 700 ml /1¼ pt black grape juice and 700 ml /1¼ pt white grape juice over the top, and stir well. Decorate the drink with seeded, peeled grapes, orange and lemon slices and sprigs of fresh mint.

Alternatively, make my refreshing Chilled cup. Put 75 g /3 oz sugar into a saucepan with 200 ml /7 fl oz water. Add the zest of 2 lemons and 2 oranges, then stir over a low heat until the sugar is dissolved. Bring to the boil, lower the heat and simmer for 3 minutes. Remove from the heat, allow to cool and then chill. Strain the syrup into a serving bowl or jug containing ice cubes, and discard the fruit zest. Squeeze the juice from the two lemons and two oranges into the bowl and add 700 ml /1¼ pt black grape juice and 575 ml /1 pt mineral water and stir. Garnish the punch with some thinly sliced cucumber and sprigs of mint.

Another idea for a non-alcoholic drink is my Cranberry punch. Make this by putting

1 L /1¾ pt cranberry juice, 300 ml /11 fl oz fresh orange juice, the juice of 3 lemons and 1 L /1¾ pt ginger ale in a large bowl or jug. Add ice cubes and stir to blend. Garnish with slices of orange and lemon, then serve.

Tasty nibbles

Fill bowls with salted nuts, crisps, cheese biscuits and dried fruits. Chop the following vegetables into bite-sized pieces: cauliflower, spring onions, carrots, cucumber, and green and red peppers, and use them as crudités to be eaten with dips.

Quick dips: my Blue cheese dip is a quick and easy recipe which serves about 12–16 people: place 225 g /8 oz crumbled blue cheese, 175 g /6 oz softened cream cheese, 60 ml /4 tbls olive oil and 10 ml /2 tsp lemon juice in a large mixing bowl and blend to a paste. Transfer to an attractive bowl when ready to serve.

For an alternative dip, try my spicy Cream cheese and avocado recipe: beat 700 g /1½ lb

cream cheese, 150 ml /5 fl oz mayonnaise, 10 ml /2 tsp chilli sauce and 10 ml /2 tsp Worcestershire sauce together in a large bowl until smooth. Season with salt. In another bowl, mash the flesh of 1 large avocado with 30 ml /2 tbls lemon juice until the mixture is pulpy. Finely chop 1 green pepper and 2 skinned tomatoes and add them to the cream cheese mixture. Add the avocado mixture, and 1 crushed garlic clove, and mix until well blended. Transfer to a serving bowl and refrigerate until needed.

Guacamole dip is one which everyone likes. Try this version of it: peel and stone 2 avocado pears. Using a wooden spoon, lightly mash the avocado flesh, together with 60 ml / 4 tbls lemon juice, 1 finely chopped garlic clove, 60 ml /4 tbls finely chopped onion and 60 ml /4 tbls finely chopped celery. Add just enough olive oil to make a smooth paste, then season to taste with salt and freshly ground black pepper. Transfer the dip to a bowl to serve.

Nuts are ideal food for parties, but if you want something slightly different, try my simple recipe for Tahini-walnuts on sticks: put 225 g /8 oz walnuts into a blender and process briefly to crush them — they should not be powdered. Add 225 ml /8 fl oz tahini, two crushed garlic cloves, 5 ml /1 tsp salt, 1.5 ml /¼ tsp cayenne pepper and 2.5 ml /½ tsp crushed coriander seeds and process until just smooth. Transfer the mixture to a bowl and slowly add about 75 g /3 oz fresh white breadcrumbs, stirring until the mixture is firm enough to hold its own shape. Form the mixture into walnut-sized balls and roll them in 75 g /3 oz lightly toasted sesame seeds. Put each ball onto a cocktail stick and chill in the refrigerator for up to 8 hours.

Unusual olives add a touch of sophistication to a party, so try making my Lemon and coriander olives — these are simple to prepare, but do make them a week or more before they are needed, to give them plenty of time to mature. First take 900 g / 2 lb black or green olives (or a mixture of both) and cut 2 or 3 shallow slits in each one. Wash and then drain them thoroughly. Put the olives into a large bowl and mix them with 30 ml /2 tbls coriander seeds. Pack the mixture into 2 large, clean jars, adding slices of lemon from time to time. Pour on olive oil to cover the olives in the jars, seal the jars and keep them in a cool place to mature. To serve, spoon the olives into bowls, discarding the lemon slices, and decorate with fresh sprigs of flat-leaved parsley.

The following recipe is a luxurious dip called Black olive caviar. To make it, use a 200 ml /7 fl oz jar of black olives. Wash the brine from the olives, stone and then chop them finely. Combine them with 30 ml / 2 tbls chopped parsley and 2 finely chopped spring onions, and mix well. In another bowl, blend together a dash of anchovy essence and 5 ml /1 tsp wine vinegar. Add 45 ml /3 tbls olive oil and freshly ground black pepper to taste, and stir until smooth. Combine this with the olive mixture and 1 finely chopped celery stick. Toss until mixed then refrigerate before serving with crackers.

A comprehensive selection of nibbles, including cheese, crudités, nuts and olives

Useful hints

● Distribute the food throughout the room so that it is always within easy reach of your guests.
● Cut a grapefruit in half and place it on a plate, cut side downwards. Use it as a base for nibbles on cocktail sticks.
● If you are serving plain olives, choose one oil-cured type and one wine-cured type.
● Put stuffed green olives and black olives on cocktail sticks with small gherkins, silverskin onions or any other pickles.
● If olives are steeped in olive oil and 3 crushed cloves of garlic for at least 4 days, they will be an unusual accompaniment to the other nibbles on the tables.
● Potato crisps are always popular, but make sure that you avoid the very strongly flavoured ones.
● Fill baskets and bowls with pretzels and bread sticks.
● Deep-fry croûtons and sprinkle them with celery salt, paprika, or salt and chopped fresh parsley.
● Cut cheese into bite-sized pieces — choose about 3 different colours and flavours such as Leiden cumin-flavoured cheese, an orange-coloured cheese such as Leicester, and a Cheddar or Edam.
● If cocktail sausages are unavailable, buy thin chipolata sausages and twist each one in the centre. Grill them or put them in a moderate oven until golden, then snip them apart. These can be served cold on cocktail sticks with spicy dips.
● Sauté mushroom caps in butter and then fill them with liver pâté.
● Small tomatoes can be halved and seeded, and then filled with a mixture of cottage cheese and chives.
● Make sandwiches before the event and then freeze them. Cut them into attractive shapes while they are still slightly frozen.
● If the party is in winter-time, try jacket potatoes — eaten with a fork — they will be easy to prepare and the dips can be used to garnish the potatoes.
● Buy or make your own Scotch eggs — cut them in half and serve them with a mustard dip, Herby mustard sauce (see page 51).
● Try stuffed vine leaves for a Mediterranean touch at your party.
● Meat balls can be made from minced beef, pork or lamb or even sausage-meat. Serve these on wooden cocktail sticks, either warm or cold with Fondue tomato sauce (see page 51).
● Stuff large, seeded, green grapes with a mixture of Gorgonzola cheese, a soft, full-fat cheese, sherry and grated onion.
● Put cubes of cheese, such as Cheddar, onto cocktail sticks with a cube of fruit such as canned pineapple.
● Serve large, seedless raisins (rinsed, drained and dried) mixed with blanched almonds in the proportion of 2:1.
● Make sure that there is a fruit bowl with a selection of fruit from which your guests can choose: apples, fresh figs, peaches, nectarines, bananas, or dessert plums and gooseberries. Avoid fruit like oranges which will need to be peeled.
● Make sure that you have enough coffee for anyone who may want it towards the end of the party.

COOKING FOR LARGE NUMBERS

Follow my 'multiplying up' recipes and learn how to cope successfully with the task of feeding a party of 18, 24, or even 30 guests. It really isn't too difficult, if you plan ahead carefully.

When you are cooking for lots of guests, the best advice to follow is to cook recipes that you are familiar with. But even when cooking tried and trusted recipes, dealing with larger numbers isn't necessarily just a matter of simple arithmetic; you can't always multiply-up ingredients in the same proportion as the number of servings.

For one thing, it is generally reckoned that portions for a buffet meal can be significantly smaller than those for a dinner party. When guests have to eat standing up, using a fork and keeping an eye on a glass of wine as well, they tend to take smaller helpings that are more comfortably manageable. Equally, at a buffet party the food is not the centre of attention in the same way it is at a formal dinner party.

If, for example, you choose a recipe which allows 225 g /8 oz boned meat per person, for a large buffet party you can confidently reduce this amount to 175 g /6 oz or even, for a cut in which there is no waste, 150 g / 5 oz. Again, the larger the party, the lower the proportion of food you need. There isn't an entirely logical explanation for this, but it is a fact that you do not have to serve 30 people ten times the amount you would serve to three.

This rule applies to certain ingredients too. Herbs and spices have the ability to flavour much larger quantities of meat, fish or sauce with practically no reduction in their aroma or pungency. On no account, for instance, increase the amount of cayenne pepper or chilli powder in direct proportion to the other ingredients.

Another important tip is, when following a recipe devised for four or six people, never attempt it all in one go for more than four times that quantity. It is better by far to make it in two batches, which will probably prove quicker and easier in the end. You will also have to consider the capacity of your casseroles, saucepans, baking dishes and flan cases.

Now, bearing these guidelines in mind, here are some recipe suggestions for dishes that can be multiplied-up quite easily for serving at large buffet parties.

First courses

Choose a dish that can be served and cleared away with the minimum of fuss. Variations on popular starters are fine for a large party. Melon balls can be shaped a day in advance, then tossed with chopped, preserved ginger and stored in the refrigerator. A sauce of thin cream flavoured with ginger syrup is delicious. Alternatively, toss the melon balls with orange or grapefruit segments, chopped herbs and a fruit juice dressing. Serve wedges or rings of melon with smoked Parma-type ham, or fill the rings with prawns or chopped smoked salmon pieces mixed together with soured cream.

Variations on savoury-filled hard-boiled eggs are easy to prepare and attractive if arranged on a bed of lettuce leaves. Scoop out the yolks and mix them with your choice of herb-flavoured cream cheese; cream cheese and curry paste; thick bechamel sauce with chopped prawns or chicken; sieved cottage cheese, banana and curry powder; mashed avocado and lemon juice — the possibilities are endless. Pipe smooth mixtures through a large star-shaped nozzle. Pile others back into the cooked egg halves and pipe a rosette of whipped cream, perhaps coloured with paprika, on top.

Cones of thinly-sliced, smoked German-style sausages make a tantalizing display. Wrap the cones, secure them with a cocktail stick and make fillings of herb or spice-flavoured cream or cottage cheese. Fill them no more than 2 hours before the party.

Liver, meat and game pâtés are always popular first courses when served with Melba toast, but herb and vegetable pâtes can offer a greater contrast with a meat-based main dish. A herb pâté can be prepared in advance and kept foil-wrapped in the refrigerator.

Prawn and mushroom mille-feuilles (see recipe) can be made in advance, the pastry stored in an airtight tin and the filling in the refrigerator. On the day of the party, heat the puff pastry in the oven for 10 minutes at 190C /375F /gas 5 to refresh it, then allow it to cool completely before sandwiching it with the fillings.

Main courses

Make this course your personal *pièce de résistance*, and choose a dish that you feel confident cooking. If pastry is your speciality, offer your guests an old favourite pie recipe with a party plus — chicken pie with green peppers; duck with black cherries; beef with chestnuts or walnuts; lamb with artichoke hearts; fish with shrimps or prawns. Make large pies in oven roasting pans — conveniently shallow, making it easy to cut the pie into portions — or alternatively, buy large-size, foil baking cases. Or, you could have a Greek-style party with a moussaka as the main dish. Stretch the more expensive ingredients by adding several layers of thinly

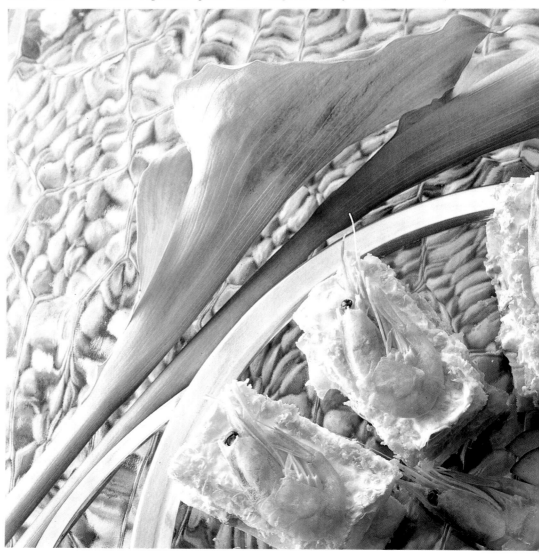

sliced potatoes, or substitute courgettes for some of the aubergines. This is helpful, as browning kilos of aubergines is usually rather time-consuming.

Pasta dishes with all their variations are perfect party pieces, although not strands of spaghetti, if you value your guests' peace of mind and your floor covering! Lasagne is a good choice, or vary the recipe with a chicken, prawn, fish or even a vegetable sauce. Lentils cooked until they are just tender and stirred into a thick and garlicky tomato sauce make an economical and tasty filling. Other shapes of pasta can be layered with a savoury sauce and a cheese topping in a similar way.

If you have the time and patience to prepare them ahead of the party, meat balls are a practical main-course idea. Make them with a mixture of minced beef and veal or pork, or chicken with veal or pork. Shallow-fry them until they are crispy-brown and serve them in a soured cream sauce or in an egg and lemon sauce.

Casseroles of all kinds, when the meat is cut into bite-sized pieces, are a perfect party choice. For a spicy dish, try my recipe for Beef curry with fennel or the appetizing Pork stroganoff (see recipes). Both these dishes can be multiplied up to serve 30 quite easily.

If you have a large electric slow cooker and can borrow another one, these can help you to eliminate all last-minute attention. Reheat the food in the slow cookers, leave them switched to low to keep warm, and the food will still be tempting when the last portion is served.

Salads and vegetables
Salads are usually more convenient than hot, cooked vegetables to serve with the main dish. Unless you have a food processor or shredding attachment to a mixer, be sure not to commit yourself to more chopping and slicing than your temper can stand! Among the salad vegetables that are quick to prepare by hand are Chinese leaves and chicory, which simply need slicing through; peppers can be sliced into strips or rings; cucumbers cut into tissue-thin slices with a mandoline cutter, tomatoes cut into slices or wedges. Three-pepper green salad (see recipe) is a dish that can be adapted for summer or winter parties.

Green salad leaves, such as lettuce, curly endive, spinach and so on, must be very thoroughly dried after washing. A plastic salad spinner is a sound investment, but without one, improvize with a bag made by tying the corners of a tea-towel together. A few good shakes usually does the trick.

Store washed and dried salad greens in the lowest part of the refrigerator, in a closed polythene bag. Have the dressing ready and then one of your few last-minute tasks will be to toss the salad just before serving.

Salads can be made infinitely more varied and interesting by the addition of ingredients such as whole, halved or flaked nuts; sultanas or raisins; sunflower or pumpkin seeds. Canned cooked pulses, such as red kidney beans (see Red kidney bean salad, page 24) white haricot beans or flageolets, well rinsed and drained, provide bulk and a smooth texture, contrasting well with crispy greens.

Lightly cooked vegetables make good salad components too — small florets of cauliflower, blanched French beans, strips of parsnip, turnips or carrots.

Pasta, potatoes and rice
What to serve as the 'foundation' of the course, rice, pasta or potatoes, often poses one of the trickiest problems. If you choose rice (use American pre-fluffed rice which does not stick), cook it by the method most familiar to you — boiled in a large pan or simmered in only twice its volume of water. Allow about 40 g /1½ oz uncooked rice per person, and cook it in manageable batches, not more than 500 g /1 lb in each pan at one time. Drained, refreshed under hot running water and drained again, the rice can be served cold or kept hot in covered dishes in a very low oven for about 2 hours. Stir it well before serving. Alternatively, you can cook the rice the day before the party, cover it closely to store it, and then refresh it in a pan of boiling water for just 3–4 minutes.

For more flavour, cook the rice in meat or vegetable stock, home-made or from cubes, or add lemon or orange juice or a bunch of herbs to the water. For flavour and colour, add 5–10 ml /1–2 tsp ground turmeric to each pan — the larger quantity is needed for the fast-boiling method of cooking rice.

Pasta shapes, too, can be kept hot or reheated in a similar way. Toss them in plenty of melted butter and chopped herbs.

If potatoes are to be your choice, be sure not to choose a cooking method that involves you in last-minute work. Jacket potatoes are firm favourites and for a large party it is enough to serve them plain, with butter, soured cream and chopped herbs as optional dressings. Duchesse potatoes, which are potatoes boiled, mashed with butter and egg yolks or cream and then piped into rosette shapes, can be prepared in advance and need only brushing with melted butter and heating through. For an alternative, consider Lyonnaise potatoes, layered in a casserole with onion and cooked in milk or cream. They can be left to cook when the party begins.

Desserts
The types of dessert you serve will, of course, depend to a large extent on the main dishes. Generally though, it is a good idea to serve one that is largely fruit based and another that is rich and creamy.

For a fruit dessert, you can opt for fresh fruit salad, but take care not to choose too many fruits that need fiddly preparation. Seeding a few grapes for decoration or colour is one thing, offering them as the principal fruit for a large number of people could turn

Prawn and mushroom mille-feuilles

out to be irritating. Fresh or frozen raspberries made into a Melba sauce contrasts perfectly with all creamy puddings. A red fruit salad of raspberries, strawberries and cherries is as delicious as it is striking; a green one of sliced kiwi fruits, greengages and melon is cool-looking and refreshing. Allow up to 100 g /4 oz fruit salad each if it is a main dessert, half that amount or less if it is one of two desserts.

Grenadine pears (see recipe on page 68), are not difficult to prepare, yet they add an air of luxury and sophistication to a meal, and are light enough to serve after a fairly substantial main course.

Meringues are a good party dessert. If you choose to make them, plan in advance how you are going to use the spare egg yolks. One egg white and egg yolk 'partnership' is a meringue pudding and a trifle — the yolks are used to enrich and set the custard topping. (Alternatively, use them in mayonnaise to dress a salad: mayonnaise can be made 5 days ahead if covered tightly with cling film.) For big meringue gateaux, consider Pavlovas or meringue bases using soft light brown sugar instead of caster sugar. The latter are made and cooked in the conventional way, but have a sticky-toffee flavour and go particularly well with a rum-flavoured cream and banana filling.

With all rich, creamy tortes and gateaux, it is best to serve them in a single or double layer at the most — triple deckers can topple precariously and embarrass the poor guest!

If pastry does not figure in your first two courses, fruit tarts are a perfect dessert for parties. Or you can try making choux buns or brandy snaps which can be made a day in advance, ready to fill no more than 3 hours before the party, with a fruit purée or cream mixture. Or serve Toasted almond cones, either on their own or with my smooth Apricot ratafia mousse (see recipes).

Beef curry with fennel, served with rice, an assortment of chutneys and pickles and sliced bananas

Prawn and mushroom mille-feuilles

 1½ hours /2 hours /2¼ hours

Serves	18	24	30
350 g /12 oz packet puff pastry	2 packets	3 packets	4 packets
flour, for dusting			
butter	50 g /2 oz	75 g /3 oz	100 g /4 oz
garlic cloves, crushed	2	3	4
button mushrooms, chopped	225 g /8 oz	350 g /12 oz	450 g /1 lb
parsley, finely chopped	30 ml /2 tbls	45 ml /3 tbls	60 ml /4 tbls
cottage cheese, sieved	225 g /8 oz	350 g /12 oz	450 g /1 lb
cream cheese	225 g /8 oz	350 g /12 oz	450 g /1 lb
salt	1.5 ml /¼ tsp	1.5 ml /¼ tsp	2.5 ml /½ tsp
freshly ground black pepper	a pinch	a pinch	1.5 ml /¼ tsp
Tabasco	5 ml /1 tsp	7.5 ml /1½ tsp	10 ml /2 tsp
prawns, boiled and peeled	225 g /8 oz	350 g /12 oz	450 g /1 lb
milk, if necessary			
soured cream, stirred	100 ml /3½ fl oz	150 ml /5 fl oz	200 ml /7 fl oz
tomato waterlilies, sliced cucumber, whole prawns, to garnish			

1 Heat the oven to 220C /425F /gas 7.

2 Divide each packet of pastry into 3 equal pieces. On a lightly floured board, roll each piece to a rectangle 11.5 × 25 cm /4½ × 10 in. Sprinkle 2 large baking sheets with cold water. Place 2 pastry strips on each baking sheet and prick the tops with a fork. Bake the pastry in the oven for 12–15 minutes or until it is crisp and golden brown. Remove the pastry and put it on a wire rack to cool. Cool the baking sheets under cold running water and then repeat the process until all the pastry is cooked.

3 Melt the butter in a large frying-pan and fry the garlic and mushrooms over a moderate heat for 3 minutes, stirring occasionally. Remove from the heat, stir in the chopped parsley and allow to cool.

4 Beat together the cottage cheese and the cream cheese and season with salt and freshly ground black pepper, then divide the mixture between two bowls.

5 Stir the Tabasco and the prawns into half the cheese mixture. Thin it with a little milk

Beef curry with fennel

 2¾ hours /3 hours /3¼ hours

Serves	18	24	30
stewing steak	3.4 kg /7½ lb	4 kg /9 lb	5 kg /11 lb
oil	225 ml /8 fl oz	250 ml /9 fl oz	300 ml /11 fl oz
onions, sliced	700 g /1½ lb	800 g /1¾ lb	900 g /2 lb
ground fennel	30 ml /2 tbls	30 ml /2 tbls	35 ml /7 tsp
ground ginger	10 ml /2 tsp	12.5 ml /2½ tsp	12.5 ml /2½ tsp
ground cloves	5 ml /1 tsp	5 ml /1 tsp	5 ml /1 tsp
ground cinnamon	5 ml /1 tsp	5 ml /1 tsp	5 ml /1 tsp
salt	15 ml /1 tbls	20 ml /4 tsp	20 ml /4 tsp
paprika	30 ml /2 tbls	30 ml /2 tbls	35 ml /7 tsp
cayenne pepper	5 ml /1 tsp	5 ml /1 tsp	5 ml /1 tsp
plain yoghurt	850 ml /1½ pt	900 ml /1¾ pt	950 ml /1 pt 18 fl oz
boiled rice, to serve			

1 Trim any fat from the beef, cut it into 5 cm /2 in cubes. In a large frying-pan, heat 60 ml /4 tbls, 75 ml /5 tbls or 90 ml /6 tbls of the oil and fry the onions over a moderate heat, stirring frequently, for 4 minutes or until they are soft and translucent. Stir in the fennel, ginger, cloves, cinnamon and salt and cook for 3 minutes, stirring.
2 Transfer the onion mixture to a large casserole (or divide between 2 casseroles).
3 Heat a little of the remaining oil in the pan and fry the meat in a single layer, in batches, so it seals and browns evenly. As each batch is finished, add it to the onions.
4 Place the casserole on the heat, add the paprika and cayenne pepper and stir well. Pour on 850 ml /1½ pt, 900 ml /1¾ pt or 1.1 L /2 pt water. Cover and lower the heat.
5 Simmer for 2 hours, stirring occasionally. If you are cooking the curry the day before the party, leave it to cool.
6 Before the party, stir in the yoghurt and heat the curry throughly. Serve with boiled rice (see Introduction).

Pork stroganoff

 1¾ hours /2 hours /2¼ hours

Serves	18	24	30
pork fillet	3.2 kg /7 lb	3.9 kg /8½ lb	4.5 kg /10 lb
butter	100 g /4 oz	150 g /5 oz	175 g /6 oz
oil	120 ml /8 tbls	150 ml /5 fl oz	175 ml /6 fl oz
garlic cloves, crushed	4	5	6
onions, sliced	225 g /8 oz	275 g /10 oz	350 g /12 oz
ground coriander	15 ml /3 tsp	20 ml /4 tsp	25 ml /5 tsp
salt	10 ml /2 tsp	10 ml /2 tsp	12.5 ml /2½ tsp
freshly ground pepper	10 ml /2 tsp	10 ml /2 tsp	10 ml /2 tsp
flour	30 ml /2 tbls	40 ml /8 tsp	45 ml /3 tbls
chicken stock, home-made or from a cube	600 ml /1 pt	750 ml /1¼ pt	900 ml /1½ pt
lemon juice	15 ml /1 tbls	15 ml /1 tbls	20 ml /4 tsp
button mushrooms, sliced	225 g /8 oz	275 g /10 oz	350 g /12 oz
soured cream	275 ml /10 fl oz	350 ml /12 fl oz	375 ml /13 fl oz
freshly chopped parsley	60 ml /4 tbls	60 ml /4 tbls	90 ml /6 tbls
rice or pasta, to serve			

1 Trim the pork and cut it into 25 mm /1 in thick slices. Pat the pork slices dry on absorbent paper. In a large frying-pan or saucepan, melt 25 g /1 oz butter and 45 ml /3 tbls oil. When it is hot, add a single layer of pork and fry it over a moderate heat until it is browned. Brown the other side. Remove the meat to a large casserole. Add more butter and oil as needed, and fry the rest of the pork.
2 Add the remaining oil to the pan and fry the garlic and onions over a moderate heat for 4–5 minutes, stirring frequently. Stir in the coriander, salt and freshly ground black pepper and fry for 2 minutes, stirring. Stir in the flour and cook for 2–3 minutes, stirring continuously, to form a pale roux.
3 Pour on the stock gradually, stirring all the time, and bring to the boil. Simmer for 3 minutes and stir in the lemon juice.
4 Pour the sauce over the meat, stir and cover. Simmer for 30 minutes.
5 Heat the remaining butter in a pan, fry the mushrooms for 3 minutes, stirring.
6 Stir the mushrooms, soured cream and half the parsley into the casserole. Adjust the seasoning. Garnish with parsley and serve with boiled rice (see Introduction) or pasta.

if necessary. Taste the mixture and add more seasoning if necessary.
6 Beat the cooled mushroom mixture into the remaining cheese mixture. Taste and adjust the seasoning if necessary.
7 Using a very sharp knife, trim the uneven edges of the pastry. Crumble and reserve the trimmings.
8 Place 2, 3 or 4 pieces of pastry side by side on a work surface. Divide the mushroom filling equally among them and level the tops. Cover each one with another piece of pastry. Spread the prawn filling over these and level the tops. Cover each one with another pastry layer.
9 Spread the soured cream over the top of each mille-feuilles. Sprinkle the reserved pastry crumbs in neat lines along each mille-feuilles, using a knife blade to guide you. Garnish with whole prawns, tomato water-lilies and slices of cucumber.
10 Carefully transfer the mille-feuilles to serving dishes and keep them in a cool place until required. To serve, cut into slices.

Three-pepper green salad

30 minutes /35 minutes /40 minutes, plus 1 hour marinating

Serves	18	24	30
Chinese leaves, trimmed and thinly sliced	1 medium head	1 large head	2 medium heads
onions, chopped	1 large	2 medium	2 large
bunches of watercress, separated into sprigs	3	4	5
basic vinaigrette (see note at end of method)	2 × basic vinaigrette	3 × basic vinaigrette	3 × basic vinaigrette
green peppers, seeded and thinly sliced	1	2	3
red peppers, seeded and thinly sliced	2	2	2
yellow peppers, seeded and thinly sliced	2	2	2

1 Put the Chinese leaves, onions and watercress in a large bowl. Toss them together well. Divide into plastic bags and chill in the lowest part of the refrigerator.
2 Mix the green, red and yellow peppers together and toss them in the vinaigrette. Cover and leave them at room temperature for at least 1 hour.
3 Remove the green salad from the refrigerator and arrange it in one or more dishes.

Arrange the sliced pepper attractively over the green salad and serve.

● To make 125 ml /4 fl oz basic vinaigrette: put 2.5 ml /½ tsp Dijon mustard into a screw top jar and add 30 ml /2 tbls wine vinegar. Add salt and freshly ground black pepper to taste and 90 ml /6 tbls olive oil. Vigorously shake the jar containing the ingredients until they form an emulsion.

Grenadine pears

45 minutes /1 hour /1¼ hours

Serves	18
sweet sparkling white wine or sparkling perry	600 ml /1 pt
sugar	100 g /4 oz
sirop de grenadine	75 ml /5 tbls
dessert pears, such as Conference	18
black grapes, seeded	225 g /8 oz

1 Put the wine or perry into a large saucepan, add the sugar and heat slowly over a low heat, stirring occasionally, until the sugar has dissolved. Bring to the boil. Stir in the grenadine.
2 Using a potato peeler, carefully peel the pears, leaving them whole and with their stalks still attached.
3 Add the pears to the pan, a few at a time. Leave enough space to turn them without damaging them. Cover the pan and simmer the pears for 3–4 minutes. Using 2 wooden spoons, turn the pears over and poach them for a further 3–4 minutes, or until they are just tender.
4 Using a slotted spoon, remove the pears from the saucepan and arrange them upright in

24	30
700 ml /1¼ pt	850 ml /1½ pt
150 g /5 oz	175 g /6 oz
90 ml /6 tbls	120 ml /8 tbls
24	30
275 g /10 oz	350 g /12 oz

a serving dish. Poach all the remaining pears.
5 When the pears have been cooked, add the grapes to the syrup and simmer them for 3 minutes. Pour the syrup and grapes over the pears. Leave to cool. Cover the pears carefully with cling film or foil and chill in the refrigerator until needed.

● Perry, a sparkling, alcoholic drink, is made from the fermented juice of pears. It will complement this dessert splendidly.
● Sirop de grenadine is a sweet cordial made from the juice of pomegranates. It is non-alcoholic, scarlet in colour and used mainly to flavour desserts, as in this recipe, or to sweeten cocktails — see Daiquiri and Cossack on page 101.

Toasted almond cones

45 minutes /1 hour /1¼ hours

Serves	18	24	30
vegetable fat, for greasing			
butter, at room temperature	100 g /4 oz	175 g /6 oz	225 g /8 oz
flour, sifted, plus extra for dusting	100 g /4 oz	175 g /6 oz	225 g /8 oz
icing sugar, sifted	100 g /4 oz	175g /6 oz	225 g /8 oz
egg whites	2	3	4
almond essence	2–3 drops	4–5 drops	5–6 drops
For the filling			
blanched almonds, flaked and toasted	50 g /2 oz	75 g /3 oz	100 g /4 oz
thick cream, whipped	225 ml /8 fl oz	275 ml /10 fl oz	350 ml /12 fl oz
whole almonds, blanched	18	24	30

1 Heat the oven to 220C /425F /gas 7. Grease and lightly flour 2 baking sheets. Beat the butter and sugar together until very soft and creamy. Beat in the egg whites, a little at a time until thoroughly blended, then gradually beat in the flour. Add the almond flavouring and beat again until smooth.
2 Drop spoonfuls of the mixture onto the prepared baking sheets and spread each one to a circle 11.5 cm /4½ in diameter.
3 Bake in the oven for 4 minutes.
4 Remove a tray from the oven, lift off one round at a time and place it on a single layer of tea-towel on the palm of one hand. Quickly wrap the biscuit into a cone shape. Stand each cone in a cup for a few minutes, then lay on a wire rack to cool completely.
5 Bake the remaining mixture in further batches and roll them up as described.
6 When the cones are completely cold, store them in an airtight container.
7 Make the filling: stir the flaked almonds into the cream. Spoon it into the cones and stick a whole almond in the top.

Apricot ratafia mousse

 overnight soaking, then 2¼ hours

Serves	18	24	30
dried apricots, soaked overnight in water	350 g /12 oz	425 g /15 oz	500 g /18 oz
powdered gelatine	45 ml /3 tbls	60 ml /4 tbls	75 ml /5 tbls
eggs, separated	9	12	16
egg yolks	2	3	4
soft, light brown sugar	175 g /6 oz	225 g /8 oz	275 g /10 oz
thick cream, whipped	425 ml /15 fl oz	600 ml /1 pt	700 ml /1¼ pt
ratafia biscuits, crushed	100 g /4 oz	175 g /6 oz	225 g /8 oz
Amaretto liqueur	90 ml /6 tbls	120 ml /8 tbls	150 ml /5 fl oz
For the topping			
ratafia biscuits, crushed	50 g /2 oz	75 g /3 oz	100 g /4 oz
thin strips of angelica	4	6–8	6–8

1 Put the apricots with their soaking liquid into a pan, bring to the boil, cover and simmer for 20 minutes or until the fruit is tender. Drain the fruit, reserving the liquid. Reserve 6 or 9 apricot halves for decoration and liquidize the remainder in a blender, in batches, with a little cooking liquid to make a thick purée. Cool.
2 Put 90 ml /6 tbls, 120 ml /8 tbls or 150 ml /5 fl oz of the cooking liquid in a bowl and sprinkle on the gelatine. Stand the bowl in a pan of hot water over a low heat for 5 minutes or until the gelatine has dissolved. Stir occasionally. Remove the bowl from the heat and briefly set aside.
3 Beat all the egg yolks and sugar together until the mixture is thick, light in colour and creamy. Pour in the gelatine in a thin, steady stream, whisking all the time.
4 Fold in the apricot purée, then the whipped cream. Stir well, then stir in the crushed ratafias and the liqueur. Set aside at room temperature for about 30 minutes, until the mixture is on the point of setting.
5 Stiffly whisk the egg whites and fold them into the mixture, using a metal spoon.
6 Turn the mixture into serving bowls and level off the tops. Put in the refrigerator and leave to set for at least one hour.
7 Before serving, sprinkle the tops with crushed ratafias to cover them completely. Arrange the reserved apricot halves and the angelica on top. Serve chilled.

● Toasted almond cones (see recipe) are the perfect acompaniment to this dessert.

COLD CANAPES & FINGER FOOD

From Glazed veal canapés with foie gras and Smoked salmon and watercress pinwheels to Ribbon sandwich fingers and Avocado barquettes, this selection of tasty recipes is diverse enough to please everyone.

Cold canapés and finger foods really come into their own at drinks parties, and the secret of a successful drinks party — one which you enjoy with your guests — is to do as much preparation as you can ahead.

Select the recipes to give a good variety of dishes. Prepare fillings the day before or early in the morning, and leave them covered in the refrigerator. Pastry cases can be made several days ahead and stored in airtight containers, or weeks ahead if you have a freezer. Other canapé bases can be made on the morning of the party and set aside until you need them. Leave the filling or topping until an hour or so before the party, as nothing is worse than a soggy base. If you introduce ideas such as my Spinach and cream cheese twirls (see recipe), you can do all the work the day before and the food is actually better for being chilled overnight.

Canapés and finger foods should be small so that they are easy to eat. At a party where there will be no forks or knives, everything must be capable of being eaten in one, two or at the most three bites. To estimate how much food you will need, allow roughly 12 'bites' per person; people with large appetites will probably eat 16–18, while the figure conscious may eat only 7–8 mouthfuls.

A tray of canapés looks most effective if the designs are kept simple. Arrange a variety of food on each plate and be lavish with your edible garnishes. Your guests should have a visual impression of colour and design, as well as anticipation of the flavour. Try these two tempting recipes:

Piped cream cheese canapés: beat 500g / 1 lb cream cheese with 100 g /4 oz butter, 2.5 ml /½ tsp curry powder, salt and pepper to taste and a little milk, if necessary, to make the mixture a piping consistency. Put the mixture in a piping bag fitted with a star nozzle. Pipe rosettes onto 40 crisp biscuits or fried-bread rounds. Top each canapé with a walnut half, half a seeded black grape, a small button mushroom slice or a rolled anchovy fillet.

Sweetcorn and pepper canapés: toast the slices of a thinly-cut medium-sized loaf of white or brown bread. Cut off the crusts and cool the slices, pressed under a heavy board to keep them flat. Using 300 g /10 oz cream cheese, spread each slice thickly. Chop a red and green pepper finely and mix well. Drain a can of sweetcorn and discard the liquid. Cover each toast slice, half with peppers and half with sweetcorn. Cutting across the pepper and corn, cut each slice into three pieces. Arrange on a serving dish and garnish with sprigs of fresh parsley.

Chess-board sandwiches

🍴 30 minutes,
plus chilling

Makes 18
275 g /10 oz butter, softened
juice of ½ lemon
5 ml /1 tsp Worcestershire sauce
2 shallots, very finely chopped
30 ml /2 tbls finely snipped fresh chives
15 ml /1 tbls finely chopped fresh parsley
5 ml /1 tsp paprika
a pinch of mild chilli seasoning
salt and freshly ground black pepper
6 slices white bread, 5 mm /¼ in thick, crusts removed
6 slices wholemeal bread, 5 mm /¼ in thick, crusts removed
parsley and sage sprigs, to garnish

1 Prepare the flavoured butter: put the butter in a large bowl with the lemon juice and Worcestershire sauce and beat until pale and creamy. Beat in the shallots, chives and parsley, the paprika and chilli seasoning, and season to taste with salt and freshly ground black pepper.
2 Spread one side of each slice of bread thickly with flavoured butter.
3 Make up 4 triple-decker sandwiches. Put 1 brown slice between 2 white, then 1 white slice between 2 brown, and repeat.
4 Cover a baking sheet with cling film and place the sandwiches on top. Cover with more cling film, place a board on top and weight it down. Chill for 1 hour.
5 Remove the cling film cover and, with a sharp knife, cut each sandwich into 4 small squares. Then cut each square into three 12 mm /½ in strips.
6 Spread one cut side of each strip with more flavoured butter. Arrange the strips, buttered sides together, in groups of 5 to make large sandwiches, alternating brown with white, so that the short edge of each pile looks like a chess-board. Make sure the top strip is placed buttered side down.
7 Place on the prepared baking sheet. Cover, weight down and chill as before.
8 Remove the cling film and slice each pile in half crossways. Arrange attractively on a serving dish and garnish with fresh parsley and sage. Serve the sandwiches as soon as possible.

Chess-board sandwiches

Vorspeisen

30 minutes

Makes 24

6 slices pumpernickel
75 g /3 oz softened butter, plus extra for
* spreading*
60 ml /4 tbls cream cheese
15 ml /1 tbls grated horseradish
150 g /5 oz rare roast fillet of beef
salt and freshly ground black pepper
30 ml /2 tbls sesame oil
150 g /5 oz Roquefort cheese
2.5 ml /½ tsp finely snipped fresh chives
2.5 ml /½ tsp finely chopped fresh chervil
2.5 ml /½ tsp finely chopped fresh tarragon
15 ml /1 tbls brandy
paprika
For the garnish
15 ml /1 tbls finely chopped fresh parsley
4 tiny sprigs of fresh parsley

1 Spread the pumpernickel slices thinly with butter. Cut each slice into 4 fingers.
2 In a bowl, blend the cream cheese with the grated horseradish. Spread this mixture over half the pumpernickel fingers.
3 Slice the rare beef very thinly and cut it into strips to fit neatly over the cheese-covered pumpernickel fingers. Season with salt and freshly ground black pepper to taste and then brush lightly with the sesame oil.
4 In a bowl, using a fork, blend the Roquefort cheese with 75 g /3 oz butter until smooth. Beat in the finely snipped chives, finely chopped chervil and tarragon, and brandy, then season to taste with pepper.
5 Mound the Roquefort mixture onto the remaining pumpernickel fingers. Sprinkle with paprika and garnish with a fine line of chopped parsley down the centre of each canapé. Transfer to a serving platter. Garnish with parsley sprigs. Serve the fingers as soon as possible.

Brie fingers

Make sure that you use ripe Brie cheese for this recipe. The inside of the cheese should be evenly firm and creamy, with no trace of a central chalky band.

1 hour 45 minutes,
including chilling

Makes 18

100 g /4 oz ripe, creamy Brie cheese
100 g /4 oz flour, plus extra for dusting
50 g /2 oz softened butter
2 egg yolks
salt
freshly grated nutmeg
cayenne pepper
milk, for brushing
a sprig of parsley or mustard and cress, to
* garnish*
For the Brie filling
50 g /2 oz ripe, creamy Brie cheese
100 g /4 oz softened butter
10 ml /2 tsp lemon juice
a pinch of cayenne pepper

1 Cut the Brie cheese into 4 pieces. Cut the rind carefully from each piece, leaving only the creamy centre. Discard the rind.
2 Put the cheese in a bowl and sift in the flour. Add the butter and egg yolks and work to a smooth dough, starting with a wooden spoon and finishing by hand. Season with salt, freshly grated nutmeg and cayenne pepper to taste. Cover the bowl with cling film and chill for at least 1 hour, or until needed.
3 Meanwhile, prepare the Brie filling. Cut the Brie into 2 pieces, then cut off and discard the rind. Cream the cheese with the butter until smooth. Add the lemon juice and cayenne pepper. Beat until smooth.
4 Heat the oven to 170C /325F /gas 3.
5 Roll out the dough on a lightly floured board to a 45×22.5 cm /18×9 in rectangle, about 3 mm /⅛ in thick. With a sharp knife, cut it into eighteen 25×15 mm /1×½ in small rectangles.
6 Brush the rectangles lightly with milk, then score the tops lightly with a fork and place on a baking sheet. Bake in the oven for 10 minutes, or until golden. Remove from the oven and leave to cool a little.
7 When the baked rectangles are cool enough to handle, split them in half horizontally. Put 10 ml /2 tsp Brie filling in the centre of each and replace the tops.
8 Arrange the brie fingers attractively on a serving dish. Garnish the dish with a bouquet of parsley or mustard and cress and serve while the Brie fingers are still warm.

Vorspeisen

Red caviar barquettes

baking the barquettes,
then 15 minutes

Makes 12

100 g /4 oz made-weight shortcrust pastry,
* defrosted if frozen*
flour, for dusting
175 g /6 oz cream cheese
45 ml /3 tbls soured cream
15 ml /1 tbls lemon juice
a pinch of cayenne pepper
salt
45 ml /3 tbls red caviar
lemon twist, to garnish

1 Heat the oven to 200C /400F /gas 6. Roll out the pastry on a floured surface and use it to line 12 barquette moulds 9 cm /3½ in long. Fill with foil and beans and bake for 10 minutes; remove the foil and beans and bake for a further 10 minutes, or until fully cooked. Leave until cold, then remove the cooked pastry from the moulds.
2 In a bowl, cream the cheese with the soured cream. Flavour with lemon juice and a pinch each of cayenne pepper and salt to taste. Fold in three-quarters of the red caviar. Chill, if not using immediately.
3 To serve, fill the cold barquettes with the mixture and garnish with the remaining caviar. Transfer to a serving dish and garnish with a twist of lemon.

Glazed veal canapés with foie gras

🕐 ⑪||| 1½ hours, overnight chilling, then 2½ hours, plus chilling

Makes 16

900 g /2 lb boned, rolled shoulder or leg of veal, barded with 50 g /2 oz pork back fat
60 ml /4 tbls olive oil
225 g /8 oz carrots, thinly sliced
1 Spanish onion, thinly sliced
bouquet garni
salt and freshly ground black pepper
125 ml /4 fl oz port
For the aspic
1 small leek, trimmed and chopped
1 celery stick, chopped
1 carrot, chopped
¼ Spanish onion, chopped
frothed white and crushed shell of 1 egg
22.5 ml /1½ tbls powdered gelatine
15 ml /1 tbls port
a few drops of red food colouring (optional)
For the foie gras slices
175 g /6 oz canned mousse de foie gras
50 g /2 oz butter, softened
15 ml /1 tbls port
50 g /2 oz walnuts, finely chopped
For the garnish
16 cocktail gherkins
lettuce leaves

1 Select a heavy, flameproof casserole that is just large enough to take the veal. Heat the olive oil in the casserole and brown the veal for about 10 minutes until it is golden all over. Add the thinly sliced carrot and onion, and the bouquet garni, and season to taste with salt and freshly ground black pepper. Pour in the port, cover the casserole and simmer very gently for 1 hour, or until it is cooked, turning the joint over occasionally and basting it with the cooking juices. To test that the veal is cooked, pierce it with a fine skewer: the juices should run clear.

2 Allow the veal to cool in the casserole. When it is cold, remove it and wrap it in muslin to make a neat, even roll, and tie it firmly in several places with string. Chill overnight. Strain and reserve the stock. Chill the reserved stock also.

3 The following day, prepare the aspic. Remove the fat from the surface of the reserved, chilled stock. Measure the stock and make it up to 700 ml /1¼ pt with water. Put the stock and water in a saucepan.

4 In another large saucepan, combine the chopped leek, celery, carrot, onion and the frothed egg white and crushed egg shell. Bring the stock to the boil and pour it onto the egg white mixture, whisking constantly.

5 Put the pan over a low heat and bring it slowly to the boil, whisking or stirring all the time. Allow a pad of foam to rise to the surface, then turn the heat down and simmer gently for 1 hour, uncovered and without stirring.

6 Line a large sieve or colander with muslin. Gently draw back the scum from one-quarter of the clarified stock using a metal spoon. Lower a ladle into this gap and ladle the clarified stock out into the muslin-lined sieve. Keep this strained stock in the refrigerator until it is needed later on.

7 Prepare the mousse de foie gras slices: cream the mousse de foie gras with the butter and port. Place the mixture on a sheet of greaseproof paper. Use the paper to roll the mousse into a neat sausage shape, about 4 cm /1½ in wide and 12.5–15 cm /5–6 in long. Roll the paper completely around the mousse and twist the ends. Chill in the refrigerator until firm.

8 Unwrap the veal, remove the string and cut it into slices, about 5 mm /¼ in thick. Remove the barding fat from each slice. Cut out rounds from each slice using a 5 cm /2 in plain cutter. You will get about 16 rounds.

9 Place 30 ml /2 tbls of the reserved stock in a separate bowl and sprinkle the gelatine over it. Leave to soften for a few minutes, then stand the bowl in a pan of simmering water until the gelatine has dissolved.

10 Stir the dissolved gelatine into the rest of the reserved strained stock and add the port. Add a few drops of red food colouring, if you wish, to give the aspic a pale pink colour. Leave to cool until syrupy (the consistency of unbeaten egg white).

11 Remove the paper from the chilled foie gras and roll it in the finely chopped walnuts so that it is evenly coated (do not coat the ends). Cut the roll into 16 slices.

12 Make the gherkin fans for decoration: cut each gherkin into 3 slices, leaving the slices attached at one end. Separate the slices to form a fan. Place each foie gras slice on a round of veal and top with a gherkin fan. Chill in the refrigerator.

13 Place the canapés on a wire rack set over a baking tray. Spoon the syrupy aspic over the canapés until each one is completely coated. Pour off the aspic that has dripped through onto the baking tray and use it again. Chill until firm.

14 Lay a few lettuce leaves on a large platter, and arrange the canapés on top.

Spinach and cream cheese twirls

🕐 ⑪||| 1¾ hours, plus overnight chilling

Makes 22–24

40 g /1½ oz butter, plus extra for greasing
225 g /8 oz frozen spinach
15 ml /1 tbls chicken stock, home-made or from a cube
15 ml /1 tbls freshly grated Parmesan cheese
1 shallot, finely chopped
30 ml /2 tbls flour
125 ml /4 fl oz milk
4 eggs, separated
salt and freshly ground black pepper
freshly grated nutmeg
For the filling
125 g /4 oz cream cheese
45 ml /3 tbls thick cream
30 ml /2 tbls lemon or lime juice
salt and freshly ground black pepper

1 Lightly butter a 30 × 20 cm /12 × 8 in Swiss roll tin and line it with a sheet of greaseproof paper. Grease the paper with a little of the butter and set the tin aside. Heat the oven to 200C /400F /gas 6.

2 Put the spinach with the chicken stock and 15 g /½ oz butter in a saucepan, and cook for 10–15 minutes or until the liquid has evaporated. Remove from the heat and stir in the grated Parmesan cheese.

3 In a separate pan, melt the remaining butter; add the finely chopped shallot and sauté for 2–3 minutes until transparent.

4 Stir in the flour and cook for 2–3 minutes to make a pale roux. Gradually pour in the milk, stirring constantly; simmer, stirring, until the sauce has thickened.

5 Add the sauce to the spinach mixture. Stir in the egg yolks and season well with salt, pepper and freshly grated nutmeg.

6 In a clean bowl, whisk the egg whites to soft peaks. With a large metal spoon, fold them into the spinach mixture and spread evenly in the prepared Swiss roll tin.

7 Cook in the oven for 20–25 minutes, or until it is springy to the touch.

8 Prepare a damp tea-towel with a lightly greased sheet of greaseproof paper on top. When the spinach layer is cooked, turn it out carefully onto the paper-lined tea-towel. Carefully remove the paper lining from the

spinach layer, edges first, and allow the steam to escape from it for about 1 minute. Then roll it up, including the tea-towel and greased paper, starting from the long side. Leave to cool.

9 Meanwhile, in a small bowl, mix the cream cheese and cream using a wooden spoon. Season with salt and freshly ground black pepper to taste, and gradually add the lemon or lime juice.

10 Gently unroll the cold spinach and spread it evenly with the cream cheese mixture.

11 Roll it up carefully, starting with a long side, omitting the tea-towel and paper. Wrap it in cling film and place in the refrigerator; leave it for at least 12 hours or up to 24 hours.

12 To serve, trim the ends and cut the roll into 15 mm /1½ in slices — it should make 22–24. Place the spinach twirls on a serving platter, cut side up, so that you can see the colour contrasts.

An attractive selection of party canapés — from front to back, Spinach and cream cheese whirls, Roquefort bites, Glazed veal canapés with foie gras and Steak tartare canapés

Roquefort bites

Roquefort cheese is delicious but expensive. This recipe makes a little go a long way.

 40 minutes

Makes 24
225 g /8 oz Roquefort cheese
125 g /4 oz butter, softened
30 ml /6 tsps mixed finely chopped fresh chives, chervil and tarragon
15 ml /1 tbls brandy
freshly ground black pepper
4 slices pumpernickel
To decorate
red and green pepper, cut into small, fine julienne strips
cucumber with the peel, cut into small, fine julienne strips
carrot, cut into small, fine julienne strips

1 In a bowl, cream the Roquefort and butter together; mix in the finely chopped fresh herbs. Add the brandy and season to taste with freshly ground black pepper.

2 Cut each slice of pumpernickel into 6 pieces. Mound a little of the Roquefort mixture onto each piece and decorate with the julienne of vegetables.

Steak tartare canapés

Steak tartare makes an unusual and exotic canapé — ideal with cocktails.

 30 minutes plus chilling and cooling, then 20 minutes

Makes 40
500 g /1 lb beef fillet
1 egg yolk
60 ml /4 tbls onion, finely chopped
2 garlic cloves, finely chopped
15 ml /1 tbls Worcestershire sauce
30 ml /2 tbls finely chopped fresh parsley
60 ml /4 tbls brandy
10 slices white bread
60 ml /4 tbls olive oil
50 g /2 oz butter
30 ml /2 tbls capers, finely chopped, and finely chopped fresh parsley, to serve

1 Mince the beef twice and combine it with the egg yolk, finely chopped onion, finely chopped garlic, Worcestershire sauce, finely chopped parsley and brandy in a mixing bowl. Mix thoroughly and chill in the refrigerator until ready to serve.

2 Cut 4 × 4 cm /1½ in diameter circles from each slice of bread. Heat the oil and butter and fry the bread circles, a few at a time, until golden. Drain on absorbent paper. Leave to cool.

3 Pile the steak mixture in a mound on top of each croûte and smooth it with a knife.

4 To serve, decorate with chopped capers and finely chopped fresh parsley.

Mouth-waterers

 30 minutes

Makes 24
75–100 g /3–4 oz butter
400 g /14 oz bought pumpernickel, about 8 slices
50 g /2 oz thinly sliced Parma ham
Dijon mustard, for spreading
50 g /2 oz Gruyère cheese, thinly sliced
50 g /2 oz watercress, trimmed and washed
75 g /3 oz kipper pâté

1 Liberally butter the first slice of pumpernickel and place a slice of Parma ham on top. Trim the edges to the shape of the bread and spread mustard over the ham.

2 Cover with a layer of Gruyère cheese slices and arrange a little watercress on top.

3 Spread another piece of pumpernickel with butter, followed by the pâté, and place it, pâté side down, on top of the watercress. Cut it into 6 pieces 25 mm /1 in wide.

4 Repeat the process with the remaining ingredients; arrange attractively on a large plate and serve.

Glazed canapé crescents

▌▌▌ 1½ hours, plus
▌▌▌ setting and chilling

Makes 18–21
7.5 ml /1½ tsp aspic powder
For the first layer
10 ml /2 tsp powdered gelatine
60 ml /4 tbls Mayonnaise (see page 84)
For the second layer
7.5 ml /1½ tsp powdered gelatine
125 g /4 oz cooked tongue, ham or pressed beef,
  chopped and pounded using a pestle and
  mortar, or finely chopped in a food processor
30 ml /2 tbls thick cream
salt and freshly ground black pepper
For the third layer
7.5 ml /1½ tsp powdered gelatine
125 g /4 oz cooked veal or chicken, chopped
  and pounded using pestle and mortar, or
  finely chopped in a food processor
30 ml /2 tbls thick cream
salt and freshly ground black pepper
For the garnish
parsley sprigs
7 stuffed green olives, sliced

1 Pour 125 ml /4 fl oz boiling water over the aspic powder and stir until it completely dissolves. Strain the aspic into another small bowl. Stand the bowl over a pan of hot water to keep the aspic liquid while you work.
2 Spoon 30 ml /2 tbls of the liquid aspic into the bottom of a 19 cm /7½ in square shallow tin. Chill until set.
3 To make the first layer: put 30 ml /2 tbls of cold water in a small bowl and sprinkle the gelatine over it. Leave the gelatine to soften for a few minutes, then place the bowl in a pan of simmering water until the gelatine has completely dissolved. Place 30 ml /2 tbls of the liquid aspic in a separate bowl and strain the dissolved gelatine onto it. Mix well until thoroughly blended, then leave to cool until it begins to set and becomes thick and syrupy. Stir in the mayonnaise, a little at a time, then pour this mixture over the layer of set aspic in the tin and return it to the refrigerator to set.
4 To make the second layer: place 30 ml / 2 tbls of cold water in a small bowl and sprinkle the gelatine over it. Soften and dissolve the gelatine in the same way as before, then place 30 ml /2 tbls of the liquid aspic in a separate bowl and strain the dissolved gelatine onto it and mix well. Stir in the tongue, ham or beef. Using a fork, whip the cream until it stands in soft peaks, then fold it into the tongue, ham or beef mixture. Season to taste with salt and freshly ground black pepper; spread the mixture over the previous layer, then return it to the refrigerator to set.
5 To make the third layer: put 30 ml /2 tbls of cold water in a small bowl and sprinkle the gelatine over it. Soften and dissolve the gelatine in the same way as before, then place the remaining 30 ml /2 tbls liquid aspic in a separate bowl and strain the dissolved gelatine into it. Mix well and stir in the veal or chicken. Using a fork, whip the

On the tray, Glazed canapé crescents and Mouth-waterers

cream until it stands in soft peaks, then fold it into the veal or chicken mixture. Season generously with salt and freshly ground black pepper. Spread this very evenly over the second layer, then return it to the refrigerator to set.
6 To serve, lay a sheet of dampened greaseproof paper on a tray. Hold a hot, damp teatowel around the tin for a few seconds to loosen the jelly, then place the tray and paper upside-down over the tin. Holding them firmly together, invert the tin and tray, then give a couple of firm shakes so that the jelly comes out, in 1 complete piece, onto the greaseproof paper.
7 To cut out crescent shapes you will need a 5 cm /2 in plain round cutter. Cut 3 circles, well apart, in a row on one side of the jelly square. Then use the cutter to 'take a bit out' of each of these circles, to form crescents. Working back from each circular hole in the jelly, cut out 5 or 6 more crescents: you will have 18–21 crescents.
8 Arrange the crescents on a large serving platter garnished with parsley sprigs. Place a slice of stuffed olive on top of each crescent and serve.

Swiss prawn tartlets

▌ 1 hour

Makes 40
575 g /1 lb 5 oz made-weight shortcrust pastry,
  defrosted if frozen
25 g /1 oz flour, plus extra for dusting
25 g /1 oz butter, plus extra for greasing
1 medium-sized onion, finely chopped
450 g /1 lb boiled, peeled prawns
100 g /4 oz Gruyère cheese
150 ml /5 fl oz milk
90 ml /6 tbls natural yoghurt or soured cream
2 medium-sized egg yolks
2.5 ml /½ tsp ground nutmeg
a few drops of anchovy essence
salt and freshly ground black pepper
1 medium-sized egg white

1 Heat the oven to 190C /375F /gas 5. Roll out the pastry very thinly on a lightly floured surface. Using a 7.5 cm /3 in cutter, cut out 40 rounds. Grease 40×5 cm /2 in tartlet tins, then line them with the pastry.
2 Melt the butter in a small saucepan over a low heat, and cook the onion until it is soft but not brown.
3 Reserve 40 of the best prawns for the garnish. Stir the remaining prawns into the onion. Divide the prawn and onion mixture among the lined tartlet tins.
4 Divide the cheese equally among the pastry cases, sprinkling it over the prawn and onion mixture.
5 Whisk together the milk, the yoghurt or the soured cream, the flour, the egg yolks, the nutmeg, the anchovy essence and the salt and freshly ground black pepper to taste. Lightly whisk the egg white until it is frothy

but not too stiff. Fold into the milk mixture. Divide it among the tartlets.

6 Bake the tartlets in the oven for 30 minutes, or until golden brown on top and the pastry is cooked and crisp. Serve warm, garnished with the reserved prawns.

York fingers

 1 hour

Makes 48
350 g /12 oz puff pastry, defrosted if frozen
flour, for dusting
15 ml /1 tbls mustard
175 g /6 oz Cheddar cheese, grated
175 g /6 oz ham, thinly sliced
beaten egg or milk, to glaze

1 Heat the oven to 200C /400F /gas 6. Roll out the pastry on a lightly floured surface to a 30 cm /12 in square.
2 Spread the mustard thinly on half the pastry, leaving a narrow border all round the outer edges. Cover the mustard with the cheese, then the ham.
3 Dampen the narrow border with cold water, then fold the bare pastry over and press the edges firmly together. Carefully transfer the pastry parcel to a baking tray. Brush the top with egg or milk, to glaze. Using a sharp knife, mark the parcel into 24 fingers. Mark lengthways down the middle, making 48 fingers.

4 Bake in the oven for 20–30 minutes or until the pastry is well risen and cooked underneath.
5 Cool the fingers slightly on the baking tray, then cut through to separate the fingers and transfer them to a serving plate.
6 Serve as soon as possible, or reheat in a hot oven for 10 minutes to crisp the pastry.

Smoked salmon and watercress pinwheels

 45 minutes

Makes about 60
1 fresh, medium-sized uncut white loaf
175 g /6 oz butter, softened
15 ml /1 tbls lemon juice
30 ml /2 tbls watercress leaves, finely chopped
350 g /12 oz smoked salmon, thinly sliced

1 Remove the top and bottom crusts from the loaf, then cut the loaf into 8 slices, lengthways. An electric carving knife, if you have one, makes this job easier.
2 Remove the remaining crusts from each slice of bread, and roll each slice lightly with a rolling pin.
3 Beat the softened butter with the lemon juice and the watercress. Spread the bread slices with the watercress butter then arrange the smoked salmon on top.
4 Roll up each slice lengthways. Wrap the rolls in cling film, to keep them in shape.
5 Either store the rolls in the refrigerator until later or, if you are preparing them well in advance, freeze them.
6 To serve, cut each roll into 8 rounds. If the rolls have been frozen, cut them while they are only partially thawed, using an electric carving knife if possible.
7 Arrange the pinwheels on serving plates and cover with cling film until needed.

Ribbon sandwich fingers

Ribbon sandwich fingers

40 minutes, plus chilling

Makes 48
5 slices white bread, 6 mm /¼ in thick
5 slices wholemeal bread, 6 mm /¼ in thick
butter, softened, for spreading
parsley sprigs, to garnish
For the egg and cheese filling
1 hard-boiled egg, roughly chopped
15 ml /1 tbls thick Mayonnaise (see page 84)
75 g /3 oz cream cheese
45 ml /3 tbls chives, finely snipped
salt and freshly ground black pepper
For the smoked salmon filling
65 g /2½ oz smoked salmon
freshly ground black pepper
a pinch of cayenne pepper
5 ml /1 tsp lemon juice
15 ml /1 tbls butter, softened
For the tuna and mustard filling
75 g /3 oz canned tuna, drained
30 ml /2 tbls grainy mustard
30 ml /2 tbls thick Mayonnaise (see page 84)
salt and freshly ground black pepper

1 Prepare the egg and cheese filling. Sieve the hard-boiled egg into a bowl. Using a wooden spoon, blend in the mayonnaise and the cream cheese. Fold in the chives. Season with salt and pepper to taste. Divide into 4 equal portions and reserve.
2 Prepare the smoked salmon filling. Using a mortar and pestle, pound the smoked salmon to a paste. Season to taste with freshly ground black pepper, cayenne pepper and lemon juice, and blend in the softened butter. Divide in half and reserve.
3 Prepare the tuna and mustard filling. In a bowl, mash the tuna fish with a fork, then blend in the mustard and mayonnaise. Season with salt and freshly ground black pepper to taste. Divide in 2 and reserve.
4 Remove the crusts from the bread and trim the slices to rectangles about 9 × 7.5 cm / 3½ × 3 in. Spread all the slices thinly with softened butter.
5 Place a slice of white bread on a board, buttered side up, and spread with a quarter of the egg and cheese filling. Take a brown slice and lay it, buttered side down, on top.
6 Spread the brown slice with half the smoked salmon filling. Cover with a slice of white bread, buttered side up.
7 Spread with half the tuna and mustard filling and place a brown slice on top, buttered side down.
8 Spread the brown slice with a little extra butter, then with another quarter of the egg and cheese filling. Finish with a white slice, buttered side down.
9 Wrap the layered sandwich in cling film and refrigerate for at least 30 minutes. Repeat with the remaining bread and fillings, starting with a brown slice.
10 To serve, slice each sandwich downwards into 8, then cut each piece into 3 sandwich fingers. Arrange on a serving platter. Garnish with parsley and serve, or cover with cling film and chill until needed.

Smoked salmon cones

🕐 🍴🍴 40 minutes, plus overnight chilling

Makes about 30 canapés
125 ml /4 fl oz thick Mayonnaise (see page 84)
15 ml /1 tbls yoghurt
1.5 ml /¼ tsp horseradish relish
100 g /4 oz boiled, peeled prawns, chopped
a pinch of salt
several drops of lemon juice
freshly ground black pepper
600 g /1¼ lb smoked salmon slices
parsley sprigs and lemon slices, to garnish

1 The day before the party, mix the mayonnaise, yoghurt, horseradish relish and chopped prawns together and season the mixture with salt, lemon juice to taste and a generous amount of black pepper.
2 Cut the salmon slices into triangles, measuring approximately 7.5×6.5×6.5 cm / 3×2½×2½ in. Fold the 2 shorter sides around your index finger, pressing the edges together to make a cone shape. It is easy to 'patch' cones and make up more cones with unused bits of salmon.
3 Use a teaspoon to fill the salmon cones with the mayonnaise mixture, then arrange the cones carefully on a serving dish, over-lapping them slightly.
4 Cover the dish with cling film and refrigerate overnight.
5 Remove the cling film just before serving, garnish the cones with the parsley sprigs and thin slices of lemon.

Avocado barquettes

🍴🍴🍴 baking the barquettes, then 15 minutes

Makes 12
100 g /4 oz made-weight shortcrust pastry, defrosted if frozen
flour, for dusting
1 large ripe avocado
20 ml /4 tsp lemon juice
1 small onion, finely chopped
salt and freshly ground black pepper
a pinch of cayenne pepper
a pinch of ground ginger
30 ml /2 tbls olive oil
10 ml /2 tsp finely chopped fresh parsley and tarragon, to garnish

1 Heat the oven to 200C /400F /gas 6. Roll out the pastry on a floured surface and use it to line 12 barquette moulds 9 cm /3½ in long. Fill with foil and beans and bake for 10 minutes. Remove the foil and beans. Bake for a further 10 minutes, or until the barquettes are fully cooked. Leave until cold, then remove from the moulds.
2 Cut the avocado in half and remove the stone. Purée the flesh in a blender, adding the lemon juice to preserve the colour.
3 Add the finely chopped onion and season to taste with salt, freshly ground black pepper, cayenne pepper and ground ginger. Blend again until smooth.
4 Add the oil to the avocado purée, drop by drop at first, then in a thin trickle, blending well between each addition.

Smoked salmon cones

Avocado barquettes

5 Fill each barquette with the avocado purée, using a fork to make an attractive pattern in the centre. Garnish with a line of finely chopped parsley and tarragon. Transfer to a serving dish and serve immediately.

Mushroom and cheese pastries

🍴🍴 1 hour 15 minutes

Makes about 50 pastries
450 g /1 lb filo pastry, defrosted if frozen
225 g /8 oz butter, melted
For the filling
45 ml /3 tbls olive oil
500 g /18 oz mushrooms, finely chopped
350 g /12 oz Parmesan cheese, grated
125 g /4 oz fresh white breadcrumbs
3 medium-sized eggs, beaten
salt and freshly ground black pepper

1 Heat the oven to 190C /375F /gas 5. Prepare the filling: heat the oil in a heavy frying-pan. Add the chopped mushrooms and sauté lightly. Transfer the mushrooms to a bowl, then thoroughly mix in the other filling ingredients and allow to cool.
2 Choose 2 very large rectangular baking dishes or roasting pans. Brush half the pastry sheets and the bottom and sides of 1 of the dishes with melted butter. Place half of the buttered pastry sheets in the bottom of the dish, folding in the edges to fit.
3 Spread half of the filling over the pastry and cover with the remaining sheets of buttered pastry, again folding in the edges to fit. Repeat this process with the remaining pastry, filling the second pan.
4 Using a sharp knife, cut through the pastry sheets diagonally in both directions to make diamond shapes. Bake for 40–50 minutes or until golden brown and crisp.

5 Either serve at once or allow the pastries to cool, then store them in the refrigerator for up to 24 hours and serve them cold, or reheat them in an oven, heated to 190C /375F /gas 5, for 10–15 minutes.

Cucumber cocktail savouries

Try ham and cottage cheese (see picture) or chicken in mayonnaise as different fillings for these savouries.

degorging the cucumber, 30 minutes draining, then 15 minutes finishing

Makes about 15
1 medium-sized cucumber
salt and freshly ground black pepper
100 g /4 oz canned sardines
1 hard-boiled egg, chopped
15 ml /1 tbls lemon juice
about 30 ml /2 tbls Mayonnaise (see page 84)
parsley, to garnish

1 Cut the cucumber into 25 mm /1 in rounds. Hollow out the centres of the cucumber rounds to make little containers, being careful not to cut right through the cucumber. Sprinkle with salt and place upside down to drain for at least 30 minutes.
2 Drain some of the oil from the sardines. Mash the sardines with the egg, adding pepper, lemon juice and enough mayonnaise to make a smooth, not too runny mixture. Wipe the cucumber dry, fill with the sardine mixture and garnish with parsley.

Above, Cucumber cocktail savouries

Below, Watercress bouchées

Watercress bouchées

25 minutes, plus chilling

Serves 4
6 slices white bread
40 g /1½ oz thinly sliced smoked salmon or ham pieces, or 20 g /¾ oz smoked salmon and 20 g /¾ oz ham
1 bunch watercress, plus extra to garnish
300 ml /10 fl oz Mayonnaise (see page 84)
3 hard-boiled eggs, finely chopped
salt and freshly ground black pepper
a pinch of cayenne pepper

1 Cut the crusts from the bread and cut each slice into four squares.
2 Use aspic cutters in a variety of shapes, such as diamonds and circles, or a very sharp knife, to cut 24 shapes from the smoked salmon or the ham or from a combination of the two.
3 Wash, drain and remove the stems and any damaged leaves from the watercress. Chop the leaves roughly.
4 Put the mayonnaise in a bowl. Fold in the watercress and eggs. Season with salt, pepper and cayenne pepper to taste.
5 Spread the watercress mixture over the bread squares to make the bouchées. Garnish each one with a diamond, circle or other shape of smoked salmon or ham. Chill, then serve garnished with watercress.

HOT SAVOURIES

When you've invited friends over for a drinks party and the weather turns chilly, there's nothing better to serve them than hot finger food. Here I suggest a colourful range of tasty morsels.

Preparing and serving hot finger food for a large number of people can be quite a time-consuming job, so select your menu carefully and plan so that nearly all the work can be done well ahead, leaving you with only the final heating and garnishing to do.

Choose the food so that its appearance is varied and the garnishes are colourful. There should be as wide a taste range as possible, and the textures should contrast pleasingly — and, for your own sake, make sure that producing it does not involve you in fiddly, last-minute preparations. Write down a good shopping list, then your own check list and a realistic timetable.

Shallow ovenproof serving dishes which you can use to pass the food around are ideal, because they save a lot of time and effort. Check early and make sure you have enough. Remember that foil can be used to hide a less-than-perfect tray, and that paper doilies can look pretty and festive if they are used on serving plates.

Do as much of the cooking and preparing as you can well in advance, to leave yourself as little as possible to do at the last minute. Do make sure that you have someone to help you in the kitchen, while the party is taking place. Cover and wrap dishes, ingredients and garnishes in cling film and make full use of your refrigerator and freezer to store your party food.

When forks are not going to be used, edible 'containers' are a convenient way of enclosing tasty, soft mixtures that would be too messy to eat otherwise. Pastry wrappers are an obvious choice, such as those used in my Garlic and cheese bundles, Smoked haddock satchels and Tomato and olive tartlets. Hollowed-out vegetables, like mushrooms and courgettes, make lovely, light containers for delicious fillings, as in my Stuffed mushrooms on croûtons and Courgette cups.

There are many other ways of preparing hot, easy-to-eat finger food. Crisp, golden croûtons are perfect bases for an endless variety of savoury concoctions, and wooden cocktail sticks make ideal skewers — and not just for mini sausages. Try my elegant Pork and fennel kebabs for an unusual and adventurous change (see recipe).

At the last minute

Decide in which order you are going to serve your hot nibbles and line up the dishes in the kitchen, ready to be popped into the oven one after the other during the party. If the food needs garnishing and/or transferring to a serving dish, have the garnish and/or dish ready.

Pass round the first batch of 'eats' early on in the party, so that guests don't drink on completely empty stomachs, and hand out napkins at the same time. Put spare napkins in convenient places around the room in case they are needed.

When you remove one dish from the oven, pop in the next one. All the recipes given take between 20 and 30 minutes to heat through. If you want to serve the batches of food at shorter intervals, pop a second dish in after 10 or 15 minutes, or put two dishes in the oven at the same time.

If you are serving food in the ovenproof serving dishes, straight from the oven, allow a few minutes' cooling to prevent the first guest burning himself with a sizzling morsel, and put the dish on a heatproof tray to protect your hands while you are passing it around.

One last word of advice: generally, it is better to pass round one or two things at a time, rather than making up a number of trays or platters of assorted food. It's much quicker and easier and, this way, you'll be sure that each guest has a chance to sample at least one bite of all the delicious food you've taken so much trouble to prepare.

Stuffed mushrooms on croûtons

Stuffed mushrooms on croûtons

🍴 1 hour,
then 25 minutes

Makes 12

15 medium-sized cup mushrooms, each about
  5 cm /2 in in diameter
135–150 ml /9–10 tbls olive oil
3 large garlic cloves, finely chopped
100 g /4 oz onion, finely chopped
2.5 ml /½ tsp dried thyme
salt and freshly ground black pepper
60 ml /4 tbls finely chopped fresh parsley
25–50 g /1–2 oz butter
45 ml /3 tbls white breadcrumbs, made with
  day-old bread
bouquets of watercress, to garnish

For the croûtons

4 slices white bread, 5 mm /¾ in thick
oil, for frying

1   Wipe the mushrooms clean with a damp
cloth. Remove the stalks from 12 of the
mushrooms, leaving the caps whole. Put the
mushroom caps in a deep bowl, dribble
about 75 ml /5 tbls oil over them, and toss
the caps in the oil until well coated. Set the
bowl aside, leaving the caps to absorb the oil.
Chop the mushroom stalks and the three
whole mushrooms finely, then set aside.
2   Over a medium heat, sauté the garlic and
onion in the remaining oil until soft but not
brown. Add the chopped mushroom mixture
and dried thyme. Turn up the heat and cook,
stirring continuously, until the liquid from
the mushrooms has evaporated. Lower the
heat, and season with salt and freshly ground
black pepper to taste. Remove the mixture
from the pan, stir in the chopped parsley and
leave to become cold.
3   Using a plain 5 cm /2 in biscuit cutter,
cut 12 rounds from the bread.
4   In a frying-pan large enough to take the
rounds of bread in a single layer, heat the oil
and sauté the bread until it is very pale gold
on both sides. Drain well on absorbent paper.
When cool and dry, arrange the croûtons on
a baking sheet.
5   Remove the mushroom caps from the
bowl. Put a tiny knob of butter inside each
cap, then spoon in the prepared mixture,
mounding it slightly in the centre. Put some
breadcrumbs and a tiny knob of butter on
top, then arrange each cap on a croûton,
hollow side up. Cover with cling film. Chill
in the refrigerator until required.
6   Heat the oven to 200C /400F /gas 6.
7   About 30 minutes before serving, transfer
the baking sheet to the oven and bake for 25
minutes, or until the caps are tender and the
croûtons golden. Transfer to a serving
platter, garnish with bouquets of watercress
and serve.

● You can vary the filling by adding one of
the following: 10 ml /2 tsp anchovy paste,
25–50 g /1–2 oz finely chopped cooked ham,
or 25–50 g /1–2 oz chopped fried bacon.

Courgette cups

🍴 1 hour, plus cooling,
then 20 minutes

Makes 20

10 courgettes, about 5–7 cm /2–2½ in
  in diameter, and 10 cm /4 in long
salt and freshly ground black pepper
3 large garlic cloves, very finely chopped
100 g /4 oz onion, finely chopped or grated
75 ml /5 tbls olive oil, plus extra for brushing
225 g /8 oz lean lamb, minced
15 ml /1 tbls oregano
2.5 ml /½ tsp dried thyme
1 red pepper halved, seeded and finely chopped,
  plus extra to garnish
50 g /2 oz cooked ham, chopped
15–25 g /½–1 oz pine nuts
45 ml /3 tbls finely chopped fresh parsley

1   Top and tail the courgettes so that they
have a flat base at either end. Halve the courgettes crossways. Using a potato peeler or an
apple corer, partially core each half, from one
end, removing all but 15 mm /½ in of the
flesh, leaving the courgette halves with a firm
base. Chop the courgette cores finely and
reserve.
2   In a large saucepan, bring lightly salted
water to the boil. Blanch the hollowed-out
courgette halves for 1–2 minutes. Drain and
refresh in cold water. Drain the courgettes
again, then stand them, base end up, on
absorbent paper to drain thoroughly.
3   Meanwhile, in a heavy-based frying-pan,
sauté the garlic and onion in the oil until soft
but not brown, stirring frequently. Add the
minced lamb. Stir to blend and cook for
about 5 minutes. Season with salt, and
freshly ground black pepper to taste, then
add the oregano and thyme. Stir to blend and
cook for a further 5 minutes.
4   Add the prepared red pepper and the
chopped courgette flesh. Increase the heat
and stir briskly until the liquid from the
courgette flesh has evaporated. If necessary,
season to taste again with salt and pepper.
Stir in the chopped ham, pine nuts and
parsley. Leave to get cold.
5   Brush the outside of the drained courgette cups lightly with olive oil. Using a
small spoon, fill the cups with the meat
mixture. Stand the cups upright, filled side
up, in a lightly oiled, shallow ovenproof
serving dish. Cover with cling film. Reserve
in a cool place until required.
6   Heat the oven to 200C /400F /gas 6.
7   Transfer the courgette cups to the oven
and bake for 20 minutes, or until heated
through. Leave until cool enough to eat.
Garnish with a little finely chopped red
pepper and serve.

Garlic and cheese bundles

🕐 30 minutes, plus chilling,
then 15 minutes

Makes 36
50 g /2 oz Gruyère cheese, freshly grated
1 garlic clove, finely chopped
30 ml /2 tbls finely chopped fresh parsley
salt and freshly ground black pepper
3 sheets filo pastry, defrosted if frozen
flour, for dusting
oil, for deep frying
parsley, to garnish

1 In a small bowl, mix the grated cheese with the finely chopped garlic and parsley and season with salt and freshly ground black pepper to taste.
2 On a lightly floured surface, cut the filo pastry into 7.5 cm /3 in squares. Place 2.5 ml /½ tsp of the cheese mixture in the centre of each square, draw the corners of each square together and twist them to form a little bundle. Cover and chill in the refrigerator until ready to use.
3 Just before serving, heat the oil to 180C /350F in a deep-fat frier. Put the bundles, about 10 at a time, in the hot oil and deep fry them for 1–2 minutes, turning them with a spoon until the pastry is golden brown. Drain well on absorbent paper. Keep warm while you fry the remaining bundles. Garnish with parsley and serve.

Butterfly prawns

🕐 20 minutes

Makes about 24
500 g /1 lb cooked prawns, in their shells
75 g /3 oz butter
20 ml /4 tsp paprika
a pinch of cayenne pepper
the juice of ½ a lemon
lemon slices, to garnish
flat-leaved parsley, to garnish

1 Remove the heads and body shells of the prawns, leaving the small tail shells still attached. Cut along the underside of each prawn, without cutting right through to the other side. Open them out as far as possible without breaking them.
2 In a large frying-pan, heat the butter. When it is melted, add the paprika and a pinch of cayenne pepper. Sauté the prawns over a high heat until they are hot and lightly coloured. Transfer to a serving dish and sprinkle the lemon juice over them. Garnish the dish with lemon slices and parsley, and serve immediately.

Pork and fennel kebabs

🕐 overnight marinating,
then 1¾ hours

Makes 20
250 g /8 oz pork fillet, all fat removed
2 fennel bulbs with leaves (reserve some of the leaves for the garnish)
salt
60 ml /4 tbls olive oil, plus extra for brushing
the juice of 1 lemon
freshly ground black pepper
20 wooden cocktail sticks
For the marinade
freshly ground black pepper
45 ml /3 tbls olive oil
the juice of 1 lemon
45 ml /3 tbls Pernod
For the garnish
lemon wedges

1 Cut the pork into 25 mm /1 in cubes and arrange them in a shallow dish.

2 To marinate the meat, sprinkle it with freshly ground black pepper. Pour the oil over the meat and toss it with your hands to coat. Pour the lemon juice and the Pernod over the top and toss the meat again. Cut off the upper stems and leaves from the fennel bulbs. Reserve half of them wrapped in cling film for the garnish. Lay the rest over the meat. Cover the dish with cling film and leave the prepared meat cubes to marinate in the refrigerator overnight.
3 Remove the fennel leaves from the meat; chop them finely and set them aside. With a slotted spoon, remove all the meat from the marinade and pat it dry with absorbent paper. Set the marinating liquid aside and season the meat to taste with salt.
4 In a frying-pan large enough to take the meat cubes in a single layer, heat the oil over

a moderate heat. Add the meat to the hot oil and cook, turning continuously, until it is lightly and evenly browned all over. Lower the heat and continue cooking the pork, turning occasionally, for 10–15 minutes, or until it is done. The juices should run clear when the meat is pierced with a skewer.

5 Remove the meat from the pan, using a slotted spoon, and leave it to get completely cold. Strain off all the fat from the pan. Return the pan to a medium to high heat. Add the marinade and, with a wooden spoon, scrape up the sediment from the bottom, stirring to blend it into the liquid. Add 15–30 ml /1–2 tbls water, and simmer the sauce until it is thick and syrupy. Strain the sauce into a bowl and stir in the reserved chopped fennel leaves. Leave it to get completely cold.

6 With a small sharp knife, trim the root of the fennel bulbs, then trim away the tough, stringy outer fibres. Discard the trimmings and cut the fennel into 40×25 mm /1 in pieces. In a small saucepan, bring some lightly salted water to the boil. Add the lemon juice and the fennel pieces. Bring the water back to the boil and then simmer for three minutes. Strain, and plunge the fennel into cold water to refresh it. Drain well and pat dry with absorbent paper. Leave to get cold.

7 Before assembling the kebabs, check the seasoning of both the meat and the sauce and, if necessary, add more salt and freshly ground black pepper. To assemble the kebabs, first thread a piece of fennel onto each cocktail stick. Follow this with a piece of pork and then another piece of fennel, so that the meat

is neatly sandwiched between the slices of fennel.

8 Brush a large, shallow, ovenproof serving dish lightly with olive oil and arrange the kebabs in the dish. Brush the meat lightly with half the sauce and reserve the remaining marinade. Cover with cling film and chill in the refrigerator until needed.

9 Make sure that the bottom shelf is low in the oven, then heat the oven to 200C /400F / gas 6.

10 Brush the kebabs lightly with olive oil, then with the remaining sauce. Transfer to the low shelf in the oven and bake for about 30 minutes. Garnish with the lemon wedges and the reserved fennel leaves, and serve the kebabs immediately.

Butterfly prawns

Smoked haddock satchels

¶¶¶ 1½ hours including chilling, then 25 minutes

Makes 25
375 g /13 oz smoked haddock fillets
600 ml /1 pt milk
25 g / 1 oz butter
30 ml /2 tbls flour
salt
freshly ground black pepper
a pinch of nutmeg
500 g /1 lb made-weight flaky pastry, defrosted
  if frozen
2.5 ml /½ tsp turmeric
a pinch of cayenne pepper
the juice of ½ a lemon
1 egg yolk mixed with 30 ml /2 tbls milk, to
  glaze
To garnish
lemon wedges
sprigs of fresh parsley

1 In a heavy-based saucepan, simmer the haddock fillets in the milk for 12–15 minutes, or until the fish flakes easily. With a slotted spoon, remove the fillets and leave them to cool. Reserve the milk.
2 Over a low heat, melt the butter in a separate heavy-based saucepan. Add the flour and cook, stirring with a wooden spoon to blend, for 2–3 minutes, to make a pale roux.
3 Gradually add the reserved milk, stirring with a wire whisk to prevent lumps forming. Raise the heat and continue whisking while the sauce comes to the boil. Lower the heat and simmer the sauce, stirring occasionally, for 15 minutes or until it reduces to a smooth, thick consistency and loses its floury taste. Season with salt, freshly ground black pepper and a pinch of nutmeg, then leave to get cold.
4 Meanwhile, roll out the pastry thinly and, with a 9 cm /3½ in plain cutter or a small saucer, cut it into 25 circles. Arrange the circles on baking sheets and refrigerate while you assemble the filling.
5 To the cooled sauce, add the turmeric, the cayenne pepper and the lemon juice. Season to taste with salt and freshly ground black pepper. Skin the fish and flake it finely. Bind the flakes together with the sauce.
6 Brush the rim of each pastry circle with the beaten yolk and milk. Reserve the remaining yolk mixture. Spoon 5 ml /1 tsp filling onto the centre of each circle of pastry. Bring the opposite sides of the circle together and press to seal. With thumb and forefingers, crimp the closed edge of each satchel into a frill. Arrange on baking sheets, cover with cling film and chill in the refrigerator for 30 minutes or until ready to cook.
7 About 45 minutes before serving, heat the oven to 220C /400F /gas 7.
8 Brush the satchels with beaten egg yolk and milk. Bake for 5 minutes, then lower the heat to 190C /375F /gas 5, and bake for a further 20 minutes, or until golden brown.
9 Transfer to a warmed serving platter. Garnish with lemon wedges and sprigs of parsley and serve.

Tomato and olive tartlets

1½ hours,
then 20 minutes baking

Makes 25
75 ml /5 tbls olive oil, plus extra for brushing
flour, for dusting
1 × shortcrust pastry (see Broccoli quiche, page
*   43)*
4 garlic cloves, peeled and finely chopped
175 g /6 oz onion, finely chopped
750 g /1½ lb ripe tomatoes, blanched, skinned,
*   seeded and chopped*
10–15 ml /2–3 tsp coriander seeds, finely
*   crushed*
5 ml /1 tsp sugar
salt
freshly ground black pepper
75–90 ml /5–6 tbls finely chopped parsley
1 large red pepper, halved and seeded
50 black olives, stoned and halved
For the garnish
parsley sprigs

1   Heat the oven to 200C /400F /gas 6.
Using a little of the olive oil, grease 25 × 6.5
cm /2½ in tartlet tins.
2   On a floured surface, roll out the pastry
to 5 mm /¼ in thick and line the tartlet tins.
Prick each pastry case with a fork. Chill in
the refrigerator for 30 minutes. Next, line the
pastry with greaseproof paper or foil, weight
with rice or dried beans, and bake blind for
20 minutes. Remove the paper and the rice
or beans. Return the pastry cases to the oven
for 5–10 minutes, or until they are pale gold
in colour. Leave them to get completely cold,
then remove from the tins.
3   In a heavy-based frying-pan, sauté the
garlic and the onion in the oil until soft but
not brown, stirring frequently with a wooden
spoon. Add the prepared tomatoes, the
coriander and the sugar. Cook over a fairly
high heat, for about 20 minutes, stirring
occasionally, until the tomatoes have reduced
to a very thick pulp that leaves the bottom of
the pan clean. Remove the pan from the heat.
Season the mixture with salt and freshly
ground black pepper to taste. Stir in the
chopped parsley and leave the mixture to
become completely cold.
4   Heat the grill to high. Grill the red
pepper halves, skin side up. When the skin
blisters, remove the pepper and wrap it in a
damp cloth, to loosen the skin. When the
halves are cool enough to handle, peel off the
skin and discard it. Cut the pepper into thin
strips and reserve.
5   Spoon the cold tomato filling into the
cold tartlet cases. Transfer to a baking sheet
and arrange the red pepper strips in a criss-
cross pattern on top of the tomato mixture.
On each tartlet place 4 pieces of black olive.
Cover with cling film and chill in the refrigerator until required.
6   Brush the tartlets lightly with oil and
bake in the oven for about 20 minutes.
7   Transfer the tartlets to a serving platter
and garnish with parsley. Serve hot.

Tomato and olive tartlets

83

OPEN SANDWICHES

Open sandwiches are a traditional feature of Scandinavian cuisine and form an important part of their famous *koldt bòrd*. Easy to make and pretty to look at, they are ideal for parties, buffets, al fresco meals, or even as a light snack.

A slice of buttered bread, a lettuce leaf or other piece of salad green and a succulent topping are the basic ingredients for a Scandinavian open sandwich or smoerrebroed. The keynote to a successful smörgåsbord (literally a cold table) is in the variety of toppings and in their presentation.

Always use high quality, fresh ingredients. Don't use sliced white bread but explore different types of bread — maybe rye, pumpernickel or black bread; or use thinly sliced crusty white bread, wholemeal, granary or crisp bread. Use good quality butter, preferably unsalted or only lightly salted. Try the many different salad leaves that can be found as well as lettuce: watercress, mustard and cress, well-shredded, raw white cabbage (particularly good with a cream cheese dressing), well-shredded, raw red cabbage (nice with pork), lamb's lettuce (slightly astringent), chicory, endive or red chicory (radicchio) which is slightly peppery to the taste.

The choice of toppings is endless — let your imagination work and make up your own combinations to suit your tastes and the season. Don't mix too many ingredients in one sandwich or the individual flavours will be lost. Whatever you choose should be attractively prepared and prettily garnished. For instance, if using slices of meat or fish arrange them overlapping either in a straight line or in a circle around the edge of the bread, and then pile your garnish in the middle. Coat with aspic for a grand finish.

Open sandwiches are inclined to be fattening. Be kind to your guests' waistlines and offer slightly more weight-conscious alternatives like a snack plate of cold meats (see page 16) or a fish platter (see page 11).

Traditionally lager is served with the Scandinavian smörgåsbord, but you may like to provide chilled white wine, mineral water or fruit juice instead. Have a look at the suggestions for punches and cocktails later in this book (pages 90–110).

Mayonnaise

Important to the success of your open sandwiches is the mayonnaise you use. It is often used as a moistening agent, either as a garnish or mixed with chopped meat or seafood. For a lighter dressing, mix an equal quantity of mayonnaise with yoghurt, or use yoghurt mixed with cream or cottage cheese. You can also vary a mayonnaise or heighten a particular flavour by using different oils or vinegars; for example make mayonnaise with lemon juice instead of vinegar, or make tarragon mayonnaise with tarragon vinegar.

Since open sandwiches are ideal for summer, the amounts of herbs given for the mayonnaise variations are for fresh herbs, which are always nicer whether for mixing or using as a garnish. If using dried herbs allow only half the given quantities.

A basic thick mayonnaise can be made quickly in an electric blender:

To make about 300 ml /10 fl oz
2 fresh egg yolks, at room temperature
15 ml /1 tbls wine vinegar
2.5 ml /½ tsp salt
2.5 ml /½ tsp dry mustard
a pinch of freshly ground black pepper
275 ml /10 fl oz olive oil

1 Blend the egg yolks, wine vinegar, salt, mustard and pepper together with 15 ml / 1 tbls cold water at maximum speed for 5 seconds or until mixed.
2 Take out the centre of the blender lid and, with the motor at maximum speed, add the olive oil in a steady but fine trickle.
3 Taste and adjust the seasoning.

● This mayonnaise will keep for up to a week in a refrigerator if kept in a screw-topped jar.

Mayonnaise variations

Add any of the following to 300 ml /10 fl oz basic mayonnaise:
Anchovy: 2 anchovy fillets, pounded.
Caper: 20 ml /4 tsp finely chopped capers.
Chilli: ½–2 seeded, finely chopped chillies.
Chives: 30 ml /6 tsp finely chopped chives.
Cucumber: 40 ml /8 tsp grated cucumber, drained of excess moisture.
Curried: 5–10 ml /1–2 tsp curry powder.
Dill: 40 ml /8 tsp finely chopped dill.
Garlic: 4 garlic cloves, crushed.
Green: 10 ml /2 tsp each of pounded parsley, marjoram and sorrel.
Green peppercorn: 20 ml /4 tsp crushed green peppercorns.
Horseradish: 10–20 ml /2–4 tsp horseradish sauce.
Lemon: use lemon juice instead of vinegar, and add grated zest of ½ lemon.
Mint: 30 ml /6 tsp pounded mint.
Mustard: 10–20 ml /2–4 tsp Dijon mustard or 10–20 ml /2–4 tsp ground mustard seed.
Onion: 20 ml /4 tsp grated onion.
Paprika: 20–30 ml /4–6 tsp paprika.
Tabasco: 3–5 ml /½–1 tsp Tabasco.
Tarragon: 30 ml /6 tsp chopped tarragon.
Tomato: 20 ml /4 tsp tomato purée.
Watercress: 30 ml /6 tsp finely chopped or pounded watercress.

Fish toppings

Here you have an enormous choice ranging from smoked salmon — best simply garnished with cucumber, to let its own taste dominate — to the subtle flavours of smoked trout and mackerel. Fresh, poached salmon is so delicious on its own that it is a pity to use it in a sandwich, but a good quality canned salmon mixed with mayonnaise makes an excellent topping.

● Slices of smoked salmon garnished with black caviar, lemon twists and a sprig of dill.

● Slices of smoked salmon rolled around asparagus tips, garnished with lemon twists and Lemon mayonnaise.
● Black caviar spread to the edges of the bread, garnished with finely chopped onion and egg white, lemon twists and sprinkled with the sieved egg yolk.
● Canned red salmon mixed with Cucumber mayonnaise, garnished with lemon and cucumber.
● Canned red salmon with a mild Tabasco mayonnaise, garnished with onion rings and sprigs of parsley.
● Fillets of smoked trout garnished with cucumber slices, Lemon mayonnaise and lemon twists.
● Fillets of smoked mackerel garnished with onion rings, Horseradish mayonnaise and orange twists.
● Fillets of pickled herring finely chopped

with onion, tossed in olive oil and sprinkled with lots of chopped fresh parsley.

● Anchovy fillets finely chopped with sweet, pickled red peppers tossed in olive oil, sprinkled with chopped onion and parsley.

● Rollmops garnished with onion rings, lemon twists and sprigs of dill.

● Prawns mixed with Garlic mayonnaise, garnished with cucumber twists, two un-shelled prawns and sprinkled with parsley.

Pork toppings

● Slices of pork, garnished with onion and red pepper rings, a spoonful of apple sauce mixed with a little mustard piled in the middle, sprinkled with bits of the crackling.

● Slices of pork spread thinly with mustard, garnished with onion rings, halved black olives and a spoonful of tomato chutney.

● Slices of pork, garnished with pickled red cabbage piled in the middle, slices of potato dressed with Mustard mayonnaise around the edge and sprinkled with finely chopped dill.

● Slices of pork, a heap of shredded raw red cabbage lightly tossed in walnut oil placed in the middle, thin slices of apple (sprinkled with lemon juice to prevent browning) around the edge and garnished with pickled walnut halves.

● Slices of pork, apple and celery tossed in a yoghurt mayonnaise lightly flavoured with mustard with a pile of cumin-stuffed olives in the middle.

Ham toppings

Use slices of ham cut from a good quality joint or any left-over cold gammon or bacon joint will be suitable.

● Slices of ham, garnished with slices of tomato and hard-boiled egg, with a spoonful of tangy Green peppercorn mayonnaise in the middle.

● Two thin slices of rolled ham stuffed with a smooth pâté, tomato slices tossed in oil wedged between the rolled ham and sprink-led with basil.

● Slices of ham on a bed of sorrel garnished with slices of tomato and bulb fennel, topped with Mustard mayonnaise, sprinkled with finely chopped sorrel.

● Parma ham garnished with thin slices of fresh fig or melon, a few black olive halves and lots of freshly ground black pepper.

Beef and tongue toppings

Ideally cold beef should be slightly pink if not actually rare, otherwise it can be very dry and tough. Both beef and tongue should be thinly sliced.

● Slices of beef garnished with slices of tomato and green pepper rings, topped with Horseradish mayonnaise.

● Slices of beef spread with Horseradish mayonnaise and rolled up, garnished with finely chopped spring onion and black olives.

● Slices of beef garnished with tomato slices topped with chopped potato in Mustard mayonnaise, sprinkled with finely chopped watercress.

● Slices of tongue, garnished with gherkin, radish and potato slices, topped with Dill mayonnaise and sprinkled with finely chopped dill, on a bed of red chicory.

● Slices of tongue garnished with cucumber and onion slices, topped with Paprika mayon-naise, sprinkled with some finely chopped red pepper.

Chicken toppings

● Slices of breast, garnished with slices of tomato and hard-boiled egg, lightly glazed with aspic.

● Slices of breast, garnished with slices of stuffed olives and rings of red peppers, glazed with aspic.

● Chopped breast in Curried mayonnaise, garnished with cucumber twists, a pinch of cayenne pepper and dill.

● Chopped breast in Lemon mayonnaise, garnished with lemon twists and red caviar on a watercress base.

● Chicken breast chopped in a Paprika mayonnaise garnished with onion rings, sliced avocado and parsley.

● Chopped breast in Horseradish yoghurt mayonnaise garnished with tomato slices and halved black olives, on a bed of chicory.

Cured sausage toppings

There are so many varieties of cured sausage to choose from that to list them all would be impossible. But the point to remember when using salami is to keep the garnish to a mini-mum: a few large green or small black olive halves, some onion rings and maybe a 5 ml / 1 tsp Basic mayonnaise. Use a green salad leaf: lettuce, mustard and cress or possibly curly endive. Some good sausages to use are mortadella, cervelat, pepperoni, milano salami, toscana, French pepper or herb salami and Danish, Hungarian or Polish salami, chorizo or Italian spinata.

Use a variety of toppings and garnishes to make these tempting open sandwiches

Prawn mayonnaise

Use unsalted butter in this recipe, if possible, to contrast with the flavour of the prawns.

 making the mayonnaise, then 15 minutes

Makes 2
100 g /4 oz boiled prawns, peeled
2 slices wholemeal bread
softened butter
2 lettuce leaves, washed and dried
1 head red chicory, separated into leaves, washed and dried

For the garnish
8 thin slices peeled cucumber
2 boiled prawns, in their shells
2 sprigs of fresh dill or fennel

For the dressing
30 ml /2 tbls thick Mayonnaise (see Introduction)
1.5 ml /¼ tsp Dijon mustard
1.5 ml /¼ tsp lemon juice
2.5 ml /½ tsp tomato ketchup
a few drops Worcestershire sauce
a few drops Tabasco
salt and freshly ground black pepper

1 Prepare the dressing. In a small bowl, blend the mayonnaise with the mustard, lemon juice and tomato ketchup. Flavour to taste with Worcestershire sauce and Tabasco. Season to taste with salt and black pepper.
2 Dry the boiled, peeled prawns on absorbent paper, pressing firmly to remove any excess moisture. Next, add the prawns to the dressing and toss until well coated.
3 Trim the crusts from the bread and butter both slices generously. Arrange 1 lettuce leaf and 2–3 red chicory leaves on each. Spoon on the prawn mixture.
4 Garnish each with cucumber, a prawn and dill or fennel. Serve as soon as possible.

Turkey asparagus

 15 minutes

Makes 2
25 g /1 oz butter, softened
15 g /½ oz Roquefort cheese, crumbled
15 ml /1 tbls finely chopped fresh parsley
lemon juice
2 slices rye or wholemeal bread
4 small lettuce leaves, washed and dried
2 slices cold roast turkey

For the garnish
2 small heads of chicory
6 canned asparagus tips, drained
½ canned pimento, drained and finely sliced
10 ml /2 tsp canned or bottled cranberries
  in syrup

1 In a small bowl, using a fork, blend the butter and Roquefort cheese until smooth. Add the finely chopped parsley and blend again until smooth. Stir in lemon juice to taste until smooth and well blended.
2 Spread each slice of bread thickly and evenly with the Roquefort butter. Place two lettuce leaves on each buttered slice, then top with a slice of turkey. Trim to shape.
3 Prepare chicory hearts for the garnish. Cut out and discard the hard part of the core, making sure the leaves still hold together. Carefully tear off the outer leaves and reserve

them for another recipe. Continue until you reveal the tiny, tender leaves which make up the 'heart'.
4 Garnish each sandwich with 3 asparagus tips, strips of pimento, a tiny chicory heart and 15 ml /1 tbls cranberries in syrup, well drained. Serve as soon as possible or chill in the refrigerator.

Tongue and mustard

 20 minutes

Makes 2
15 g /½ oz butter, softened
5 ml /1 tsp Dijon mustard
2 small slices wholemeal bread, toasted
2 slices cold cooked tongue

From left to right, Prawn mayonnaise, Turkey asparagus and Tongue and mustard

For the garnish
2 gherkin fans (see note below)
2 sprigs of watercress
4 canned mandarin segments, drained

1 In a small bowl, combine the softened butter and the mustard until well blended.
2 Trim the crusts and spread the toast evenly with mustard butter. Place each slice of tongue on a piece of toast and trim it to fit.
3 Garnish each open sandwich with a gherkin fan, a sprig of watercress and 2 mandarin segments. Serve as soon as possible or chill until ready to serve.

● Gherkin fans: cut gherkins 3 times lengthways, almost to stalk end. Open like a fan.

Beef tartare with egg yolk and onion

Only use top quality beef and make sure no trace of fat is left, since it will affect the taste of the sandwich.

 20 minutes

Makes 2
100 g /4 oz fillet steak, all fat removed, then finely chopped
1 spring onion, green part only, thinly sliced
4 ml /¾ tsp Dijon mustard
a small pinch of paprika
salt
freshly ground black pepper
2.5 ml /½ tsp Worcestershire sauce
a dash of Tabasco
2 slices rye or wholemeal bread
softened butter
2 medium-sized onion rings
2 small egg yolks
For the garnish
5 ml /1 tsp cooked beetroot, chopped
2 small capers, drained
2.5 ml /½ tsp onion, finely chopped
5 ml /1 tsp horseradish, grated

1 Prepare the raw beef patties. In a bowl, mix the finely chopped beef, sliced spring onion tops, Dijon mustard, paprika, salt and freshly ground black pepper, Worcestershire sauce and Tabasco to taste. Mix until well blended.
2 Shape the beef mixture into two even-sized patties that will fit neatly over the slices of bread.
3 Butter the slices of bread generously and place a beef patty on each slice.
4 With a teaspoon, make a small depression in the centre of each patty. Place 1 onion ring over it and slip an egg yolk into the hollow through the onion ring.
5 Garnish with a sprinkling of chopped beetroot, 1 caper, a little chopped onion and a sprinkling of grated horseradish. Serve as soon as possible or cover with cling film and refrigerate until needed.

Sardine and scrambled egg

 15 minutes

Makes 2
2 slices wholemeal bread
softened butter
2 lettuce leaves, washed and dried
2 canned sardines in oil, drained
For the scrambled egg
1 egg
salt
freshly ground black pepper
5 ml /1 tsp thick cream or water
a knob of butter
For the garnish
2 stuffed olives, thinly sliced
2 tomato wedges

1 Prepare the scrambled egg: break the egg into a small bowl. Season to taste with salt and freshly ground black pepper and mix well with a fork to combine the yolk and white. Stir in the thick cream or water.
2 Place half the knob of butter in a small, heavy-based saucepan and heat it until it sizzles. Swirl it around the base of the pan.
3 Add the egg mixture, reduce the heat and stir with a wooden spoon until the mixture is thick and creamy.
4 Remove the pan from the heat, still stirring. Fold in the remaining butter and leave the scrambled egg to get cold.
5 Trim the crusts from the bread and butter both slices generously.
6 Place a lettuce leaf on each buttered slice of bread, with the hollow side up. Next, spoon half the scrambled egg into the hollow of each lettuce leaf.
7 Arrange a sardine on top and garnish with the sliced stuffed olives and a tomato wedge. Serve as soon as possible.

Rare beef on coleslaw

 20 minutes, plus chilling

Makes 2
2 slices rye bread
softened butter
4 lettuce leaves, washed and dried
2 slices rare roast beef
½ small carrot, cut in julienne strips
½ black olive, cut in slivers
10 ml /2 tsp sesame oil
For the coleslaw
50 g /2 oz green cabbage, finely shredded
30 ml /2 tbls soured cream
5 ml /1 tsp lemon juice
¼ small garlic clove, finely chopped
5 ml /1 tsp horseradish, grated
2.5 ml /½ tsp Dijon mustard
a pinch of paprika
a pinch of cayenne pepper
salt
freshly ground black pepper

1 Prepare the coleslaw. Wash the finely shredded cabbage. Drain and shake it dry. Wrap in a clean tea-towel and chill.
2 Make the dressing. In a medium-sized bowl, combine the soured cream, the lemon juice, finely chopped garlic, grated horse-radish and Dijon mustard. Season to taste with paprika, cayenne pepper, salt and freshly ground black pepper. Chill in the refrigerator until needed.
3 Two hours before serving, place the cabbage in the bowl with the dressing. Toss until well coated then chill.
4 Just before serving, trim the crusts from the slices of bread and butter them generously then arrange 2 lettuce leaves on top of each.
5 Evenly spread the chilled coleslaw on the buttered bread.
6 Fold each slice of beef in half and place over the coleslaw. Top with the carrot julienne and olive slivers. Brush the beef with sesame oil. Serve as soon as possible.

Raw beef with caviar

 preparing the garnish and the beef, then 5 minutes

Makes 2
1 slice pumpernickel
unsalted butter, softened
40 g /1½ oz raw fillet of beef, very finely chopped, and chilled
10 ml /2 tsp black caviar, or lumpfish roe
2 radish accordions, to garnish, (see note below)

1 Cut the slice of pumpernickel in half. Spread generously with unsalted butter.
2 Spread a good layer of the finely chopped chilled beef, about 5 mm /¼ in thick, on top of the butter, smoothing it evenly.
3 Top with black caviar and garnish with a radish accordion. Serve as soon as possible.

● Radish accordions: wash and trim the radishes. Cut thinly across, but not quite through each one, then drop the accordions in iced water to open out.
● Buy pumpernickel thinly sliced in packets or tins, it will then keep for two weeks in a refrigerator.

Curried cheese, ham and peaches

 10 minutes

Makes 2
2 slices of rye bread
softened butter
50 g /2 oz cream cheese
25 g /1 oz cooked ham, finely chopped
5 ml /1 tsp Mayonnaise (see Introduction)
2.5 ml /½ tsp curry paste
salt and freshly ground black pepper
4 small lettuce leaves
½ canned peach, drained and sliced
1 ring of green pepper, cut into very thin slices
For the garnish
½ cocktail gherkin, cut into 4 round slices
2 sprigs of watercress

1 Trim the crusts from the bread, and then butter lightly.
2 In a bowl, blend together the cream cheese, finely chopped cooked ham, mayonnaise, curry paste and season with salt and freshly ground black pepper, to taste.
3 Place 2 lettuce leaves, hollow side up, on each slice of bread and divide the cheese and ham mixture between the slices. Spread it out smoothly.
4 Arrange a line of peach slices neatly down the centre of each sandwich, over-lapping slightly. Place a strip of green pepper around the top edge of each slice.
5 Garnish with the gherkin rounds and watercress sprigs. Serve as soon as possible or cover and refrigerate until needed.

From the left clockwise, Curried cheese, ham and peaches; Raw beef with caviar; Rare beef on coleslaw; Beef tartare with egg yolk and onion; Sardine and scrambled egg

WHAT TO DRINK

Ice-cool wine cups and punches are the perfect answer for a buffet party. They are simple to make, so try some of the recipes in this chapter and surprise — and delight — your guests.

Your party drinks can be as exciting and exotic or as classic as you wish to make them: the only rule is that the drink should flow and allow the party atmosphere to develop as quickly as possible. At the beginning it is important to keep your guests' glasses fully charged.

What to serve

Offer beer or cider if your menu lends itself to these drinks. Wine is a very safe all-rounder. However, sparkling wines are festive but tend to be expensive, and chilling vast quantities of white wine can be a problem. A cheaper alternative is a wine punch or cup, excellent for large parties — see my recipes for Summer wine bowl, Wine and sherry punch bowl and White wine punch. There are many variations so that you can choose the flavours and mixtures that will complement the food. The wine cups can be adapted to suit everyone, from dry white wine cups (see Pineapple cooler) to rich fruity red ones (see Queen Charlotte cup). It is a waste to use a vintage champagne in a punch. Instead, buy cheap non-vintage champagne or sparkling wines, and chill them well (see recipes for Champagne cup and Rothschild cup). Add soda water only at the last moment; for sweet wine cups try using fizzy lemonade.

Brandy, curaço, maraschino, grenadine, chartreuse and crème de menthe are the most commonly used additions. Gin can be added,

but never too much. Remember that a big block of ice melts more slowly than ice cubes, but your ice will be much clearer if you boil your water before freezing it. Make decorative ice cubes by freezing small pieces of fruit or tiny sprigs of mint in each one.

Garnish your punches with fruit, but remember that you are making a drink and not a dessert! Use herbs — lemon balm, sweet verbena, borage with its pretty blue flowers and all the different mints: spearmint, applemint, eau-de-cologne mint and lemon mint. Even rose petals can be used as an attractive garnish. Do remember to wash them all thoroughly before use.

Punches are generally quick to assemble and can be made in large jugs which keep the flow of drink going. The rule is to mix the initial punch on the strong side, then increase the proportion of soda water to alcohol as the evening progresses.

In cold weather a welcoming, warming punch or a mull (see Mulled spiced wine) is a splendid greeting for your guests as they arrive.

Cocktails (see pages 100–107), do not have to be the result of an elaborate mixing and shaking and straining procedure, wonderful though that ritual may be. Many simple cocktails can be speedily assembled in a punch bowl or a pitcher, and are practical to prepare for a large crowd. Try a heady 'swizzle', based on white rum (see recipe) it is guaranteed to bring a lively note to any party. Or make my Pineapple punch (see recipe) with one of the white rum liqueurs.

Chilled mineral water, served with ice, is becoming increasingly popular; allow at least six bottles for 30 people. Some guests, particularly those who have to drive home, will welcome soft drinks, such as grapefruit or tomato juice, so lay in a good supply of these. One or two suggestions for alcohol-free drinks can be found on page 62.

If you are serving punch, the initial welcoming drink can be poured directly into glasses, but after that you will need large serving jugs to carry it around to the guests. A long spoon in each jug will be a great help to cope with any floating garnish. Somehow the garnish always seems to get trapped in the lip of the jug, blocking the flow of the liquid and causing it to spill or flop untidily into the glass. Use the spoon to draw aside the garnish as you are pouring out the drink.

Wines

Look for good wines, not necessarily fine wines of great subtlety and expense. Many wine shops and supermarkets run monthly promotions; see what is on offer and buy single bottles to try out before you buy in bulk. Reasonably priced dry white wines include a Sauvignon Blanc, a Pinot Chardonnay, a Soave or a bone-dry Muscadet. Frascati and Vinho Verde, both light and

fresh tasting, are good summer buffet wines. Riesling, Vouvray, Anjou Blanc and Piesporter are good medium dry wines.

Popular light-bodied red wines include Côtes du Rhône, young Beaujolais, Chianti Classico and, if you like a sparkle, Lambrusco. If you want a medium-bodied red with some extra depth try a Cabernet Sauvignon, a Côtes de Ventoux, a Côtes du Rousillon, Rioja, Barbaresco or Barola.

Serving temperatures

On a hot day, or in a hot room, wine should be served slightly cooler than is normally recommended. Chill white wines to about

Summer wine bowl

Soft fruits, steeped in Grand Marnier, then combined with chilled sparkling wine will make a beautiful summer punch.

Makes 12–14 drinks
225 g /8 oz strawberries or raspberries
3 peaches, peeled, halved and stoned
the zest of 1 orange, cut into julienne strips
50 g /2 oz sugar
the juice of 1 orange
175 ml /6 fl oz Grand Marnier
a block of ice or ice cubes
2 × 75 cl bottles dry sparkling wine, chilled
500 ml /18 fl oz sparkling mineral water, chilled (optional)

1 Hull the strawberries or raspberries. Leave the small strawberries whole and halve or slice any large ones. Slice the peaches thinly.
2 Arrange the fruit and orange zest in the bottom of a large shallow dish. Add the sugar and pour the orange juice and the Grand Marnier over the fruit in the bowl. Leave to macerate at room temperature for at least 1 hour.
3 Put a block of ice or plenty of ice cubes in a large punch bowl. Transfer the macerated strawberries or raspberries, peaches and juices to the punch bowl.
4 Just before serving, add the chilled, dry sparkling wine and, if you like a slightly weaker drink, then also the chilled sparkling mineral water.

Wine and sherry punch bowl

Makes 20 drinks
100 g /4 oz sugar
150 ml /5 fl oz lemon juice
½ × 75 cl bottle dry sherry
75 ml /3 fl oz brandy (optional)
2 L /3½ pt dry white wine
350 ml /12 fl oz strong tea, strained
1 L /1¾ pt soda water
ice cubes, to serve
cucumber slices, to serve
cucumber twists, to garnish

1 Mix together the sugar and lemon juice until the sugar has dissolved. Pour the mixture into a large bowl or jug.
2 Add the sherry, and the brandy, if using. Stir well.
3 Add the white wine and the strained tea to the bowl or jug. Mix together thoroughly and refrigerate for at least an hour, until ready to serve.
4 Just before serving, add the soda water to the bowl or jug. Float the cucumber slices on top of the punch bowl. Put an ice lump in each glass and ladle in some of the drink, with a slice or two of cucumber.
5 Garnish the glasses attractively with cucumber twists.

● Make the drink stronger by adding more sherry and wine, to taste, or make it weaker by adding more soda water or extra ice to the punch bowl.

8–10C /46–50F; this ensures a pleasant crispness. Put them in a bath, sink or portable baby's bath, even clean dustbins. Half fill the container with cold water and add ice blocks, if you can get them. Serve sparkling white wines and champagne several degrees colder than you serve white wine: ice is a must.

If you want to serve a chilled wine, this need not exclude a red. But choose young, light and medium-bodied reds and chill them to 10–12C /50–53F. Decant young reds into big jugs to give them a chance to open up and reveal their fruitiness.

Individual ice buckets are useful if you

Summer wine bowl

have them. Wine-coolers do away with ice, because they keep a bottle of pre-chilled wine at its chilled temperature for 1–3 hours.

Closing the party
If you have not specified a time for the party to end on your invitation, either you can serve just one last drink — a 'Late nighter' (see page 108) — or, as a gentle hint to one and all, you can make coffee. Remember that some people may prefer a decaffeinated coffee last thing at night so, if it is possible, offer a choice.

Sangria

This is the authentic Spanish recipe for a very popular drink which has many different versions.

Makes 8–10 drinks
2 oranges, sliced thinly
2 lemons, sliced thinly
150 ml /5 fl oz brandy
a block of ice
75 cl bottle red wine, chilled
600 ml /1 pt soda water, chilled

1 Marinate the orange and the lemon slices in the brandy for at least 1 hour, in the refrigerator.
2 Put a block of ice into a large jug, add the marinated fruit and brandy and stir in the wine. Top up with soda water and serve in wine glasses.

Hock cup

Makes 16–18 drinks
2 × 75 cl bottles Rhine wine (hock), chilled
75 cl bottle medium-dry sparkling German wine, chilled
150 ml /5 fl oz cognac
10 ml /2 tsp crème de menthe
20 ml /4 tsp gin
ice cubes
3 peaches, stoned and sliced
225 g /8 oz fresh strawberries, hulled and sliced
sprigs of lemon mint

1 Mix the hock, sparkling wine, cognac, crème de menthe and gin in a large punch bowl.
2 Add the ice cubes to the punch bowl and then float the fruit and sprigs of lemon mint on top. Serve in hock glasses.

Pineapple cooler

Makes 12–14 drinks
crushed ice
700 ml /1¼ pt pineapple juice, chilled
75 cl bottle dry white wine, chilled
50 g /2 oz icing sugar
1.4 L /2½ pt soda water, chilled
the zest of 1 orange, cut thinly in a long twist
the zest of 1 lemon, cut thinly in a long twist
sprigs of eau-de-cologne mint
ice cubes, to serve

1 Half-fill a large jug with crushed ice and pour in the pineapple juice and white wine. Add the sugar and stir well.
2 Top up the jug with soda water, stir again and then add the orange and lemon zests. Float the sprigs of eau-de-cologne mint on top of the drink. Serve in tall glasses with a lump of ice in each glass.

Champagne cup

Makes 14–16 drinks
crushed ice
2 × 75 cl bottles non-vintage dry champagne, chilled
75 ml /3 fl oz brandy
75 ml /3 fl oz curaçao
25 ml /1 fl oz lemon juice
700 ml /1¼ pt soda water, chilled
25 ml /5 tsp icing sugar
2 nectarines, sliced
225 g /8 oz raspberries, hulled
sprigs of mint, to garnish

1 Stand a punch bowl in a larger bowl filled with crushed ice. Mix all the liquid ingredients together in the punch bowl, adding the soda water last.
2 Stir in the sugar: be careful the liquid does not spill over — since it will be very effervescent.
3 Add the nectarines and raspberries, garnish with the mint sprigs and serve immediately in champagne glasses.

Sherry cobbler

Makes 10–12 drinks
6 oranges, sliced thinly
3 lemons, sliced thinly
½ a medium-sized pineapple, peeled and cubed
crushed ice
sugar
75 cl bottle dry sherry, chilled
500 ml /18 fl oz sparkling mineral water, chilled
sprigs of mint

1 Put the orange and lemon slices and pineapple chunks in layers in a large punch bowl and put between each layer of fruit a layer of crushed ice and a sprinkling of sugar.
2 Pour in the sherry and the mineral water and stir well. Add the mint sprigs.
3 Pour the drink into wine glasses, making sure each glass has some fruit, mint and ice. Serve with 2 straws in each glass.

Loving cup

This is an adaptation of an Eighteenth-century recipe, which was served to celebrate a betrothal. The violets are a symbol of everlasting love.

Makes 10–12 drinks
75 cl bottle light red wine
75 cl bottle non-vintage dry champagne
150 ml /5 fl oz curaçao
100 g /4 oz icing sugar
the zest of 1 lemon, cut thinly in a long twist
the zest of 1 orange, cut thinly in a long twist
ice cubes
225 g /8 oz sweet black grapes, skinned, cut in half and seeded
a handful of crystallized violets

1 Put all the ingredients, except the grapes and crystallized violets, into a large punch bowl and allow them to stand for 1 hour in the refrigerator.
2 Add plenty of ice cubes, the black grapes, and the crystallized violets and then serve the cup immediately.

Queen Charlotte cup

Makes 10–12 drinks
a block of ice
75 cl bottle robust red wine, chilled
375 ml /13 fl oz grenadine or raspberry syrup
1.1 L /2 pts mineral water
1 medium-sized cucumber, thinly sliced

1 Put a block of ice in a large jug and pour the wine and grenadine or raspberry syrup over it.
2 Add the mineral water and stir well. Float the cucumber slices on top and then serve in wine glasses.

Rothschild cup

Makes 10–12 drinks
225 g /8 oz strawberries, hulled and washed
100 g /4 oz icing sugar
crushed ice
75 cl bottle non-vintage dry champagne, chilled

1 Put the strawberries and icing sugar into a blender and purée them.
2 Half-fill long glasses with crushed ice and pour a little of the strawberry purée over the crushed ice in each glass. Top up each glass with the chilled champagne, stir and serve immediately.

Red wine cup

Makes 20–25 drinks
2 × 75 cl bottles young red wine, chilled
375 ml /13 fl oz dry sherry, chilled
60 ml /4 tbls sugar
ice cubes
700 ml /1¼ pts soda water
For the decoration
8 kiwi fruit, peeled and sliced
half a cucumber, cut into julienne strips 5 cm / 2 in long
the zest of one lemon, cut in one long strip
sprigs of mint

1 Pour the wine and sherry over the sugar in a large bowl. Stir well to dissolve it.
2 Add plenty of ice cubes, then pour in the soda water, stirring.
3 Float the kiwi fruit, the cucumber strips, the lemon zest and sprigs of mint on top of the bowl and serve immediately.

Claret punch

Punches were introduced from the West Indies to England in the 18th century when making them became a great drawing-room ritual. Limes were always used in cold punches, replacing the lemons which were used in hot punches.

Makes 20–25 drinks
3 × 75 cl bottles young claret, chilled
75 cl bottle port, chilled
375 ml /13 fl oz cognac, chilled
100 g /4 oz icing sugar
the juice of 6 oranges
the juice of 4 limes
1 L /1¾ pt soda water
a block of ice
4 limes, thinly sliced
1 small melon, quartered and the flesh scooped into small balls

1 Mix the claret, port and cognac in a large punch bowl.
2 Dissolve the sugar in the orange juice and lime juice and add to the bowl.
3 Pour in the soda water and stir well. Add a block of ice and float the fruit on top. Serve immediately.

Mulled spiced wine

This is a warming, welcoming drink to serve your guests on a chilly evening.

Makes 10–12 drinks
1 orange, halved, and each half stuck with cloves
16 cloves
1 orange, sliced
½ a lemon, sliced
4 dried figs, halved
50 g /2 oz sugar
90 ml /6 tbls thin honey
8 cinnamon sticks
2 × 75 cl bottles red wine
375 ml /13 fl oz tawny port
For the garnish
12 almonds, coarsely chopped
50 g /2 oz raisins
1 orange, thinly sliced

1 Put the orange halves studded with the cloves, the orange slices, the lemon slices and the figs, with the sugar, honey and cinnamon sticks into a heavy-based saucepan and pour in the wine.
2 Stir with a wooden spoon over a low heat, until the sugar has dissolved. Increase the heat and simmer for 10 minutes. Remove from the heat, cover and leave to stand for about 30 minutes.
3 Place a sieve over a large bowl and strain the wine carefully into the bowl, discarding the contents of the sieve.
4 Return the wine to the saucepan and heat gently. Add the port and heat through. Keep the wine warm over a low heat until you are ready to serve it. Take care not to let the liquid boil.
5 Just before serving, transfer the hot wine to a warm punch bowl and add the almonds, raisins and orange slices. Ladle the wine into individual glasses and float some of the garnish on the top of each one.

● If possible, keep the punch bowl warm by placing it on an electric warming tray or over a candle warmer. Or you could keep the wine warm in the saucepan on top of the stove and transfer it to jugs for serving. In this case put the garnish in the jugs, or just garnish the individual glasses.

White rum swizzle

Serve this as a sophisticated opening drink. Follow it with something lighter, perhaps even non-alcoholic.

Makes 25 drinks
crushed ice or ice cubes
2½ × 70 cl bottles of white rum, chilled
225 ml /8 fl oz fresh lime juice
225 ml /8 fl oz grenadine
5 ml /1 tsp Angostura bitters
For the garnish
1 large orange, quartered and sliced
2 lemons, halved and sliced
slices of pineapple
sugar, for the glasses
swizzle sticks

1 Fill a large pitcher or punch bowl two-thirds full with crushed ice or ice cubes. Pour in the rum, the fresh lime juice, grenadine and the Angostura bitters. Stir well to mix the ingredients thoroughly. Add the slices of orange, lemon and pineapple.
2 Pour into glasses, preferably chilled and with the rims sugar-frosted. Add a swizzle stick and ice to each drink and garnish.

Pineapple punch

Makes 25 drinks
crushed ice or ice cubes
2 × 70 cl bottles Malibu or CocoRibe liqueur, chilled
350 ml /12 fl oz lemon juice, chilled
1 L /1¾ pt pineapple juice, chilled
For the garnish
2 lemons, halved and sliced
pineapple cubes

1 Fill a large pitcher or punch bowl two-thirds full of crushed ice or ice cubes. Pour in the liqueur, lemon and pineapple juices and stir well.
2 Embellish with the lemon and pineapple

White rum swizzle

cubes. Ladle or pour into glasses, adding ice and some of the garnish to each glass.

White wine punch

Makes 20–25 drinks
3 × 75 cl bottles dry white wine
75 cl bottle dry sherry
375 ml /13 fl oz brandy
425 ml /15 fl oz fresh lime juice
100 g /4 oz icing sugar
600 ml /1 pt strong tea
1 L /1¾ pt soda water, chilled
sprigs of borage leaves and flowers

1 Mix all the ingredients except the soda water and borage in a large punch bowl. Chill for 2 hours.
2 Add the soda water, stir well and float the borage leaves and blue flowers on top. Serve in wine glasses.

Cocktails

BEGINNERS' GUIDE

The deliciously wicked world of cocktails — and cocktail parties — is fashionable once again. Here is a glossary of terms for the uninitiated, plus details of the spirits and mixers you'll need to make your party sparkle.

The word cocktail has a rather glamorous image, which is hardly surprising considering the vast range of tastes, colours and exotic names such as Blue Lady, Shanghai Lil, Whizz-bang and Fallen Angel. Cocktails can be long or short, sweet or sour, iced or warmed, simple or elaborate. They range in alcoholic strength from the pleasantly mild to the positively lethal!

When to serve cocktails

In the 1920s and 1930s — the cocktail heyday — there was a 'happy hour' for cocktails, after work. Nowadays things are more flexible, although happy hours are still popular. In the late morning before lunch, or in the evening before dinner, try one of my delicious concoctions as an aperitif. Or conjure up something special for after dinner; my selection of Late-nighters (see pages 108–109) will give you some exciting ideas. If you are having friends round for a drink on a hot summer's evening, it is better to serve them something long, cool and refreshing, such as Pineapple cooler (see page 92) and Summer wine bowl (see page 91).

Cocktails are ideal when you are entertaining on a small scale. Mix the drinks in front of your guests, since part of the fun of cocktails is seeing them being assembled. See my chapter on Bar techniques (pages 98–99) for tips on how best to make and present your drinks.

Do remember that while one or two cocktails are an excellent aperitif before a meal, too many will spoil your appetite and enjoyment of the food and wine which follow.

If you are entertaining a large crowd, I suggest you stick to wine cups or simple punches, which are easier to assemble and serve in large quantities than individual cocktails. Jugs of chilled Sangria, White wine punch and Rothschild cup are just some of the tantalizing suggestions in my chapter on What to drink (see pages 90–94).

Setting up a bar

Experiment to find out which cocktails you and your drinking companions prefer. The half bottles of spirits and miniature-sized liqueurs that are available are ideal for this, so that even your disasters need not turn out to be too costly!

Before you assemble your ingredients it is as well to know what a cocktail is: usually, it is composed of three things — a base, a modifier and a flavouring and/or colourant. The base is the predominant ingredient and is usually a spirit; the modifier takes away the harshness of the spirit (it can be a vermouth, wine, fruit juice or thick cream, for example); the flavouring or colourant may be a syrup, liqueur or, for a savoury cocktail, a sauce like Worcestershire sauce.

Spirits

Your choice of spirits will depend on your personal preference. The following spirits are the base of a wide variety of cocktails included in my chapter on Happy hour ideas (see pages 100–107).

Rum: it has a fairly strong, distinctive taste; it goes well with many liqueurs and makes excellent fruit punches. There are three types

of rum: dark (brown), white (colourless) and golden. Among the best-known rum-based cocktails are Daiquiri, made with white rum, lime juice and grenadine syrup (see page 101), and Pina colada from Puerto Rico, a blend of golden rum, pineapple juice and coconut cream (see page 104).

Vodka is a versatile spirit because it lacks a distinct flavour. It gives a kick to fruit punches and is the basic ingredient in many well-known cocktails such as Bloody Mary, a mixture of vodka and tomato juice (see page 39), Harvey Wallbanger (page 103) and Screwdriver (see page 106), both made with vodka and orange juice.

Gin is the classic cocktail spirit, with its fragrant, juniper-scented taste. It forms the base for many well-known cocktails such as White lady (see page 107) and Singapore sling (see page 106), both made with Cointreau, and — most famous of all — Dry Martini (see page 102), which is gin mixed with vermouth.

Whisky: include at least one type of whisky in your selection of spirits. Start with Scotch and gradually build up your stock of bottles to include Irish, Canadian and bourbon. Well-known whisky-based cocktails include Manhattan (see page 104) and Whisky sour (see page 107).

Brandy is a very useful ingredient in the making of punches and cups, as well as cocktails. Try my refreshing Hock cup (page 92) and Claret punch (see page 93). Famous brandy cocktails include Brandy Alexander (see page 108) and Prairie oyster, brandy with lemon juice and a raw egg yolk, one of the traditional revivers suggested in my Hair of the dog chapter (see page 110).

Liqueurs

There is an enormous variety of liqueurs available — evocatively named, exotically bottled — and even the most basic list of popular cocktails involves quite a few.

Begin by experimenting with a good range of miniatures, including Triple Sec and Cointreau (orange liqueurs from the West Indies and France respectively); crème de cacao (chocolate and vanilla-flavoured liqueur which is either dark brown or white); Galliano (a sweet, yellow Italian liqueur with a hint of vanilla) and Amaretto (an Italian almond liqueur).

To add variety, try crème de menthe (mint-flavoured liqueur, either green or white); apricot brandy; crème de cassis (a blackcurrant-flavoured liqueur from France); curaço (a West Indian liqueur made from the peel of dried green oranges and available in green, blue and white as well as the more usual orange); and Tia Maria (a coffee liqueur from Jamaica).

Syrups and other additions

These are non-alcoholic, usually inexpensive and come in a great variety of flavours. Keep a good stock of syrups: flavours include strawberry, cherry, raspberry, blackcurrant, grenadine (pomegranate), orgeat (almond), mint and banana. Fruit syrups are ideal for making non-alcoholic cocktails for people who may be driving.

You may also find it useful to keep some made-up sugar syrup, called *gomme*. It is

---

Guide to cocktail terms

Cocktail making has a colourful language all of its own. Here are a few of the most commonly used terms.

Collins: the 'tallest' of mixed drinks, John and Tom are both made with dry gin but there is also Mike (Irish whiskey), Jack (apple brandy), Pedro (rum) and Pierre (cognac).

Daiquiri: originally a daiquiri was a white rum and lime juice mixture, but frozen fruit daiquiris are now popular. These are made from rum, fruit or fruit juice, such as strawberry, and a complementary liqueur blended together.

Fizz: a drink made from a spirit shaken with ice and 'fizzed' with a splash of soda or sparkling mineral water.

Flip: a cocktail made with eggs.

Frappé: a drink served over finely crushed ice. Crème de menthe frappé is probably the most well known.

Julep: is a long, cool, sweet drink, usually flavoured with mint. The base can be whisky, brandy, rum or bourbon.

Martini: the most famous of cocktails, basically dry gin with a hint of dry vermouth. It is the quantity of the 'hint of vermouth' that makes all the difference.

Mull: a hot wine punch.

On the rocks: served on ice cubes.

Punch: hot or cold drink of spirits and/or wines or cider with spices, fruit juices, fruit and sugar.

Rickey: a medium-sized drink based usually on gin with lime added and topped with soda. It should be fairly dry.

Sling: a sweetish, long drink composed of gin and sometimes cherry brandy. It is usually topped up with water. The most famous are Gin sling and Singapore sling (see pages 102 and 106).

Smash: like a mint julep but shorter. The base is either whisky or brandy.

Sour: a spirit shaken with lemon juice and sugar or a sweet fruit liqueur. Sours are usually served on the rocks.

Straight up: served without ice (though the ice will have been used in the mixing and strained out).

Toddy: a hot drink made with a spirit base and hot water.

A selection of exotic and colourful cocktails and their garnishes

better than using just sugar in a recipe as time is not needed for it to dissolve. To make it, bring to the boil equal parts of sugar and water and simmer them for a minute; allow the syrup to cool and then bottle it.

Fruit juices are definitely best when they are home-made; use a citrus squeezer or a blender attachment. If you use canned, frozen or carton juices because you are catering for large numbers of people, then always buy the best quality.

Wine-based cocktails

Cocktail mixes are available in both liquid and powder form. All you need do is add the alcohol.

Wines: table wines (both red and white), fortified wines (port and sherry), vermouths and sparkling wines all make excellent bases for cocktails. Buck's fizz (champagne and orange juice) is perfect for a celebration breakfast (lunch, tea or dinner!) and Champagne cocktail (champagne with brandy) will give any party a lift. Kir (crème de cassis and dry white wine) and Oscar Wilde (white wine with soda water) make refreshing summer afternoon or evening tipples.

BAR TECHNIQUES

Many people love drinking cocktails but lack the know-how to make them for themselves at home. This chapter gives you information on the utensils needed, and how to use them.

Choosing the right equipment and using it correctly are second nature to the professional barman, but it is surprising how quickly you can learn the tricks of the trade. Follow this guide to equipment, mixing methods and presentation to recreate the stylish cocktail era of the Twenties at home.

Equipment

Once you have decided on the particular cocktails you want to drink, the next step is assembling the equipment necessary to make them. If you do not have them already, you will have to buy some items, but there are others you can improvize.

A mixing jug is an essential piece of equipment, although you may well be able to make do with a water jug. It should have a good lip for pouring, and is best made of clear glass so you can see the results you are achieving.

A mixing spoon is necessary for stirring cocktails in a jug. The best mixing spoons are about 25 cm /10 in long, with an oval bowl and a spiral handle which won't slip when wet, but you can use any long-handled spoon you happen to have.

A cocktail shaker is one piece of equipment it's difficult to improvize. Shakers come in all styles and shapes. A Boston shaker is the simplest of all, as it consists of a glass tumbler and a stainless steel tumbler which fits, upside down, over the top of the glass one. It is ideal for many cocktails, although it doesn't have a strainer to retain the ice when pouring. Other shakers can be all metal or have a glass tumbler and a metal lid which fits over the top of the tumbler with a pouring hole, a cap, and a built-in strainer. The glass tumbler can also be used as a mixing jug.

A strainer, usually metal, is necessary if you want to prevent the ice ending up in the glass, and you are not using a shaker with a built-in strainer. Strainers usually have a rolled wire edge which stops splashing and spills.

A blender is the most expensive piece of equipment you will need but, of course, it is useful for cooking too. Ideally it should be capable of crushing ice, although you can always do this by wrapping ice cubes in a clean tea-towel and smashing them with a hammer, wooden mallet or meat tenderizer. Hand-operated or electric ice crushers are available as well, but unless you are going into cocktail making in a big way, these are not vital pieces of equipment.

A spirit measure is useful: the standard measure is 40 ml /1½ fl oz — sometimes called a jigger. Although you can improvize with a liqueur glass or, less elegantly, an egg

cup, the important thing is to use the same measure consistently throughout a recipe so that the proportions are correct. Another alternative for measuring spirits is an automatic pouring measure, which fits on the bottle and measures as it pours.

Other useful items for cocktail making are: an insulated ice bucket, ice tongs, several ice trays and bags for making ice in the freezer, a good corkscrew and a bottle opener, a solid chopping board and a sharp knife for preparing the garnishes.

Glasses

Having the right glasses makes all the difference to the presentation of your cocktails. You probably have wine, beer, champagne, sherry and brandy glasses, and these can all

Mixing methods

Here are the basic ways to mix cocktails.
Stirring is the simplest method, and it requires no equipment other than a jug — preferably glass — and a long spoon. It is the best method for recipes that include wine or vermouth — like a Manhattan or a Martini — as it allows the mix to remain clear.

To make a stirred cocktail, simply put the ice, crushed or cubed, into the jug. Add the rest of the ingredients and stir briskly with a large spoon. If the recipe includes soda or sparkling wine, stir gently so as not to flatten the bubbles. The cocktail is sufficiently chilled as soon as the glass feels cold and begins to 'sweat'. Strain the drink to serve it.
Shaking: this produces a colder drink than stirring and makes the cocktail cloudy. Put the ice, crushed or cubed, into the cocktail shaker, add the other ingredients and shake briskly, supporting the base of the shaker with one hand and holding the lid with the other, just in case it comes loose.
Blending: this is necessary when a recipe includes fruit or eggs. Using an electric

Top right, a citrus squeezer. Clockwise from lemons, strainer, ice tongs, insulated bucket, spirit measures, cocktail shaker, cocktail glass with swizzle sticks, mixing jug and spoon

blender makes a frothier drink than shaking; don't add soda or any other fizzy ingredient until after blending, or you may get a more violent fizz than you bargained for! It's better to use crushed ice so you don't put too much strain on the blender.

Floating: this is similar to the action of pouring cream on top of Irish coffee. It's the method used to float a high-proof spirit or cream on top of a cocktail, as in a Harvey Wallbanger when Galliano is floated on top of vodka and orange juice; or when a layered drink is constructed by pouring the heaviest liquid in first and then the other ingredients in order of density over the back of a spoon placed against the side of the glass. It's vital to follow the order given in the recipe (although if you do make a mistake you can put the drink in the refrigerator where it will separate out into layers).

Muddling: this is the method used when you need to crush ingredients with a spoon to dissolve them. In a mint julep, for example, you crush the sugar and mint before adding the whisky and soda.

be pressed into service. Below are descriptions of the most common glasses mentioned in cocktail recipes. You may not wish to buy all of these, so you can approximate with what you already have.

Rocks or Old fashioned glass is a medium-sized tumbler (and it is sometimes quite simply called a tumbler). It usually has a 125–150 ml /4–5 fl oz capacity and slightly flared sides.

Highball or Collins glass is a tall, usually straight-sided, glass that holds 275–450 ml / 10–16 fl oz.

Martini or cocktail glasses have a saucer or a V-shaped bowl and a long stem. They are designed in this way so that you can hold them by the stem, which means the drink stays cold longer. They usually hold about 175 ml /6 fl oz.

Paris goblet is a classic 'U' shaped glass, holding either 125 ml /4 fl oz, 175 ml / 6 fl oz or 225 ml /8 fl oz.

Large goblet, or Hoffman goblet, is usually found in 275 ml /10 fl oz size, and is suitable for larger, more exotic cocktails.

Glasses should always be kept spotlessly clean. Wash and rinse them in very hot water

and then dry them straight away on a clean tea-towel. It's a good idea to chill the glasses in the refrigerator for at least an hour before using them. This will keep the finished drink cooler for longer.

Frosting a glass
A simple and attractive way to decorate glasses is to frost them, either with sugar for sweet cocktails or with salt for drinks such as Margaritas. To frost a glass with sugar, first dip the rim of the glass in egg white or water, and then lightly in caster sugar — you may have to dip it in the sugar several times to get a good, even coating. For added decoration, you can dip the rim of the glass in a saucer of food colouring (red, green or blue) and then dip it in the caster sugar, which will then be coloured.

To frost a glass with salt, hold the glass upside down (so the juice doesn't run down the sides of the glass) and wipe the rim of the glass with a wedge of lemon or lime, then dip it into fine salt.

Garnishes
There are many ways to garnish cocktails and there are lots of special decorations you can buy — from paper parasols to brightly-coloured spoons. On the whole, though, the edible garnishes are the most pleasing, but do remember to keep them relevant to the cocktail with which they are being served.

● Simple green olives, on a cocktail stick if wished, are the perfect accompaniment to the classic Dry Martini (see page 102), and just by changing the garnish to a pearl onion, you have a different drink — a Gibson.

● A small stick of celery is just right in a Bloody Mary, especially if you have added celery salt to the flavourings (see page 39).

● For fruit garnishes, try orange slices with a Harvey Wallbanger (see page 103), and strawberries with a Strawberry daiquiri (see page 101). You can also thread a cocktail stick with a selection of different-coloured fruit for a punch.

● Some garnishes add to the drink itself, not just to appearance. A sprig of mint on a crème de menthe frappé or a mint julep gives the drink a delicious smell as you drink it. A sprinkling of powdered cinnamon is lovely on any coffee-based cocktail, and a White Russian (see page 109) and a Brandy Alexander (see page 108) just aren't complete without freshly grated nutmeg on the top.

Hints and tips
● Prepare your ice well in advance; make cubes in ice trays, then store them in plastic bags in the freezer. Crushed ice will keep in the freezer too, but you may have to break it up again before use.

● Keep a box full of lemon slices and some curls of citrus fruit zest in the freezer — they not only look attractive but also help to chill the drinks too.

● If you are planning to return home with friends, put the glasses in the refrigerator to chill before you go out; you can frost them, too, ready to serve.

● Cocktails are strong! Provide nibbles (see pages 62 and 63) to eat with them.

HAPPY HOUR IDEAS

The two previous chapters have prepared the way; now comes the difficult part — choosing which of these splendid cocktails to mix. You'll find something here to suit all tastes and occasions.

The gorgeous concoctions in this chapter are listed alphabetically for your convenience. They serve one, so if you are making a cocktail in a shaker, simply multiply up the quantity you require, depending on how many people you are serving and how big your shaker is. Alternatively, your cocktail may be mixed in the glass, in which case just follow the recipe for each individual glass.

The huge variety of drinks here range from the exotic (such as Brandy crusta and Piña colada) to the simple (Gin sour; Whisky Mac), and from the elegant (Blue lady; Vodkatini) to the flamboyant (Shanghai Lil).

I also include classic favourites like Dry Martini, White lady and John Collins. You'll find another favourite — Bloody Mary — in my Brunch section (see page 39).

If the weather is hot and you want a refreshing, long cocktail, try Bourbon cooler; if you want to impress your guests, serve eye-catching drinks with intriguing names such as American beauty, Knickerbocker extra, Last tango and Yellow daisy.

American beauty

25 ml /1 fl oz brandy
2.5 ml /½ tsp crème de menthe
2.5 ml /½ tsp orange juice
2.5 ml /½ tsp grenadine
2.5 ml /½ tsp dry vermouth
ice, for shaking
25 ml /1 fl oz port

1 Shake together vigorously the brandy, crème de menthe, orange juice, grenadine, dry vermouth and ice. Strain them into a goblet, top up with port and serve.

Ingredients for cocktails

Americano

50 ml /2 fl oz sweet vermouth
25 ml /1 fl oz Campari
ice cubes
soda water
a slice of orange, to garnish

1 Pour the sweet vermouth and Campari over ice cubes into a tulip wine glass. Add a splash of soda water and serve, garnished with a slice of orange.

Balalaika

caster or icing sugar, to frost (optional)
25 ml /1 fl oz vodka
15 ml /½ fl oz lemon juice
15 ml /½ fl oz Cointreau
ice, for shaking
a slice of orange, to garnish

1 If wished, frost the rim of a cocktail glass.
2 Shake together vigorously the vodka, lemon juice, Cointreau and ice. Strain into the cocktail glass and serve, garnished with an orange slice.

Blue lady

caster or icing sugar, for frosting (optional)
25 ml /1 fl oz dry gin
25 ml /1 fl oz blue curaçao
15 ml /1/2 fl oz lemon juice
5 ml /1 tsp egg white
ice, for shaking

1   If wished, frost the rim of a cocktail glass.
2   Shake together vigorously the gin, curacao, lemon juice, egg white and ice. Strain them into the glass and serve.

Bourbon cooler

crushed ice, to serve
50 ml /2 fl oz bourbon
75 ml /3 fl oz lemon juice
pineapple juice

1   Half fill a tall glass with crushed ice. Pour the bourbon and lemon juice over the ice, then top up with pineapple juice and serve with straws.

Brandy crusta

caster or icing sugar, to frost (optional)
a thin spiral of lemon zest, to garnish
ice, for shaking and serving
25 ml /1 fl oz brandy
5 ml /1 tsp Cointreau
2.5 ml /1/2 tsp maraschino
2.5 ml /1/2 tsp lemon juice
a dash of Angostura bitters
a slice of orange, to garnish

1   If wished, frost the rim of a 150 ml /5 fl oz goblet. Suspend the lemon spiral from the rim of the goblet, and half fill the goblet with ice.
2   Shake together vigorously the brandy, Cointreau, maraschino, lemon juice, bitters and ice. Strain into the goblet and garnish with a slice of orange. Serve with a straw.

Bronx

25 ml /1 fl oz gin
15 ml /1/2 fl oz red vermouth
15 ml /1/2 fl oz dry vermouth
50 ml /2 fl oz fresh orange juice

1   Shake and strain into a cocktail glass.

Churchill

25 ml /1 fl oz whisky
10 ml /2 tsp lemon juice
10 ml /2 tsp Cointreau
10 ml /2 tsp sweet vermouth
ice cubes, for shaking

1   Shake together vigorously the whisky, lemon juice, Cointreau, sweet vermouth and ice cubes. Strain the ingredients into a cocktail glass land then serve.

Deep purple

City slicker

25 ml /1 fl oz brandy
15 ml /1/2 fl oz Cointreau
ice, for shaking
cherry on a cocktail stick, to garnish

1   Shake together vigorously the brandy, Cointreau and ice. Strain into a cocktail glass and serve, garnished with a cherry.

Cossack

caster or icing sugar, to frost (optional)
25 ml /1 fl oz vodka
25 ml /1 fl oz brandy
25 ml /1 fl oz lemon juice
10 ml /2 tsp grenadine
ice, for shaking

1   If wished, frost the rim of a cocktail glass.
2   Shake together vigorously the vodka, brandy, lemon juice, grenadine and ice. Strain into the cocktail glass and serve.

Daiquiri

Originally from Cuba, this cocktail can be made with fresh lemons if limes are not available — but double the quantity.

25 ml /1 fl oz white rum
15 ml /1/2 fl oz lime juice
15 ml /1/2 fl oz grenadine
ice cubes

1   Shake the ingredients thoroughly until very cold, then strain them into a cocktail glass and serve.

● There are many variations of Daiquiri made with fruit juice syrups in place of grenadine; if you use strawberry syrup the drink becomes a strawberry daiquiri.
● Frozen daiquiri is made with crushed ice in a blender.

Deep purple

40 ml /1½ fl oz white rum
40 ml /1½ fl oz crème de cassis
10 ml /2 tsp Parfait Amour
15 ml /1 tbls lemon juice
ice cubes
dry sparkling white wine, to fill
a slice of lemon, to garnish

1   Shake the white rum, crème de cassis, Parfait Amour and lemon juice with ice. Strain into a 225 ml /8 fl oz Paris goblet.
2   Pour sparkling white wine into the goblet until the foam reaches the rim. Serve garnished with a slice of lemon and a straw.

Dry Martini

The most celebrated and one of the simplest cocktails, the dry Martini is the only mixed drink to have whole books devoted to it. It was most probably created around 1910 in the Knickerbocker Hotel, New York City, and named after the head barman there, Signor Martini.

50 ml /2 fl oz dry gin
a few drops of extra-dry vermouth
a slice of lemon
a green olive, to garnish (optional)

1 Stir the gin and vermouth together, and strain into a chilled cocktail glass.
2 Squeeze the lemon over the drink. Garnish it with a green olive on a stick, if wished, and serve.

● For a Gibson, serve it with a pearl onion.
● Vodka may be substituted for the gin.

Fallen angel

caster or icing sugar, for frosting (optional)
50 ml /2 fl oz dry gin
25 ml /1 fl oz lemon juice
5 ml /1 tsp crème de menthe
a dash of Angostura bitters
crushed ice, for shaking

1 If wished, frost the rim of a cocktail glass.
2 Shake together the dry gin, lemon juice, crème de menthe, Angostura bitters and crushed ice. Strain them into the cocktail glass and serve.

Fibber McGee

caster or icing sugar, for frosting (optional)
50 ml /2 fl oz dry gin
25 ml /1 fl oz unsweetened grapefruit juice
25 ml /1 fl oz sweet vermouth
2 dashes of Angostura bitters
ice, for stirring
a twist of lemon peel, to serve

1 If wished, frost the rim of a glass.
2 In a glass jug, using a long-handled spoon, stir together the dry gin, grapefruit juice, sweet vermouth, Angostura bitters and the ice.
3 Strain and serve the cocktail with a twist of lemon peel.

Flying high

50 ml /2 fl oz dry gin
25 ml /1 fl oz orange juice
25 ml /1 fl oz cherry brandy
10 ml /2 tsp lemon juice
a dash of Angostura bitters
1 medium-sized egg white
ice, for shaking

1 Shake together vigorously the gin, orange juice, cherry brandy, lemon juice, bitters, egg white and ice.
2 Strain into a goblet and serve.

Fun and games

caster or icing sugar, for frosting (optional)
25 ml /1 fl oz dry gin
15 ml /1½ fl oz blackcurrant syrup
15 ml /1½ fl oz lemon juice
a dash of Angostura bitters
ice, for shaking
a slice of lemon, to garnish

1 If wished, frost the rim of a cocktail glass with sugar.
2 Shake together vigorously the gin, blackcurrant syrup, lemon juice, Angostura bitters and ice.
3 Strain into the glass and serve, garnished with a lemon slice.

Gimlet

50 ml /2 fl oz gin
50 ml /2 fl oz lime cordial
crushed ice
ice cubes (optional)
a twist of lemon peel

1 Shake the gin, lime cordial and crushed ice and strain either into a cocktail glass or onto ice cubes in a tall glass. Decorate with a twist of lemon peel.

Gin fizz

25 ml /1 fl oz gin
juice of ½ large lemon
10 ml /2 tsp caster sugar
soda water

1 Shake the gin, lemon juice and caster sugar and strain them into a wine goblet. Top with soda water and serve.

Gin-gin

25 ml /1 fl oz dry gin
25 ml /1 fl oz ginger wine
25 ml /1 fl oz orange juice
ice, for shaking

1 Shake together vigorously the gin, ginger wine, orange juice and ice. Strain them into a cocktail glass and serve.

Gin rickey

50 ml /2 fl oz gin
5 ml /1 tsp grenadine
ice cubes
juice of ½ lime or small lemon
soda water

Clockwise from left on the tray, White lady, Dry Martini (with olive on a stick), Gin rickey (with frosted rim), Gimlet, Bronx at the front. From left to right on the table, Singapore sling (with straw and orange slice), Negroni, John Collins and Horse's neck

1   If wished, frost the rim of a cocktail glass.
2   Shake together vigorously the vodka, Pernod and ice until very cold. Strain into the cocktail glass and serve, garnished with a cherry on a cocktail stick.

John Collins

This drink is said to be named after a popular waiter at an hotel in Conduit Street, London, in the early Nineteenth century.

25 ml /1 fl oz gin
10 ml /2 tsp caster sugar
juice of ½ a lemon
ice cubes
soda water

1   Mix the gin, caster sugar and lemon juice on-the-rocks in a large tumbler. Top with soda water and serve.

Knickerbocker extra

caster or icing sugar, to frost (optional)
50 ml /2 fl oz dark rum
15 ml /½ fl oz Cointreau
15 ml /½ fl oz raspberry syrup
15 ml /½ fl oz lemon juice
15 ml /½ fl oz orange juice
ice, for shaking

1   If wished, frost the rim of a goblet.
2   Shake together vigorously the rum, Cointreau, raspberry syrup, lemon and orange juices and ice. Strain into the goblet and serve.

Last tango

caster or icing sugar, for frosting (optional)
25 ml /1 fl oz dry gin
15 ml /½ fl oz sweet vermouth
15 ml /½ fl oz dry vermouth
10 ml /2 tsp Cointreau
5 ml /1 tsp lemon juice
ice, for shaking

1   If wished, frost the rim of a goblet.
2   Shake together vigorously the gin, the vermouths, the Cointreau, the lemon juice and the ice. Strain them into the goblet and then serve.

Loch Lomond

25 ml /1 fl oz whisky
5 ml /1 tsp caster sugar
a dash of Angostura bitters
ice, for shaking

1   Shake together vigorously the whisky, sugar, Angostura bitters and ice. Strain them into a glass and serve.

1   Mix the gin and grenadine on-the-rocks, then add the lime or lemon juice and a splash of soda water and serve.

Gin sling

50 ml /2 fl oz gin
10 ml /2 tsp caster sugar
juice of 1 lemon
a dash of Angostura bitters
ice cubes

1   Mix the ingredients on-the-rocks in a Highball glass. Top with water and serve.

Gin sour

50 ml /2 fl oz gin
25 ml /1 fl oz lemon juice
5 ml /1 tsp caster sugar

1   Shake the ingredients, strain into a cocktail glass and serve.

Harvey Wallbanger

This drink was named after a legendary California bar-fly who banged on the nearest wall when he wanted a fresh drink!

50 ml /2 fl oz vodka
25 ml /1 fl oz orange juice
25 ml /1 fl oz Galliano

1   Shake the ingredients, strain them into a cocktail glass and serve.

● Substitute Strega for the Galliano, if wished.

Horse's neck

a spiral of lemon zest
50 ml /2 fl oz gin
ginger ale

1   Hang the lemon spiral from the rim of a tall glass. Pour the gin into the glass on-the-rocks. Top with ginger ale.

● Substitute any other spirit for the gin, try whisky, brandy or light rum.

Iceberg

caster or icing sugar, to frost (optional)
50 ml /2 fl oz vodka
2.5 ml /½ tsp Pernod
ice, for shaking
cherry on a cocktail stick, to garnish

Manhattan and Manhattan skyscraper

Manhattan

A similar cocktail to Manhattan is said to have been invented in 1846 in Maryland, U.S., to revive a wounded duellist! However, in the 1890s the sweet vermouth replaced sugar in the recipe and the drink was subsequently named Manhattan.

25 ml /1 fl oz bourbon
15 ml /½ fl oz dry vermouth
15 ml /½ fl oz sweet vermouth
a dash of Angostura bitters
ice, for stirring
cherry on a cocktail stick, to garnish

1 In a glass jug, using a long-handled spoon, stir together the bourbon, vermouths, bitters and ice. Strain them into a cocktail glass and serve, garnished with a cherry on a cocktail stick.

● For a Manhattan skyscraper, pour 50 ml / 2 fl oz bourbon and 25 ml /1 fl oz dry vermouth over crushed ice, if wished, in a 200 ml /7 fl oz glass. Add a dash of Angostura bitters, mix the ingredients thoroughly and top with ginger ale.

Margarita

a slice of lemon
salt
ice cubes
25 ml /1 fl oz tequila
juice of 1 lime or lemon
25 ml /1 fl oz orange curaçao

1 Rub the rim of a chilled glass with the lemon slice, then dip the rim in salt. Shake off any excess.
2 Half fill a cocktail shaker with ice cubes. Combine the tequila, lime or lemon juice and orange curacao in the shaker; cover and then shake.
3 Strain the cocktail into the prepared glass and serve.

Mary Pickford

caster or icing sugar, to frost
25 ml /1 fl oz white rum
25 ml /1 fl oz unsweetened pineapple juice
5 ml /1 tsp grenadine
2.5 ml /½ tsp maraschino
ice, for shaking
cherry on a cocktail stick, to garnish

1 Frost the rim of a cocktail glass.
2 Shake together vigorously the rum, pineapple juice, grenadine, maraschino and ice. Strain the cocktail into the prepared glass and serve, garnished with a cherry on a cocktail stick.

Midnight vodka

25 ml /1 fl oz vodka
50 ml /2 fl oz blackcurrant syrup
15 ml /1 tbls lemon juice
ice cubes
soda water
lemon slices, to garnish

1 In a small tumbler mix the vodka, blackcurrant syrup and lemon juice on-the-rocks. Add a splash of soda water and garnish with lemon slices.

Negroni

50 ml /2 fl oz gin
25 ml /1 fl oz Campari
25 ml /1 fl oz red vermouth
soda water
an orange slice

1 Mix the gin, Campari and vermouth on-the-rocks in a tall goblet. Top with soda water and add the orange slice.

Old fashioned

2 ice cubes
50 ml /2 fl oz bourbon
10 ml /2 tsp sugar
4 dashes of Angostura bitters
a cocktail cherry, to garnish
a twist of lemon peel, to garnish

1 Put the ice cubes into a glass tumbler (about 150 ml /5 fl oz capacity). Pour the bourbon over these and add the sugar and the Angostura bitters. Stir it with a cocktail stirrer. Garnish the tumbler with a cherry and a twist of lemon peel and serve with a cocktail stirrer.

● To make an Old fashioned special, add 2 cherries and a fresh, or canned, pineapple cube to the glass and top with soda water, before garnishing with the cherry and twist of lemon peel.

Orange blossom

caster or icing sugar, for frosting (optional)
50 ml /2 fl oz dry gin
50 ml /2 fl oz orange juice
ice, for shaking

1 If wished, frost the rim of a cocktail glass.
2 Shake together vigorously the dry gin, orange juice and ice. Strain into the glass and then serve.

Piña colada

The Spanish name of this long drink from Puerto Rico means a 'soaked or drenched pineapple'.

125 ml /4 fl oz pineapple juice
50 g /2 oz coconut cream
50 ml /2 fl oz golden rum
125 ml /4 fl oz crushed ice
a piece of pineapple, to garnish
a maraschino cherry, to garnish

1 Put the pineapple juice, coconut cream, rum and crushed ice into a blender and blend for a few seconds. Pour unstrained into a tumbler, garnish with the pineapple and cherry and serve.

Midnight vodka

Screwdriver

50 ml /2 fl oz vodka
25 ml /1 fl oz orange juice
2.5 ml /½ tsp caster sugar (optional)

1   Shake all the ingredients together, strain them into a cocktail glass and serve.

● As an alternative, fill a tumbler with ice and pour the vodka and orange juice over it.

Shanghai Lil

caster or icing sugar, to frost (optional)
50 ml /2 fl oz dark rum
25 ml /1 fl oz lemon juice
5 ml /1 tsp Pernod
5 ml /1 tsp grenadine
crushed ice, for shaking
a cherry on a cocktail stick, to garnish

1   If wished, frost the rim of a cocktail glass.
2   Shake together vigorously the dark rum, lemon juice, Pernod, grenadine and crushed ice. Strain into the cocktail glass and serve, garnished with a cherry on a cocktail stick.

Sidecar

caster or icing sugar, to frost (optional)
25 ml /1 fl oz brandy
15 ml /½ fl oz lemon juice
15 ml /½ fl oz Cointreau
ice, for shaking

1   If wished, frost the rim of a cocktail glass.
2   Shake together vigorously the brandy, lemon juice, Cointreau and ice. Strain into the cocktail glass and serve.

Singapore sling

This is a relic of British imperial grandeur from the celebrated Raffles Hotel.

50 ml /2 fl oz gin
juice of a large lemon
10 ml /2 tsp caster sugar
ice cubes
soda water
15 ml /½ fl oz Cointreau
15 ml /½ fl oz cherry brandy
a slice of orange, to garnish

1   Mix the gin, lemon juice and caster sugar on-the-rocks in a tall glass. Fill nearly to the top of the glass with soda water.
2   Add the Cointreau and cherry brandy. Decorate with the orange slice and serve the drink with straws.

Southern

2 ice cubes
50 ml /2 fl oz bourbon
2.5 ml /½ tsp Benedictine
2.5 ml /½ tsp grenadine
2.5 ml /½ tsp lemon juice
a cherry on a cocktail stick, to garnish
a twist of lemon peel, to garnish

1   Place the ice cubes in a glass tumbler. Add the bourbon, Benedictine, grenadine and lemon juice and stir together.
2   Serve, garnished with a cherry on a cocktail stick and a twist of lemon peel.

Stone fence

ice cubes
50 ml /2 fl oz whisky
150 ml /5 fl oz sweet cider

1   Put the ice cubes in a tall glass, pour the whisky and sweet cider over them. Stir well and serve.

Sunshade

caster or icing sugar, to frost (optional)
25 ml /1 fl oz white rum
25 ml /1 fl oz dry vermouth
25 ml /1 fl oz pineapple juice
2.5 ml /½ tsp grenadine
crushed ice, for stirring

Vodkatini

1   If wished, frost the rim of a cocktail glass.
2   In a glass jug, using a long-handled spoon, stir together vigorously the white rum, dry vermouth, pineapple juice, grenadine and crushed ice. Strain into the cocktail glass and serve.

Twentieth century

caster or icing sugar, for frosting (optional)
25 ml /1 fl oz dry gin
15 ml /½ fl oz Lillet
15 ml /½ fl oz crème de cacao
15 ml /½ fl oz lemon juice
ice, for shaking

1   If wished, frost the rim of a cocktail glass.
2   Shake together vigorously the gin, Lillet, crème de cacao, lemon juice and ice. Strain into the glass and serve.

Vodkatini

75 ml /3 fl oz vodka
10 ml /2 tsp dry vermouth
ice, for stirring
a twist of grapefruit peel, to garnish
a green olive, to garnish

1   In a glass jug, using a long-handled spoon, mix together the vodka, vermouth and ice. Strain into a cocktail glass. Squeeze the piece of grapefruit peel to release the oils. Serve, garnished with the peel and a single green olive.

Volga boatman

caster or icing sugar, to frost (optional)
25 ml /1 fl oz vodka
25 ml /1 fl oz cherry brandy
25 ml /1 fl oz orange juice
ice, for shaking

1   If wished, frost the rim of a cocktail glass with sugar.
2   Shake together vigorously the vodka, cherry brandy, orange juice and ice. Strain into the cocktail glass and serve.

Waldorf

caster or icing sugar, to frost (optional)
25 ml /1 fl oz whisky
25 ml /1 fl oz Pernod
25 ml /1 fl oz sweet vermouth
ice, for shaking

1   If wished, frost the rim of a cocktail glass.
2   Shake together vigorously the whisky, Pernod, sweet vermouth and ice. Strain into the cocktail glass and serve.

Whisky Mac

50 ml /2 fl oz whisky
50 ml /2 fl oz ginger wine, chilled

1   Mix the whisky and ginger wine together in a cocktail glass and serve.

Margarita (page 104)

Whisky sour

75 ml /3 fl oz whisky
juice of half a lemon
7.5 ml /1½ tsp caster sugar
crushed ice, for shaking
soda water
a slice of orange, to garnish
a cherry on a cocktail stick, to garnish

1 Shake the first 4 ingredients together, then strain them into a small tumbler. Add a dash of soda water.
2 Serve, garnished with an orange slice and a cherry on a cocktail stick.

White lady

25 ml /1 fl oz gin
15 ml /½ oz Cointreau
15 ml /½ fl oz lemon juice
5 ml /1 tsp egg white

1 Shake the ingredients together and strain into a cocktail glass.

Whizz-bang

caster or icing sugar, to frost (optional)
25 ml /1 fl oz whisky
15 ml /½ fl oz dry vermouth
2.5 ml /½ tsp Pernod
2.5 ml /½ tsp grenadine
a dash of orange bitters
ice, for shaking

1 If wished, frost the rim of a cocktail glass.
2 Shake together vigorously the whisky, vermouth, Pernod, grenadine, bitters and ice. Strain into a cocktail glass and serve.

Yankee invigorator

50 ml /2 fl oz brandy
200 ml /7 fl oz strong, cold black coffee
50 ml /2 fl oz port
10 ml /2 tsp sugar
1 medium-sized egg
ice, for shaking

1 Shake together vigorously the brandy, coffee, port, sugar, egg and ice, until cold. Strain into a very tall (575 ml /1 pt) glass.

Yellow daisy

caster or icing sugar, for frosting (optional)
25 ml /1 fl oz dry gin
15 ml /½ fl oz vermouth
15 ml /½ fl oz Grand Marnier
ice, for shaking
a cherry on a cocktail stick, to garnish

1 If wished, frost the rim of a cocktail glass.
2 Shake together vigorously the gin, vermouth, Grand Marnier and ice. Strain into the glass and serve, garnished with a cherry on a cocktail stick.

LATE NIGHTERS

Shake up and sample some of these luscious, sweet and creamy cocktails with their alluring names and exotic flavours. It won't take much to tempt your guests to taste these marvellous drinks.

Delicious indulgences, these creamy, sweet cocktails in which liqueurs or cream or both feature, are still as popular as ever. Served as alcoholic cordials they can add an exotic touch to the end of a day or enliven the start of a party. They are best avoided as aperitifs, though — their sweetness deadens the palate. All the recipes contained in this section are for single servings.

Buy small bottles of the liqueurs at first, until you have decided which cocktails you prefer and have perfected your techniques making them.

Most of these cocktails should be served in cocktail glasses, although a 75ml /3 fl oz stemmed glass may be used for the shortest,

Platinum blonde and Silk stockings

simplest mixes, and some longer drinks require goblets — stemmed glasses holding up to 200 ml /7 fl oz.

Barbary coast

25 ml /1 fl oz whisky
15 ml /½ fl oz dry gin
15 ml /½ fl oz white rum
15 ml /½ fl oz crème de cacao
15 ml /½ fl oz thick cream
5 ml /1 tsp lemon juice
ice cubes, for shaking

1 Shake together vigorously the whisky, gin, rum, crème de cacao, cream, lemon juice and ice. Strain into a goblet and serve.

Booster

25 ml /1 fl oz Cointreau
25 ml /1 fl oz brandy
1 medium-sized egg white
ice cubes, for shaking
freshly grated nutmeg, for dusting

1 Shake together the Cointreau, brandy, egg white and ice.
2 Strain into a glass and dust with nutmeg.

Brandy Alexander

fine caster or icing sugar, for frosting (optional)
25 ml /1 fl oz crème de cacao
25 ml /1 fl oz brandy
25 ml /1 fl oz thick cream
ice cubes, for shaking

1 If wished, dip the rim of a glass in cold water, then dip it in the sugar to frost.
2 Shake together vigorously the crème de cacao, brandy, cream and ice. Strain into the glass and serve at once.

Copperino

25 ml /1 fl oz Galliano
25 ml /1 fl oz Kahlua
25 ml /1 fl oz thick cream
ice cubes, for shaking
freshly grated nutmeg, for dusting

1 Shake together vigorously the Galliano, Kahlua, cream and ice.
2 Strain the cocktail into a glass, dust with grated nutmeg and serve at once.

Deb's delight

50 ml /2 fl oz apricot brandy
50 ml /2 fl oz vodka
15 ml /½ fl oz anisette
To serve
crushed ice
thick cream

1 Stir together the apricot brandy, the vodka and the anisette. Pour this onto the crushed ice in a tumbler.

2 Top up the glass with the thick cream and serve the cocktail immediately, to be drunk through straws.

Grasshopper

fine caster or icing sugar, for frosting (optional)
25 ml /1 fl oz crème de menthe
25 ml /1 fl oz white crème de cacao
25 ml /1 fl oz thick cream
ice cubes, for shaking

1 If wished, dip the rim of a glass in cold water, then dip it in the sugar to frost.
2 Shake together vigorously the crème de menthe, crème de cacao, cream and ice. Strain into the glass and serve at once.

Platinum blonde

25 ml /1 fl oz white rum
25 ml /1 fl oz Cointreau
5 ml /1 tsp sugar
10 ml /2 tsp thick cream
ice cubes, for shaking

1 Shake together the rum, Cointreau, sugar, cream and ice. Strain into a cocktail glass and serve at once.

Silk stockings

25 ml /1 fl oz tequila
25 ml /1 fl oz white crème de cacao
50 ml /2 fl oz thick cream
5 ml /1 tsp grenadine
crushed ice, for mixing
powdered cinnamon, to serve

1 In a blender mix the tequila, crème de cacao, cream, grenadine and ice.
2 Strain into a glass, dust the surface of the drink with powdered cinnamon and serve the cocktail at once.

Snowball

50 ml /2 fl oz advocaat
5 ml /1 tsp lemon juice
To serve
crushed ice
fizzy lemonade
a slice of lemon

1 In a tall glass, mix the advocaat and lemon juice with the crushed ice.
2 Top up with lemonade, decorate with a slice of lemon and serve.

Stinger

25 ml /1 fl oz crème de menthe
25 ml /1 fl oz brandy
15 ml /1 tbls lemon juice
ice cubes, for shaking

1 Shake together vigorously the crème de menthe, brandy, lemon juice and ice. Strain into a glass and serve at once.

Strawberry fair

25 ml /1 fl oz dry gin
30 ml /2 tbls thick cream
5 ml /1 tsp sugar
4 strawberries
crushed ice, for mixing

1 In a blender mix the gin, cream, sugar, 3 strawberries and ice.
2 Strain into a goblet and decorate with a strawberry. Serve at once.

Sundowner

lemon juice, for frosting (optional)
fine caster or icing sugar, for frosting (optional)
50 ml /2 fl oz Van der Hum
25 ml /1 fl oz brandy
15 ml /1 tbls orange juice
15 ml /1 tbls lemon juice
ice cubes, for shaking

1 If wished, dip the rim of a glass in lemon juice, then dip it into the sugar to frost.
2 Shake together vigorously the Van der Hum, brandy, orange and lemon juices and ice. Strain into the glass and serve.

Sunset

25 ml /1 fl oz crème de banane
25 ml /1 fl oz blue curaçao
25 ml /1 fl oz thick cream
25 ml /1 fl oz lemon juice
ice cubes, for shaking

1 Shake the crème de banane, blue curaçao, cream, lemon juice and ice. Strain into a glass and serve at once.

White Russian

50 ml /2 fl oz Kahlua
25 ml /1 fl oz vodka
To serve
crushed ice
thick cream

1 Pour the Kahlua and vodka over the crushed ice in a tumbler.
2 Top up with cream and serve the cocktail immediately, with straws.

Widow's kiss

fine caster or icing sugar, for frosting (optional)
25 ml /1 fl oz yellow chartreuse
25 ml /1 fl oz Benedictine
25 ml /1 fl oz calvados
2 dashes of Angostura bitters
ice cubes, for shaking
a strawberry or a cherry, to garnish

1 If wished, dip the rim of a glass in cold water, then dip it in the sugar to frost.
2 Shake together vigorously the chartreuse, Benedictine, calvados, bitters and ice.
3 Strain into the glass and decorate with a strawberry or a cherry. Serve at once.

HAIR OF THE DOG

You enjoyed the party! Comes the morning after and you're feeling terrible, sandpaper behind the eyes and a splitting headache. There's help at hand in this selection of comforting concoctions.

Prairie oyster

This is not the time for major decisions like 'Never again', but practical measures. The first step is to recognize that alcohol — apart from its enjoyable effects — actually depletes the body of essential vitamins and minerals. These have to be replaced as soon as possible. Try a 1-gram tablet of effervescent vitamin C in water — much easier to swallow than the 40 oranges it represents. A tablet of vitamin B-complex will also help. Both are available from chemists and health food stores. Also available from health food stores are oyster essence tablets — much less expensive than real oysters and sadly less pleasant to swallow, but they are said to work wonders on hangovers.

Liquid comfort
Vitamin tablets or capsules are a sound idea from a health point of view and an antidote

to 'morning after' miseries. But it's important to deal with the dehydrating effects of alcohol.

Drink lots of cold water to help wash away the poisons, and when your taste buds crave something a little more appetizing, try one of these simple but effective remedies: ice cold lager, for example, will give your whole system a short, sharp shock. Similarly, mix 30 ml /2 tbls powdered yeast into 300 ml/ 10 fl oz Guinness, for a real booster, or add a splash of champagne or sparkling dry white wine to your Guinness for a Black Velvet with a difference — and a much brighter day.

You can also pamper yourself — or let yourself be pampered, if someone in the house is sympathetic — with a sophisticated concoction (see recipes), balanced to nurse or kick you back into the land of the living. There are no miracles — only time will cure your hangover — but any of these cocktails will help you to suffer in comfort.

Hair of the dog

25 ml /1 fl oz whisky
15 ml /1 tbls clear honey
30 ml /2 tbls thick cream
crushed ice

1 Combine the ingredients in an electric blender. Blend until smooth.
2 Transfer to a glass and serve.

● To make the Hair of an Old English sheepdog, double the quantities.

Life enhancer

25 ml /1 fl oz Fernet Branca (Italian bitters)
25 ml /1 fl oz Campari
juice of 1 lemon
quinine tonic water, to taste
ice cubes

1 Combine all the ingredients in a shaker. Cover and shake.
2 Transfer to a chilled glass and serve.

Corpse reviver

25 ml /1 fl oz brandy
25 ml /1 fl oz Fernet Branca (Italian bitters)
25 ml /1 fl oz white crème de menthe
crushed ice

1 In a shaker, combine the brandy, Fernet Branca and white crème de menthe, then cover and shake.
2 Half fill a glass with crushed ice and pour the mixture over it. Serve immediately.

Prairie oyster

This traditional, effective reviver is definitely not for the faint-hearted. It's best drunk with closed eyes and in one gulp.

1 egg yolk, unbroken
25 ml /1 fl oz brandy
5 ml /1 tsp Worcestershire sauce
5 ml /1 tsp lemon juice
a dash of Tabasco, to taste

1 Gently drop the egg yolk into a glass, using a spoon. Take care not to break it.
2 Pour the brandy, Worcestershire sauce, lemon juice and Tabasco, to taste, over the yolk. Serve immediately.

The cardinal

This smooth, invigorating mixture is a red wine variation of the better known Kir, traditionally made with a white burgundy and crème de cassis.

10 ml /2 tsp crème de cassis
150 ml /5 fl oz red wine

1 Pour the crème de cassis into a wine glass.
2 Add the red wine, stir, then serve.

Index